Sounding the Shallows

Sounding the Shallows

A Confederate Companion for the Maryland Campaign of 1862

Joseph L. Harsh

THE KENT STATE UNIVERSITY PRESS

Kent, Ohio, & London

Library of Congress Catalog Card Number 98-53995
ISBN 0-87338-640-x (cloth)
ISBN 0-87338-641-8 (paper)
Manufactured in the United States of America

06 05 04 03 02 01 00 5 4 3 2 1

Library of Congress Cataloging-in-Publication Data
Harsh, Joseph L.
Sounding the shallows : a Confederate companion for the Maryland campaign of 1862 / Joseph L. Harsh.
p. cm.
Companion vol. to: Taken at the flood.
Includes bibliographical references (p.) and index.
ISBN 0-87338-640-x (cloth : alk. paper)∞ — ISBN 0-87338-641-8 (paper : alk. paper)∞
1. Maryland Campaign, 1862—Miscellanea. 2. Lee, Robert E. (Robert Edward), 1807–1870—Military leadership—Miscellanea. 3. Confederate States of America—Military policy—Miscellanea. I. Harsh, Joseph L. Taken at the flood. II. Title.
E474.61.H372 2000
973.7'336—dc21 98-53995

British Library Cataloging-in-Publication data are available.

With love,

for

Trudy, Laura, Drew, Greg

&

Margaret Lucille Harsh (1911–1995)

&

Joseph Paul Harsh (1913–1975)

There is a tide in the affairs of men
Which, taken at the flood, leads on to fortune.
Omitted, all the voyage of their life
Is bound in shallows and in miseries.

—William Shakespeare, *Julius Caesar*, IV.3

Contents

Preface

This is a book of many questions and scant answers. It charts the depths and shallows of a third of a century of sporadic study that culminated in a focused seven-year research project. It is intended to be a companion to *Taken at the Flood: Robert E. Lee and Confederate Strategy in the Maryland Campaign of 1862*.

Even the most respectable historical narratives are composed of interpretations, educated guesses, informed speculations, and (regrettably) few facts. Sometimes, statements about mundane matters—such as weather, headquarters sites, and if an individual was on horseback or not—are, unavoidably, speculations based on contradictory, ambiguous, and fragmentary evidence. Always, statements about larger, critical matters—such as the motivation of leaders, the causes of events, and the meaning of results—must be interpretations. Such are the inescapable consequences of the nature of historical study.

Rather than despairing at such a state of affairs, the historian might take heart. For one thing, there is no danger that we will ever exhaust our subject. Even if the seemingly unending stream of newly discovered sources were to dry up, we can always continue to reinterpret, reexamine, and reconsider the works of each other. On another, more serious level, the essential ambiguity of history ought to compel us to view our own efforts—no matter how long in years or careful in execution—as no more than a contribution toward an evolving understanding of the past.

It is my belief that because of the nature of our craft, the historian owes two overriding obligations to his audience. The first is to make our interpretations as educated, informed, and objective as possible. The second is to lay out fully and clearly the bases for the interpretations, so that those who follow, whether their own studies cause them to confirm or to reject the conclusions, will not have to start again at the beginning.

In deference to both obligations, and as an integral part of the preparation for writing *Taken at the Flood*, I attempted to identify those areas that would for any reason pose a problem in constructing the narrative. The topics on the list I compiled included: issues that had in the past been the subject of controversy among historians (Why did Lee cross the Potomac?); points of contradictory testimony by eyewitnesses (Was there fog at Harpers Ferry on the morning of September 15?); new questions that occurred to me during the research that seemed never to have been covered by historians (Did Lee know, when he dictated S.O. 191, that McClellan commanded the opposing army?); and running topics that provided consistent details for the entire project (day-by-day weather in the Maryland campaign and a revised table of organization for the Army of Northern Virginia).

Each topic became the subject of a research study. These studies assumed a variety of forms, including lists, charts, calendars, statistical tables, chronologies, rosters, itineraries, identifications of obscure persons and places, and historiographical essays. Before starting to write, I had compiled forty research studies; by the time I had finished, the number had grown to nearly three hundred.

Where possible I condensed and incorporated the results of the research studies into the endnotes of *Taken at the Flood*. For convenience, a list of those already published, with reference to their locations, is given in chapter 11. The remainder of the studies either resisted condensation or, even when abridged, were still unwarrantably long for endnotes. It is these remainders that are here presented as research appendixes.

None of the research offered here should be considered definitive. In no instance do I claim to have rendered the "last word" on a subject. It is my more modest hope that I have been able to contribute a "first word" by identifying problem areas, laying bare the sources I have been able to discover, and pointing out a direction for future research.

To the list of those named in *Taken at the Flood* to whom I am indebted for their assistance, I need to add John Frye, curator of the Western Maryland Room of the Washington County Free Library in Hagerstown. John provided invaluable help in locating population figures for small Maryland towns.

In addition to my wife and children, this book is dedicated to my parents, Margaret Lucille and Joseph Paul Harsh.

CHAPTER ONE

Confederate Almanac for the Maryland Campaign of 1862

INTRODUCTION

Almanac information (sunrise, sunset, moon phase) is from the 1862 edition of Jonathan Gruber's farmers' almanac for Hagerstown and area.[1] Frederick weather station information (temperature, precipitation, clouds, wind, and barometer) is from Weather Bureau Records in the National Archives.[2] Cloud cover is expressed on a scale from 1 to 10, with 1 being cloudless and 10 fully overcast. Wind force is given in miles per hour. These are the only extant weather statistics scientifically gathered in the western Maryland region at the time. Information from the Georgetown, D.C., station will be included in a Federal Almanac in a future study.

The personal observations are taken from Confederate diaries, letters, and memoirs. They are included for two reasons. First, the scientific records do not describe marching conditions, nor do they reflect human reactions to the weather. Hence, some days that record moderate temperatures in the seventies were nonetheless perceived as "very warm" and "hot" by the soldiers. Second, weather conditions sometimes varied even a short distance from Frederick. For example, note that despite the widespread observations of rain on September 12, no precipitation was recorded in Frederick. Because of this, the personal observations are grouped by command, and an attempt is made to identify the location of each unit.

Monday, September 1

Almanac

Sunrise: 5:32 A.M.
Sunset: 6:28 P.M.
Moon's phase: first quarter

Frederick Weather Station

Temperature	7:00 A.M.: 70.5°		
	2:00 P.M.: 74.5°		
	9:00 P.M.: 66.5°		
Precipitation	Time: 1:30 to 7:00 P.M.		Amount: 1.375 inches
Clouds	7:00 A.M.	Degree: 10	Type: cumulo-stratus
	2:00 P.M.	Degree: 10	Type: nimbus
	9:00 P.M.	Degree: 2	Type: cirro-stratus
Wind	7:00 A.M.	Direction: SW	Force: 2
	2:00 P.M.	Direction: S	Force: 3
	9:00 P.M.	Direction: N	Force: 2
Barometer	7:00 A.M.: 29.640	2:00 P.M.: 29.428	9:00 P.M.: 29.405

Firsthand Observations

CHANTILLY AREA

Jackson's Command:

". . . a terrific storm of rain, thunder and lightning." Night: "It was very cold and we suffered a good deal; we also got very wet." Pleasant Valley to Chantilly Plantation.[3]

"It lasted but a short time, but it came down in torrents." Chantilly.[4]

". . . a driving thunderstorm." Chantilly.[5]

"A beating shower of rain poured upon us during the engagement and for a good portion of the night, blinding and drenching those actually engaged, and almost drowning the line in reserve, who lay on the ground for protection from bullets." Chantilly.[6]

"... in a pouring rain ... cold, wet and hungry." Chantilly.[7]

"It rained heavily during the entire battle." Chantilly.[8]

"The most pelting rain I was ever in." Chantilly.[9]

"... a pouring rain." Chantilly.[10]

"The rain fell in perfect torrents." Chantilly.[11]

Longstreet's Command:

"... a sharp engagement in a driving rain." Chantilly.[12]

"... raining in torrents ... the drowning summer's storm. ... In the wet, showery, drowning rain, we had to spend the night." Chantilly.[13]

D. H. Hill's Division:

"A cold rain swept over the field at this time, beating directly into the faces of our troops." Chantilly.[14]

Stuart's Division:

"The rain was pouring down in torrents." Chantilly.[15]

GAINESVILLE AREA

D. H. Hill's Division:

"This evening it rained. We all got wet." Gainesville to [near Little River Turnpike.][16]

"Had a very hard rain in the evening & got gloriously wet." Gainesville.[17]

McLaws's Division:

"Clear and pleasant." [But see entry for Sept. 2] Warrenton Springs to Warrenton to Greenville on Manassas Gap RR.[18]

Walker's Division:

"We had hardly stopped for the night, when it commenced raining very hard and continued so for more than an hour. We all got a good drenching." One mile north of Culpeper.[19]

Tuesday, September 2

Almanac

Sunrise: 5:33 A.M.
Sunset: 6:27 P.M.
Moon's phase: one day after first quarter

Frederick Weather Station

Temperature	7:00 A.M.: 58.0°			
	2:00 P.M.: 65.0°			
	9.00 P.M.: 55.0°			
Precipitation	Time:	Amount:		
Clouds	7:00 A.M.	Degree: 3	Type: cirro-stratus	
	2:00 P.M.	Degree: 0	Type: 0	
	9:00 P.M.	Degree: 0	Type: 0	
Wind	7:00 A.M.	Direction: NW	Force: 3	
	2:00 P.M.	Direction: NW	Force: 4	
	9:00 P.M.	Direction: 0	Force: 0	
Barometer	7:00 A.M.: 29.603	2:00 P.M.: 29.640		9:00 P.M.: 29.820

Firsthand Observations

CHANTILLY AREA

Longstreet's Command:

"The weather is now clear and cool." Chantilly.[20]

Jackson's Command:

"A fine day; there was a frost at night." Chantilly.[21]

MANASSAS AREA

McLaws's Division:

"Clear and Cool. Rained last night." From Greenville to Sudley Mill, ca. 8 miles.[22]

Wednesday, September 3

Almanac

Sunrise: 5:35 A.M.
Sunset: 6:25 P.M.
Moon's phase: two days after first quarter

Frederick Weather Station

Temperature	7:00 A.M.: 52.0°			
	2:00 P.M.: 66.0°			
	9:00 P.M.: 57.5°			
Precipitation	Time:	Amount:		
Clouds	7:00 A.M.	Degree: 0	Type: 0	
	2:00 P.M.	Degree: 0	Type: 0	
	9:00 P.M.	Degree: 0	Type: 0	
Wind	7:00 A.M.	Direction: 0	Force: 0	
	2:00 P.M.	Direction: NW	Force: 2	
	9:00 P.M.	Direction: 0	Force: 0	
Barometer	7:00 A.M.: 29.966	2:00 P.M.: 29.980		9:00 P.M.: 30.000

Firsthand Observations

LEESBURG AREA

Jackson's Command:

"A fine day." Chantilly to Dranesville.[23]

D. H. Hill's Division:

"The moon shown brightly." Marching through Leesburg.[24]

McLaws's Division:

"Clear and pleasant." Sudley Mill to Leesburg to Big Spring.[25]

Thursday, September 4

Almanac

Sunrise: 5:36 A.M.
Sunset: 6:24 P.M.
Moon's phase: half-moon waxing

Frederick Weather Station

Temperature	7:00 A.M.: 53.0°			
	2:00 P.M.: 69.0°			
	9:00 P.M.: 62.0°			
Precipitation	Time:	Amount:		
Clouds	7:00 A.M.	Degree: 0	Type: 0	
	2:00 P.M.	Degree: 0	Type: 0	
	9:00 P.M.	Degree: 0	Type: 0	
Wind	7:00 A.M.	Direction: 0	Force: 0	
	2:00 P.M.	Direction: 0	Force: 0	
	9:00 P.M.	Direction: 0	Force: 0	
Barometer	7:00 A.M.: 30.078	2:00 P.M.: 30.070		9:00 P.M.: 30.075

Firsthand Observations

LEESBURG AREA

Jackson's Command:

"A very fine day; cool at night." Dranesville to Leesburg to Big Spring.[26]

McLaws's Division:

"Clear and pleasant." Big Spring.[27]

Friday, September 5

Almanac

Sunrise: 5:37 A.M.
Sunset: 6:23 P.M.
Moon's phase: half-moon waxing

Frederick Weather Station

Temperature	7:00 A.M.: 56.5°			
	2:00 P.M.: 76.0°			
	9:00 P.M.: 66.0°			
Precipitation	Time:	Amount:		
Clouds	7:00 A.M.	Degree: 0	Type: 0	
	2:00 P.M.	Degree: 0	Type: 0	
	9:00 P.M.	Degree: 0	Type: 0	
Wind	7:00 A.M.	Direction: 0	Force: 0	
	2:00 P.M.	Direction: 0	Force: 0	
	9:00 P.M.	Direction: 0	Force: 0	
Barometer	7:00 A.M.: 30.055	2:00 P.M.: 30.000		9:00 P.M.: 29.965

Firsthand Observations

BUCKEYSTOWN AREA

Jackson's Command:

"A very fine bright day, but quite warm." Crossed Potomac; to Buckeystown, Three Springs.[28]

Saturday, September 6

Almanac

Sunrise: 5:39 A.M.
Sunset: 6:21 P.M.
Moon's phase: two days before full moon

Frederick Weather Station

Temperature	7:00 A.M.: 61.0°			
	2:00 P.M.: 80.0°			
	9:00 P.M.: 71.0°			
Precipitation	Time:	Amount:		
Clouds	7:00 A.M.	Degree: 0	Type: 0	
	2:00 P.M.	Degree: 1	Type: 0	
	9:00 P.M.	Degree: 2	Type: 0	
Wind	7:00 A.M.	Direction: SE	Force: 2	
	2:00 P.M.	Direction: W	Force: 1	
	9:00 P.M.	Direction: 0	Force: 0	
Barometer	7:00 A.M.: 29.935	2:00 P.M.: 29.890		9:00 P.M.: 29.850

Firsthand Observations

FREDERICK AREA

Jackson's Command:

"A fine warm day, but very dusty and unpleasant in the roads." Three Springs to Best's Grove.[29]

"... I sit here on the banks of the Monocacy under the full, unclouded moon." Monocacy Junction.[30]

LEESBURG AREA

D. H. Hill's Division:

"... a beautiful morning." Vicinity of Lovettsville.[31]

McLaws's Division:

"Clear and warm." Big Spring to cross Potomac to one mile on road to Frederick.[32]

Walker's Division:

"This is a very warm day and the men straggle very much." Just north of Leesburg.[33]

Sunday, September 7

Almanac

Sunrise: 5:40 A.M.
Sunset: 6:20 P.M.
Moon's phase: one day before full moon

Frederick Weather Station

Temperature	7:00 A.M.: 65.5°		
	2:00 P.M.: 81.0°		
	9:00 P.M.: 73.0°		
Precipitation	Time:	Amount:	
Clouds	7:00 A.M.	Degree: 0	Type: 0
	2:00 P.M.	Degree: 0	Type: 0
	9:00 P.M.	Degree: 10	Type: 0
Wind	7:00 A.M.	Direction: 0	Force: 0
	2:00 P.M.	Direction: SW	Force: 3
	9:00 P.M.	Direction: SE	Force: 2
Barometer	7:00 A.M.: 29.935	2:00 P.M.: 29.870	9:00 P.M.: 29.878

Firsthand Observations

FREDERICK AREA

Jackson's Command:

"Very warm." Best's Grove.[34]

McLaws's Division:

"Clear and warm." From one mile north of Potomac to Buckeystown to Monocacy Junction.[35]

Monday, September 8

Almanac

Sunrise: 5:41 A.M.
Sunset: 6:19 P.M.
Moon's phase: full moon (Harvest Moon)

Frederick Weather Station

Temperature	7:00 A.M.: 67.5°			
	2:00 P.M.: 80.0°			
	9:00 P.M.: 75.0°			
Precipitation	Time:	Amount:		
Clouds	7:00 A.M.	Degree: 0	Type: 0	
	2:00 P.M.	Degree: 0	Type: 0	
	9:00 P.M.	Degree: 0	Type: 0	
Wind	7:00 A.M.	Direction: 0	Force: 0	
	2:00 P.M.	Direction: W	Force: 2	
	9:00 P.M.	Direction: 0	Force: 0	
Barometer	7:00 A.M.: 29.900	2:00 P.M.: 29.828		9:00 P.M.: 29.866

Firsthand Observations

FREDERICK AREA

McLaws's Division:

"Clear and warm." Monocacy Junction.[36]

Tuesday, September 9

Almanac

Sunrise: 5:43 A.M.
Sunset: 6:17 P.M.
Moon's phase: one day after full moon

Frederick Weather Station

Temperature:	7:00 A.M.: 67.5		
	2:00 P.M.: 78.0		
	9:00 P.M.: 71.0		
Precipitation	Time:	Amount:	
Clouds	7:00 A.M.	Degree: 1	Type: cirro-stratus
	2:00 P.M.	Degree: 0	Type: 0
	9:00 P.M.	Degree: 0	Type: 0
Wind	7:00 A.M.	Direction: W	Force: 1
	2:00 P.M.	Direction: N	Force: 3
	9:00 P.M.	Direction: SW	Force: 2
Barometer	7:00 A.M.: 30.000	2:00 P.M.: 30.000	9:00 P.M.: 30.050

Firsthand Observations

FREDERICK AREA

Jackson's Command:

"It is very warm." Best's Grove.[37]

"We have had hot days lately, but this is a fall afternoon." Monocacy Junction.[38]

McLaws's Division:

"Clear and pleasant." Monocacy Junction.[39]

Wednesday, September 10

Almanac

Sunrise: 5:44 A.M.
Sunset: 6:16 P.M.
Moon's phase: two days after full moon

Frederick Weather Station

Temperature	7:00 A.M.: 64.5°		
	2:00 P.M.: 77.0°		
	9:00 P.M.: 73.0°		
Precipitation	Time:	Amount:	
Clouds	7.00 A.M.	Degree: 9	Type: cirro-stratus
	2:00 P.M.	Degree: 5	Type: cirro-stratus
	9:00 P.M.	Degree: 3	Type: cirro-stratus
Wind	7:00 A.M.	Direction: NE	Force: 2
	2:00 P.M.	Direction: NE	Force: 2
	9:00 P.M.	Direction: 0	Force: 0
Barometer	7:00 A.M.: 30.101	2:00 P.M.: 30.025	9:00 P.M.: 30.060

Firsthand Observations

FREDERICK TO BOONSBORO AREA

Longstreet's Command:

". . . a bright, beautiful day." Monocacy Junction to Frederick to [some point on National Road].[40]

Jackson's Command:

"A very warm day. . . . Very warm." Best's Grove to western slope of South Mountain, near Boonsboro.[41]

McLaws's Division:

"Clear and pleasant." Monocacy Junction to Frederick to Middletown.[42]

Thursday, September 11

Almanac

Sunrise: 5:45 A.M.
Sunset: 6:15 P.M.
Moon's phase: half-moon waning

Frederick Weather Station

Temperature	7:00 A.M.: 70.0°		
	2:00 P.M.: 75.5°		
	9:00 P.M.: 71.5°		
Precipitation	Time:	Amount:	
Clouds	7:00 A.M.	Degree: 10	Type: cirro-stratus
	2:00 P.M.	Degree: 10	Type: cirro-stratus
	9:00 P.M.	Degree: 4	Type: cirro-stratus
Wind	7:00 A.M.	Direction: N	Force: 2
	2:00 P.M.	Direction: N	Force: 3
	9:00 P.M.	Direction: 0	Force: 0
Barometer	7:00 A.M.: 30.050	2:00 P.M.: 29.960	9:00 P.M.: 29.935

Firsthand Observations

BOONSBORO TO MARTINSBURG AREA

Jackson's Command:

"A warm day; showers in the P.M." Boonsboro to Williamsport to Hammond's Mill.[43]

BOONSBORO AREA

D. H. Hill's Division:

". . . showery all night." Just east of Turner's Gap.[44]

CRAMPTON'S GAP AREA

McLaws's Command:

"Warm and raining. Very disagreeable marching." Middletown to Burkittsville to near Brownsville.[45]

POINT OF ROCKS AREA

Walker's Division:

"This has been a cloudy & drizzly day." In Virginia, one mile south of Point of Rocks.[46]

FREDERICK AREA

Stuart's Division:

"A steady falling rain." Urbana, implied pre-11:00 A.M.[47]

Friday, September 12

Almanac

Sunrise: 5:46 A.M.
Sunset: 6:14 P.M.
Moon's phase: half-moon waning

Frederick Weather Station

Temperature	7:00 A.M.: 70.0°			
	2:00 P.M.: 78.5°			
	9:00 P.M.: 75.0°			
Precipitation	Time:	Amount:		
Clouds	7:00 A.M.	Degree: 4	Type: cirro-stratus	
	2:00 P.M.	Degree: 3	Type: cirro-stratus	
	9:00 P.M.	Degree: 3	Type: cirro-stratus	
Wind	7:00 A.M.	Direction: NW	Force: 1	
	2:00 P.M.	Direction: W	Force: 3	
	9:00 P.M.	Direction: W	Force: 1	
Barometer	7:00 A.M.: 29.815	2:00 P.M.: 29.790	9:00 P.M.: 29.950	

Firsthand Observations

MARTINSBURG AREA

Jackson's Command:

"It rained last night and laid the dust, and this is quite a pleasant day." Hammond's Mill to Hedgesville to Martinsburg.[48]

BOONSBORO AREA

D. H. Hill's Division:

"This was a very warm day, and we suffered for water very much." Crossed Turner's Gap to beyond Boonsboro.[49]

"... foggy" in morning. Just beyond Boonsboro.[50]

"Had another rain this evening." Beyond Boonsboro, within 6 miles of Hagerstown.[51]

CRAMPTON'S GAP AREA

McLaws's Command:

"Clear and warm." Brownsville to Solomon's Gap and down Elk Ridge to Maryland Heights.[52]

Saturday, September 13

Almanac

Sunrise: 5:48 A.M.
Sunset: 6:12 P.M.
Moon's phase: two days before last quarter

Frederick Weather Station

Temperature	7:00 A.M.: 67.5°		
	2:00 P.M.: 73.0°		
	9:00 P.M.: 62.5°		
Precipitation	Time:	Amount:	
Clouds	7:00 A.M.	Degree: 5	Type: cirro-stratus
	2:00 P.M.	Degree: 0	Type: 0
	9:00 P.M.	Degree: 0	Type: 0
Wind	7:00 A.M.	Direction: NW	Force: 3
	2:00 P.M.	Direction: NW	Force: 3
	9:00 P.M.	Direction: NW	Force: 2
Barometer	7:00 A.M.: 29.990	2:00 P.M.: 29.978	9:00 P.M.: 30.022

Firsthand Observations

HARPERS FERRY AREA

Jackson's Command:

"A warm day." Martinsburg to Halltown to Loudoun Heights.[53]

McLaws's Command:

"Clear and warm." Maryland Heights.[54]

BOONSBORO AREA

D. H. Hill's Division:

". . . marching by moonshine untill we came to Boonville." Vicinity of Boonsboro.[55]

Sunday, September 14

Almanac

Sunrise: 5:49 A.M.
Sunset: 6:11 P.M.
Moon's phase: one day before last quarter

Frederick Weather Station

Temperature	7:00 A.M.: 58.0°		
	2:00 P.M.: 73.0°		
	9:00 P.M.: 65.5°		
Precipitation	Time:	Amount:	
Clouds	7:00 A.M.	Degree: 3	Type: cirro-stratus
	2:00 P.M.	Degree: 10	Type: cirro-stratus
	9:00 P.M.	Degree: 0	Type: 0
Wind	7:00 A.M.	Direction: N	Force: 2
	2:00 P.M.	Direction: 0	Force: 0
	9:00 P.M.	Direction: 0	Force: 0
Barometer	7:00 A.M.: 30.095	2:00 P.M.: 30.078	9:00 P.M.: 30.113

Firsthand Observations

HAGERSTOWN TO TURNER'S GAP AREA

Longstreet's Command:

"Hot day and troops tired." Harpers Ferry area.[56]
"The day was hot and the road dusty." Harpers Ferry area.[57]
"We marched . . . over a hot and dusty road." Harpers Ferry area.[58]

Jackson's Command:

"We had a cold night on the mountain. . . . A warm day." Loudoun Heights to Keyes Ford.[59]

McLaws's Command:

"Cloudy and cool." Maryland Heights.[60]

Monday, September 15

Almanac

Sunrise: 5:50 A.M.
Sunset: 6:10 P.M.
Moon's phase: last quarter

Frederick Weather Station

Temperature	7:00 A.M.: 62.5°		
	2:00 P.M.: 79.0°		
	9:00 P.M.: 71.0°		
Precipitation	Time:	Amount:	
Clouds	7:00 A.M.	Degree: 2	Type: cumulo-stratus
	2:00 P.M.	Degree: 5	Type: cumulus
	9:00 P.M.	Degree: 0	Type: 0
Wind	7:00 A.M.	Direction: 0	Force: 0
	2:00 P.M.	Direction: NW	Force: 1
	9:00 P.M.	Direction: 0	Force: 0
Barometer	7:00 A.M.: 30.050	2:00 P.M.: 29.950	9:00 P.M.: 29.885

Firsthand Observations

HARPERS FERRY AREA

Jackson's Command:

"The morning was still and clear." Harpers Ferry.[61]

McLaws's Command:

"Clear and warm." Maryland Heights.[62]

Walker's Division:

". . . smoke and fog. . . . A very warm day, and quite dusty." Keyes Ford to Harpers Ferry to Charlestown.[63]

"Owing to a heavy mist, which concealed Harper's Ferry from view, we did not open fire until after 8 o'clock." Loudoun Heights.[64]

". . . the enemy's position was entirely concealed by a dense fog clinging to the sides of the mountain far below." Loudoun Heights.[65]

Tuesday, September 16

Almanac

Sunrise: 5:52 A.M.
Sunset: 6:08 P.M.
Moon's phase: one day after last quarter

Frederick Weather Station

Temperature	7:00 A.M.: 70.0°		
	2:00 P.M.: 75.0°		
	9:00 P.M.: 67.0°		
Precipitation	Time:	Amount:	
Clouds	7:00 A.M.	Degree: 10	Type: cirro-cumulus
	2:00 P.M.	Degree: 10	Type: cirro-stratus
	9:00 P.M.	Degree: 10	Type: nimbus
Wind	7:00 A.M.	Direction: N	Force: 3
	2:00 P.M.	Direction: NE	Force: 3
	9:00 P.M.	Direction: NE	Force: 2
Barometer	7:00 A.M.: 29.950	2:00 P.M.: 29.957	9:00 P.M.: 29.980

Firsthand Observations

SHARPSBURG AREA

Longstreet's Command:

Several veterans' anecdotes about heavy morning fog: Lee paces in it on Boonsboro Pike; Nelson Miles carries out scout across Antietam under its cover.[66]

"About nine a light rain began to fall and continued most of the night." Sharpsburg.[67]

"A light rain began to fall at nine o'clock." Sharpsburg.[68]

Stuart's Division:

"A fine drizzling rain, which began to fall about daybreak, wet us to the skin, and, chilled." Sharpsburg.[69]

HARPERS FERRY AREA

Jackson's Command:

"A very warm and dusty day." Charlestown to Harpers Ferry to Halltown.[70]

McLaws's Command:

"Cloudy and warm." Maryland Heights to Harpers Ferry and late to near Shepherdstown.[71]

"Cloudy and warm." Maryland Heights to Harpers Ferry and late to near Shepherdstown.[72]

Wednesday, September 17

Almanac

Sunrise: 5:53 A.M.
Sunset: 6:07 P.M.
Moon's phase: two days after last quarter

Frederick Weather Station

Temperature 7:00 A.M.: 65.0°
2:00 P.M.: 74.5°
9:00 P.M.: 69.5°

Precipitation	Time:	Amount:	
Clouds	7:00 A.M.	Degree: 10	Type: nimbus
	2:00 P.M.	Degree: 10	Type: cirro-stratus
	9:00 P.M.	Degree: 0	Type: 0
Wind	7:00 A.M.	Direction: NE	Force: 2
	2:00 P.M.	Direction: W	Force: 2
	9:00 P.M.	Direction: 0	Force: 0
Barometer	7:00 A.M.: 29.957	2:00 P.M.: 29.902	9:00 P.M.: 29.887

Firsthand Observations

SHARPSBURG AREA

D. H. Hill's Division:

"I often looked at the sun and longed for night to come." Sharpsburg.[73]

"The day was clear and beautiful, with scarcely a cloud in the sky." Sharpsburg.[74]

McLaws's Division:

"Clear and warm." Boteler's Ford to Sharpsburg.[75]

Walker's Division:

Shell falls in midst of 49th N.C. (Ransom), killing and wounding 13; coming from east of Antietam, men thought signal station directed it by "bayonets, glistening in the setting sunset."[76]

HARPERS FERRY AREA

Jackson's Command:

"The day was very warm and the dust excessive." Halltown to Charlestown to Shepherdstown.[77]

Thursday, September 18

Almanac

Sunrise: 5:54 A.M.
Sunset: 6:06 P.M.
Moon's phase: three days after last quarter

Frederick Weather Station

Temperature	7:00 A.M.: 71.0		
	2:00 P.M.: 79.0		
	9:00 P.M.: 72.5		
Precipitation	Time: 5:15 to 6:.00 P.M.		Amount: 0.156 inches
Clouds	7:00 A.M.	Degree: 10	Type: cumulo-stratus
	2:00 P.M.	Degree: 8	Type: cirro-cumulus
	9:00 P.M.	Degree: 0	Type: 0
Wind	7:00 A.M.	Direction: SW	Force: 3
	2:00 P.M.	Direction: SW	Force: 2
	9:00 P.M.	Direction: 0	Force: 0
Barometer	7:00 A.M.: 29.850	2:00 P.M.: 29.758	9:00 P.M.: 29.785

Firsthand Observations

SHARPSBURG AREA

Longstreet's Command:

"The fog was dense, and the camp-fires burning alongside the road were blinding. . . . I rode away in the fog." Sharpsburg, implied between 9 and midnight.[78]

Jackson's Command:

"The day was quite warm until the P.M. when there was a heavy thunder storm." Shepherdstown to Sharpsburg; reconnaissance up Potomac.[79]

McLaws's Division:

"Cloudy and raining." [See entry for Sept. 19.] Sharpsburg to Boteler's Ford.[80]

Walker's Division:

"It rained all next day." Sharpsburg.[81]

Stuart's Division:

"A fine rain, which had been falling all evening." Sharpsburg.[82]

". . . it was very dark and a heavy fog arose from the river, wrapping everything in an impenetrable veil of mist." Potomac River.[83]

Friday, September 19

Almanac

Sunrise: 5:56 A.M.
Sunset: 6:04 P.M.
Moon's phase: four days before new moon

Frederick Weather Station

Temperature	7:00 A.M.: 66.0°		
	2:00 P.M.: 75.5°		
	9:00 P.M.: 65.5°		
Precipitation	Time:	Amount:	
Clouds	7:00 A.M.	Degree: 1	Type: cirrus
	2:00 P.M.	Degree: 4	Type: cirro-cumulus
	9:00 P.M.	Degree: 0	Type: 0
Wind	7:00 A.M.	Direction: 0	Force: 0
	2:00 P.M.	Direction: W	Force: 2
	9:00 P.M.	Direction: 0	Force: 0
Barometer	7:00 A.M.: 29.880	2:00 P.M.: 29.890	9:00 P.M.: 29.950

Firsthand Observations

SHEPHERDSTOWN TO MARTINSBURG AREA

Jackson's Command:

Army crossed Potomac by 8 A.M., "having been covered by the fog." Shepherdstown to 3 miles in the direction of Martinsburg.

"A fine warm day." Shepherdstown to 3 miles in the direction of Martinsburg.[84]

McLaws's Division:

"Rained last night very hard." Boteler's Ford to within 2 miles of Martinsburg.[85]

Saturday, September 20

Almanac

Sunrise: 5:57 A.M.
Sunset: 6:03 P.M.
Moon's phase: three days before new moon

Frederick Weather Station

Temperature	7:00 A.M.: 62.5°		
	2:00 P.M.: 74.0°		
	9:00 P.M.: 66.0°		
Precipitation	Time:	Amount:	
Clouds	7:00 A.M.	Degree: 10	Type: cirro-stratus
	2:00 P.M.	Degree: 10	Type: nimbus
	9:00 P.M.	Degree: 0	Type: 0
Wind	7:00 A.M.	Direction: NE	Force: 3
	2:00 P.M.	Direction: NE	Force: 1
	9:00 P.M.	Direction: 0	Force: 0
Barometer	7:00 A.M.: 29.953	2:00 P.M.: 29.915	9:00 P.M.: 29.944

Firsthand Observations

MARTINSBURG AREA

Jackson's Command:

"The day was very pleasant." From camp to Martinsburg and toward Williamsport to where road from Tabler's Mill joins turnpike.[86]

McLaws's Division:

"Clear and warm." From camp to crossroads with Winchester turnpike; then back to camp.[87]

Sunday, September 21

Almanac

Sunrise: 5:58 A.M.
Sunset: 6:02 P.M.
Moon's phase: two days before new moon

Frederick Weather Station

Temperature	7:00 A.M.: 57.5°		
	2:00 P.M.: 65.0°		
	9:00 P.M.: 63.5°		
Precipitation	Time:	Amount:	
Clouds	7:00 A.M.	Degree: 3	Type: cirro-stratus
	2:00 P.M.	Degree: 0	Type: 0
	9:00 P.M.	Degree: 0	Type: 0
Wind	7:00 A.M.	Direction: W	Force: 1
	2:00 P.M.	Direction: NE	Force: 3
	9:00 P.M.	Direction: 0	Force: 0
Barometer	7:00 A.M.: 30.022	2:00 P.M.: 30.014	9:00 P.M.: 30.052

Firsthand Observations

MARTINSBURG AREA

McLaws's Division:

"Clear and warm." Marched to north bank of Opequon Creek.[88]

Monday, September 22

Almanac

Sunrise: 5:59 A.M.
Sunset: 6:01 P.M.
Moon's phase: one day before new moon

Frederick Weather Station

Temperature	7:00 A.M.: 56.5		
	2:00 P.M.: 73.0		
	9:00 P.M.: 62.0		
Precipitation	Time:	Amount:	
Clouds	7:00 A.M.	Degree: 0	Type: 0
	2:00 P.M.	Degree: 3	Type: cirro-cumulus
	9:00 P.M.	Degree: 0	Type: 0
Wind	7:00 A.M.	Direction: W	Force: 1
	2:00 P.M.	Direction: W	Force: 2
	9:00 P.M.	Direction: S	Force: 1
Barometer	7:00 A.M.: 30.075	2:00 P.M.: 30.045	9:00 P.M.: 30.058

Firsthand Observations

MARTINSBURG AREA

Jackson's Command:

"The days are getting quite cool." Second day at Tabler's Mill, on south bank of Opequon Creek.[89]

McLaws's Division:

"Clear and warm, night very cool." Camp on the Opequon.[90]

Tuesday, September 23

Almanac

Sunrise: 6:01 A.M.
Sunset: 5:59 P.M.
Moon's phase: new moon

Frederick Weather Station

Temperature	7:00 A.M.: 56.0°
	2:00 P.M.: 72.5°
	9:00 P.M.: 63.0°

Precipitation	Time:	Amount:	
Clouds	7:00 A.M.	Degree: 0	Type: 0
	2:00 P.M.	Degree: 0	Type: 0
	9:00 P.M.	Degree: 0	Type: 0
Wind	7:00 A.M.	Direction: 0	Force: 0
	2:00 P.M.	Direction: W	Force: 1
	9:00 P.M.	Direction: 0	Force: 0
Barometer	7:00 A.M.: 30.040	2:00 P.M.: 29.923	9:00 P.M.: 29.883

Firsthand Observations

MARTINSBURG AREA

Jackson's Command:

"A fine Sept. day." Tabler's Mill.[91]

McLaws's Division:

"Clear and warm." Moved camp to near Martinsburg Road.[92]

Wednesday, September 24

Almanac

Sunrise: 6:02 A.M.
Sunset: 5:58 P.M.
Moon's phase: one day after new moon

Frederick Weather Station

Temperature	7:00 A.M.: 58.0°		
	2:00 P.M.: 69.0°		
	9:00 P.M.: 60.5°		
Precipitation	Time: 11:00 A.M. to 1 P.M.		Amount: 0.230 inches
Clouds	7:00 A.M.	Degree: 1	Type: cirrus
	2:00 P.M.	Degree: 8	Type: cumulo-stratus
	9:00 P.M.	Degree: 1	Type: cirro-stratus

Wind	7:00 A.M.	Direction: W	Force: 1
	2:00 P.M.	Direction: W	Force: 1
	9:00 P.M.	Direction: 0	Force: 0
Barometer	7:00 A.M.: 29.695	2:00 P.M.: 29.695	9:00 P.M.: 29.850

Firsthand Observations

MARTINSBURG AREA

Jackson's Command:

"We had quite a shower in the P.M." Tabler's Mill to near Martinsburg.[93]

Thursday, September 25

Almanac

Sunrise: 6:03 A.M.
Sunset: 5:57 P.M.
Moon's phase: two days after new moon

Frederick Weather Station

Temperature	7:00 A.M.: 50.0°		
	2:00 P.M.: 63.0°		
	9:00 P.M.: 52.0°		
Precipitation	Time:	Amount:	
Clouds	7:00 A.M.	Degree: 0	Type: 0
	2:00 P.M.	Degree: 0	Type: 0
	9:00 P.M.	Degree: 0	Type: 0
Wind	7:00 A.M.	Direction: NW	Force: 2
	2:00 P.M.	Direction: SW	Force: 2
	9:00 P.M.	Direction: 0	Force: 0
Barometer	7:00 A.M.: 29.945	2:00 P.M.: 29.887	9:00 P.M.: 29.900

Firsthand Observations

MARTINSBURG AREA

Jackson's Command:

"It has been a delightful day." Camp near Martinsburg.[94]

Friday, September 26

Almanac

Sunrise: 6:04 A.M.
Sunset: 5:56 P.M.
Moon's phase: three days after new moon

Frederick Weather Station

Temperature	7:00 A.M.: 44.0°			
	2:00 P.M.: 65.0°			
	9:00 P.M.: 52.5°			
Precipitation	Time:	Amount:		
Clouds	7:00 A.M.	Degree: 0	Type: 0	
	2:00 P.M.	Degree: 0	Type: 0	
	9:00 P.M.	Degree: 0	Type: 0	
Wind	7:00 A.M.	Direction: W	Force: 1	
	2:00 P.M.	Direction: W	Force: 3	
	9:00 P.M.	Direction: 0	Force: 0	
Barometer	7:00 A.M.: 29.930	2:00 P.M.: 29.895		9:00 P.M.: 29.910

Firsthand Observations

MARTINSBURG AREA

Jackson's Command:

"Day cool and sad." Camp near Martinsburg.[95]

Saturday, September 27

Almanac

Sunrise: 6:06 A.M.
Sunset: 5:54 P.M.
Moon's phase: three days before first quarter

Frederick Weather Station

Temperature	7:00 A.M.: 45.0°		
	2:00 P.M.: 70.0°		
	9:00 P.M.: 64.5°		
Precipitation	Time:	Amount:	
Clouds	7:00 A.M.	Degree: 0	Type: 0
	2:00 P.M.	Degree: 6	Type: cirrus
	9:00 P.M.	Degree: 10	Type: cirrus
Wind	7:00 A.M.	Direction: 0	Force: 0
	2:00 P.M.	Direction: W	Force: 3
	9:00 P.M.	Direction: 0	Force: 0
Barometer	7:00 A.M.: 29.925	2:00 P.M.: 29.880	9:00 P.M.: 29.910

Firsthand Observations

MARTINSBURG AREA

Jackson's Command:

"Quite warm." From Martinsburg to Bunker's Hill.[96]

Sunday, September 28

Almanac

Sunrise: 6:07 A.M.
Sunset: 5:53 P.M.
Moon's phase: two days before first quarter

Frederick Weather Station

Temperature	7:00 A.M.: 62.5°		
	2:00 P.M.: 74.0°		
	9:00 P.M.: 63.5°		
Precipitation	Time:	Amount:	
Clouds	7:00 A.M.	Degree: 10	Type: cirro-stratus
	2:00 P.M.	Degree: 2	Type: cirrus
	9:00 P.M.	Degree: 0	Type: 0
Wind	7:00 A.M.	Direction: NE	Force: 3
	2:00 P.M.	Direction: W	Force: 2
	9:00 P.M.	Direction: 0	Force: 0
Barometer	7:00 A.M.: 29.840	2:00 P.M.: 29.728	9:00 P.M.: 29.738

Firsthand Observations

BUNKER HILL AREA

Jackson's Command:

"A fine day." Bunker Hill.[97]

Monday, September 29

Almanac

Sunrise: 6:08 A.M.
Sunset: 5:52 P.M.
Moon's phase: one day before first quarter

Frederick Weather Station

Temperature	7:00 A.M.: 55.5°		
	2:00 P.M.: 75.0°		
	9:00 P.M.: 68.5°		
Precipitation	Time:	Amount:	
Clouds	7:00 A.M.	Degree: 0	Type: 0
	2:00 P.M.	Degree: 5	Type: cirrus
	9:00 P.M.	Degree: 4	Type: cirro-stratus

Wind	7:00 A.M.	Direction: 0	Force: 0	
	2:00 P.M.	Direction: NW	Force: 3	
	9:00 P.M.	Direction: W	Force: 1	
Barometer	7:00 A.M.: 29.733	2:00 P.M.: 29.720		9:00 P.M.: 29.762

First-hand Observations

WINCHESTER AREA

Jackson's Command:

"Very warm, dry and dusty." Bunker Hill to Winchester and back.[98]

Tuesday, September 30

Almanac

Sunrise: 6:10 A.M.
Sunset: 5:50 P.M.
Moon's phase: first quarter

Frederick Weather Station

Temperature	7:00 A.M.: 61.0°		
	2:00 P.M.: 78.0°		
	9:00 P.M.: 69.5°		
Precipitation	Time:	Amount:	
Clouds	7:00 A.M.	Degree: 5	Type: cirrus
	2:00 P.M.	Degree: 4	Type: cirrus
	9:00 P.M.	Degree: 8	Type: cirro-stratus
Wind	7:00 A.M.	Direction: NW	Force: 1
	2:00 P.M.	Direction: W	Force: 2
	9:00 P.M.	Direction: W	Force: 1
Barometer	7:00 A.M.: 29.860	2:00 P.M.: 29.850	9:00 P.M.: 29.935

Firsthand Observations

WINCHESTER AREA

Jackson's Command:

". . . a fine day." Winchester and vicinity.[99]

CHAPTER TWO

Organization of the Army of Northern Virginia in the Maryland Campaign, September 2–22, 1862

Introduction

Since annotated commentary immediately follows, the organization of this material has not been cluttered with notes. The basic structure and information for the table is from Carman, "Maryland Campaign," chapter 11. Carman himself had expanded and amended the table in *OR*, vol. 19, 1:803–10.

The table presented here differs even from Carman, however, in the following respects. (1) The army is divided into thirds, not halves Substantial evidence indicates that the divisions of D. H. Hill, R. H. Anderson, McLaws, and Walker were not incorporated into the commands of Longstreet and Jackson until the close of the campaign. (2) Forty-five problematic units (i.e., some questions exist about the units' presence) have been included in square brackets. The information covered about each is included in the commentary at the appropriate place. Also, a checklist of such units may be found in Table 2 in chapter 3. (3) Included is fuller information on unit commanders: additional individuals, additional notes on the commanders' fates in the campaign, and, wherever possible, full names replacing the intitials used by Carman. This information has been taken from Krick, *Lee's Colonels: A Biographical Register of the Field Officers of the Army of Northern Virginia*, 3d rev. ed. (Dayton, Ohio: Morningside Bookshop, 1991); William C. Davis, ed., *The Confederate Generals*, 6 vols. (N.p.: National Historical Society, 1991); and Lee A. Wallace, Jr., *A Guide to Virginia Military Organizations, 1861–1865*, 2d rev. ed. (Lynchburg: H. E. Howard, Inc., 1986). (4) The number of companies in units smaller than regiments has been taken from Joseph H. Crute, Jr., *Units of the Confederate States Army* (Midlothian, Va.: Derwent Books, 1987).

Army of Northern Virginia in the Maryland Campaign, September 2–22, 1862

Gen. Robert Edward Lee, commanding

Longstreet's Command

Maj. Gen. James Longstreet, commanding
Escort: Independent Company, South Carolina Cavalry, Capt. James Doby

D. R. JONES'S DIVISION

Brig. Gen. David Rumph Jones

Toombs's Brigade

Brig. Gen. Robert Augustus Toombs (injured 9/18)
Col. Henry Lewis Benning
2d Georgia, Lt. Col. William R. Holmes (killed 9/17)
Maj. James Alpheus Skidmore Harris (wounded 9/17)
Capt. Abner McCoy Lewis
15th Georgia, Col. William Terrell Millican (mortally wounded 9/17)
Capt. Thomas H. Jackson
17th Georgia, Capt. J. A. McGregor (*vice* Benning)
20th Georgia, Col. John B. Cumming

G. T. Anderson's Brigade

Col. George Thomas Anderson
1st Georgia (Regulars), Col. William Joseph Magill (wounded 9/17)
Capt. Richard Alexander Wayne
7th Georgia, Col. George H. Carmical
8th Georgia, Col. John R. Towers
9th Georgia, Lt. Col. John Clark L. Mounger (wounded 9/17)
11th Georgia, Maj. Francis Hamilton Little
Capt. Joseph S. Stokes (commanding left wing of regiment at Martinsburg 9/17)

Drayton's Brigade

Brig. Gen. Thomas Fenwick Drayton

50th Georgia, Lt. Col. Francis Kearse
51st Georgia
15th South Carolina, Col. William Davie DeSaussure
[3d South Carolina Battalion (7 companies), Maj. George Sholter James (killed 9/14)]
[Phillips's Georgia Legion (9 companies)]

Kemper's Brigade

Brig. Gen. James Lawson Kemper
1st Virginia, Capt. George F. Newton
Maj. William Hanery Palmer
7th Virginia, Maj. Arthur Herbert (17th Virginia)
Capt. Philip S. Ashby
11th Virginia, Maj. Adam Clement (wounded 9/14)
17th Virginia, Col. Montgomery Dent Corse (wounded 9/17)
24th Virginia, Col. William Richard Terry

Jenkins's Brigade

Col. Joseph Walker
1st South Carolina (Volunteers), Lt. Col. Daniel Livingston (wounded 9/17)
2d South Carolina Rifles, Lt. Col. Robert Anderson Thompson
5th South Carolina, Capt. Thomas Chisholm Beckham
6th South Carolina, Capt. E. B. Cantey (wounded 9/17)
4th South Carolina Battalion (5 companies), Lt. W. T. Field
Palmetto (S.C.) Sharpshooters (12 companies), Capt. A. H. Foster (wounded 9/17)
Capt. F. W. Kirkpatrick

Pickett's Brigade

Col. Eppa Hunton
Brig. Gen. Richard Brooke Garnett
8th Virginia, Col. Eppa Hunton
18th Virginia, Maj. George Craighead Cabell
19th Virginia, Col. John Bowie Strange (killed 9/14)
Lt. William Nathaniel Wood (adjutant)
Capt. J. L. Cochran
Capt. B. Brown

28th Virginia, Capt. William Lewis Wingfield
56th Virginia, Col. William Dabney Stuart
Capt. John Blair McPhail, Jr. (wounded 9/14)

Artillery

[Fauquier (Va.) Artillery, Capt. Robert Mackey Stribling]
[Goochland (Va.) Artillery, Capt. Walter D. Leake]
[Loudoun (Va.) Artillery, Capt. Arthur Lee Rogers]
Wise (Va.) Artillery, Capt. James S. Brown (wounded 9/17)

HOOD'S DIVISION

Brig. Gen. John Bell Hood

Hood's Brigade

Col. William Tatum Wofford
18th Georgia, Lt. Col. Solon Zackary Ruff
Hampton (S.C.) Legion, Lt. Col. Martin Witherspoon Gary
1st Texas, Lt. Col. Philip Alexander Work
4th Texas, Lt. Col. Benjamin F. Carter
5th Texas, Capt. Ike N. M. Turner

Law's Brigade

Col. Evander McIvor Law
4th Alabama, Lt. Col. Owen Kenan McLemore (mortally wounded 9/14)
Capt. Lawrence Houston Scruggs (wounded 9/17)
Capt. William McKendree Robbins
2d Mississippi, Col. John Marshall Stone (wounded 9/17)
Lt. Moody
11th Mississippi, Col. Philip Frank Lidell (mortally wounded 9/16)
Lt. Col. Samuel Butler (mortally wounded 9/17)
Maj. Taliaferro Sidney Evans (killed 9/17)
6th North Carolina, Maj. Robert Fulton Webb (wounded 9/17)

Artillery

Maj. Bushrod Washington Frobel
German (S.C.) Artillery, Capt. William K. Bachman
Palmetto (S.C.) Artillery, Capt. Hugh R. Garden
Rowan (N.C.) Artillery, Capt. James Reilly

EVANS'S DIVISION

Brig. Gen. Nathan George Evans

Evans's Brigade

Col. Peter Fayssoux Stevens (wounded 9/17)
17th South Carolina, Col. Fitz William McMaster
18th South Carolina, Col. William Henry Wallace
22d South Carolina, Lt. Col. Thomas C. Watkins (mortally wounded 9/14)
Maj. Miel Hilton
23d South Carolina, Capt. S. A. Durham (wounded 9/14)
Lt. E. R. White
Holcombe (S.C.) Legion, Col. Peter Fayssoux Stevens (wounded 9/17)
Macbeth (S.C.) Artillery, Capt. Robert Boyce

Longstreet's Artillery Reserve
Washington (La.) Artillery
Col. James Burdge Walton
1st Company, Capt. Charles Winder Squires
2d Company, Capt. John B. Richardson
3d Company, Capt. Merritt Buchanan Miller
4th Company, Capt. Benjamin Franklin Eshleman

Jackson's Command

Maj. Gen. Thomas Jonathan Jackson, commanding
Escort: Company H, 4th Virginia Cavalry (Black Horse Troop), Capt. Robert Randolph
White's Virginia Cavalry (3 companies), Capt. Elijah Viers White

JACKSON'S (STONEWALL) DIVISION

Brig. Gen. John Robert Jones (wounded 9/17)
Brig. Gen. William Edwin Starke (killed 9/17)
Col. Andrew Jackson Grigsby

Stonewall (Winder's) Brigade

Col. Andrew Jackson Grigsby (27th Va.)
Lt. Col. Robert Davison Gardner (wounded 9/17)
Maj. Hazael Joseph Williams
2d Virginia, Capt. Raleigh Thomas Colston
4th Virginia, Lt. Col. Robert Davison Gardner
5th Virginia, Maj. Hazael Joseph Williams
Capt. E. L. Curtis (wounded 9/17)
27th Virginia, Capt. Frank C. Wilson
33d Virginia, Capt. Jacob Burner Golladay (wounded 9/17)

J. R. Jones's Brigade

Col. Bradley Tyler Johnson
Brig. Gen. John Robert Jones
Capt. John Edmund Penn (42d Va.; wounded 9/17)
Capt. A. C. Page (wounded 9/17)
Capt. Robert Woodson Withers
21st Virginia, Capt. A. C. Page
42d Virginia, Capt. Robert Woodson Withers
Capt. D. W. Garrett
48th Virginia, Capt. John H. Candler
1st (Irish) Virginia Battalion (5 companies), Lt. C. A. Davidson

Taliaferro's Brigade

Col. Edward Tiffin Harrison Warren (10th Va.)
Col. James W. Jackson (wounded 9/17)
Col. James Lawrence Sheffield
47th Alabama, Col. James W. Jackson
Maj. James McDonald Campbell
48th Alabama, Col. James Lawrence Sheffield
10th Virginia
23d Virginia
37th Virginia, Lt. Col. John F. Terry (wounded 9/17)

Starke's Brigade

Brig. Gen. William Edwin Starke (killed 9/17)
Col. Jesse Milton Williams (wounded 9/17)

Col. Leroy Augustus Stafford (wounded 9/17)
Col. Edmund Pendleton
1st Louisiana, Lt. Col. Michael Nolan (wounded 9/17)
Capt. W. E. Moore
2d Louisiana, Col. Jesse Milton Williams
9th Louisiana, Col. Leroy Augustus Stafford
Lt. Col. William Raine Peck
10th Louisiana, Capt. Henry D. Monier
15th Louisiana, Col. Edmund Pendleton
Coppens's (1st Zouave, La.) Battalion (6 companies)

Artillery

Maj. Lindsay Mayo Shumaker
Alleghany (Va.) Artillery, Capt. Joseph Carpenter
Baltimore (Md.) Artillery, Capt. John Bowyer Brockenbrough
Danville (Va.) Artillery, Capt. George Washington Wooding
Eighth Star (Va.) Artillery, Capt. William H. Rice
Hampden (Va.) Artillery, Capt. William Henderson Caskie
Lee (Va.) Artillery, Capt. Charles J. Raine
Rockbridge (Va.) Artillery, Capt. William Thomas Poague
Lt. Archibald Graham
Winchester (Va.) Artillery, Capt. Wilfred Emory Cutshaw

EWELL'S DIVISION

Brig. Gen. Alexander Robert Lawton (wounded 9/17)
Brig. Gen. Jubal Anderson Early

Early's Brigade

Brig. Gen. Jubal Anderson Early
Col. William Smith (wounded 9/17)
13th Virginia, Capt. F. V. Winton
25th Virginia, Capt. R. D. Lilley
31st Virginia
44th Virginia, Capt. David W. Anderson (wounded 9/17)
49th Virginia, Col. William Smith (wounded 9/17)
Lt. Col. Jonathan Catlett Gibson (wounded 9/17)
52d Virginia, Col. Michael Garber Harmon
58th Virginia

Trimble's Brigade

Capt. W. F. Brown (commanding at Chantilly; killed 9/1)
Col. James Alexander Walker (13th Va.; wounded 9/17)
15th Alabama, Capt. Isaac Ball Feagin (wounded 9/19)
12th Georgia, Capt. James G. Rodgers (killed 9/17)
Capt. John Thomas Carson
21st Georgia, Maj. Thomas Coke Glover (wounded 9/17)
Capt. James Cooper Nisbit
21st North Carolina, Capt. F. P. Miller (killed 9/17)
1st North Carolina Battalion (2 companies of sharpshooters; attached to 21st N.C.)

Hays's Brigade

Brig. Gen. Harry Thompson Hays
5th Louisiana, Col. Henry Forno
6th Louisiana, Col. Henry B. Strong (killed 9/17)
7th Louisiana
8th Louisiana, Lt. Col. Trevanion D. Lewis (wounded 9/17)
14th Louisiana

Lawton's Brigade

Col. Marcellus Douglass (13th Ga.; killed 9/17)
Maj. John Hollinger Lowe
Col. John Hill Lamar (31st Ga.)
13th Georgia, Capt. D. A. Kidd
26th Georgia
31st Georgia, Lt. Col. John Terrell Crowder (wounded 9/17)
Maj.. John Hollinger Lowe
38th Georgia, Capt. W. H. Battey (killed 9/17)
Capt. Peter Brennan
Capt. John W. McCardy
60th Georgia, Maj. Waters Burras Jones
61st Georgia, Maj. Archibald Philip McRae (killed 9/17)

Artillery

Maj. Alfred Ranson Courtney
[Charlottesville (Va.) Artillery, Capt. James McDowell Carrington]
Chesapeake (Md.) Artillery, Capt. William Brown

Courtney (Va.) Artillery, Capt. Joseph White Latimer
Johnson's (Va.) battery, Capt. John R. Johnson
Louisiana Guard Artillery, Capt. Louis E. D'Aquin
1st Maryland Battery, Capt. William F. Dement
Staunton (Va.) Artillery (Balthis's battery), Lt. Asher W. Garbor

A. P. HILL'S (LIGHT) DIVISION

Brig. Gen. Lawrence O'Bryan Branch (while Hill was under arrest)
Maj. Gen. Ambrose Powell Hill
Escort (company of Cobb Legion): Capt. G. J. Wright, Lt. C. H. Camfield

Branch's Brigade

Brig. Gen. Lawrence O'Bryan Branch (killed 9/17)
Col. James Henry Lane
7th North Carolina, Col. Edward Graham Haywood
18th North Carolina, Lt. Col. Thomas James Purdie
28th North Carolina, Col. James Henry Lane
Maj. William James Montgomery
33d North Carolina, Lt. Col. Robert Frederick Hoke
37th North Carolina, Capt. William Groves Morris

Archer's Brigade

Brig. Gen. James Jay Archer (ill 9/17)
Col. Peter Turney
5th Alabama Battalion (6 companies), Capt. Charles M. Hooper
19th Georgia, Maj. James Henry Neal
Capt. Tilghman Willis Flynt (wounded 9/17)
Capt. F. M. Johnston
1st Tennessee (Provisional Army), Col. Peter Turney
7th Tennessee, Maj. Samuel G. Shepard
Lt. G. A. Howard
14th Tennessee, Col. William McComb (wounded 9/17)
Lt. Col. James W. Lockert

Gregg's Brigade

Brig. Gen. Maxcy Gregg (wounded 9/17)
1st South Carolina (Provisional Army), Maj. Edward McCrady, Jr., Col. Daniel Heyward Hamilton, Sr.

1st South Carolina Rifles, Lt. Col. James Monroe Perrin (wounded 9/17)
12th South Carolina, Col. Dixon Barnes (mortally wounded 9/17)
Lt. Col. Cadwallader Jones
Maj. William Hart McCorkle
13th South Carolina, Col. Oliver Evans Edwards
14th South Carolina, Lt. Col. William Dunlap Simpson

Pender's Brigade

Brig. Gen. William Dorsey Pender
[Lt. Richard Henry Brewer]
16th North Carolina, Lt. Col. William A. Stowe
22d North Carolina, Maj. Christopher Columbus Cole
34th North Carolina, Lt. Col. John Lewis McDowell
38th North Carolina

Field's Brigade

Col. John Mercer Brockenbrough
40th Virginia, Lt. Col. Fleet William Cox
47th Virginia, Lt. Col. John Warner Lyell
55th Virginia, Maj. Charles Nicholas Lawson
22d Virginia Battalion (6 companies), Maj. Edward Poinsett Tayloe

Thomas's Brigade

Col. Edward Lloyd Thomas
14th Georgia, Col. Robert Warren Folsom
35th Georgia
45th Georgia, Maj. Washington Leonidas Grice
49th Georgia [Lt. Col. Seaborn M. Manning]

Artillery

Maj. Reuben Lindsay Walker
[Branch (N.C.) Artillery, Capt. A. C. Latham]
Crenshaw's (Va.) battery, Capt. William G. Crenshaw
Fredericksburg (Va.) Artillery, Capt. Carter Moore Braxton
Letcher (Va.) Artillery, Capt. Greenlee Davidson
[Middlesex (Va.) Artillery, Capt. William C. Fleet]
Pee Dee (S.C.) Artillery, Capt. David Gregg McIntosh
Purcell (Va.) Artillery, Capt. William Johnson Pegram

Unattached Divisions

R. H. ANDERSON'S DIVISION

Maj. Gen. Richard Heron Anderson (wounded 9/17)
Brig. Gen. Roger Atkinson Pryor

Armistead's Brigade

Brig. Gen. Lewis Addison Armistead (wounded 9/17)
Col. James Gregory Hodges
9th Virginia, Capt. William James Richardson
Capt. James Jasper Phillips
14th Virginia, Col. James Gregory Hodges
38th Virginia, Col. Edward Claxton Edmonds
53d Virginia, Capt. W. G. Pollard (killed 9/17)
Capt. Harwood
57th Virginia
[5th Virginia Battalion]

Mahone's Brigade

Lt. Col. William Allen Parham
6th Virginia, Capt. John R. Ludlow
12th Virginia, Capt. John Richard Lewellen (wounded 9/14)
16th Virginia, Maj. Francis David Holliday (captured 9/14)
41st Virginia
[61st Virginia]

Wright's Brigade

Brig. Gen. Ambrose Ransom Wright (wounded 9/17)
Col. Robert Harris Jones (wounded 9/17)
Col. William Gibson
44th Alabama, Lt. Col. Charles Alexander Derby (killed 9/17)
Maj. William Flank Perry
3d Georgia, Capt. Reuben Battle Nisbit (wounded and captured 9/17)
Capt. John T. Jones
22d Georgia, Col. Robert Harris Jones
Capt. Lawrence D. Lallerstedt (wounded 9/17)
48th Georgia, Col. William Gibson

Wilcox's Brigade

Brig. Gen. Cadmus Marcellus Wilcox
Col. Alfred Cumming (10th Ga.; wounded 9/17)
Maj. Hilary Abner Herbert
Capt. James McCullough Crow

8th Alabama, Maj. Hilary Abner Herbert

9th Alabama, Maj. Jeremiah Henry Johnston (wounded 9/17)
Capt. James McCullough Crow
Lt. A. C. Chisholm

10th Alabama, Capt. G. C. Whatley (killed 9/17)

11th Alabama, Maj. Jno. Christopher Columbus Sanders

Pryor's Brigade

Brig. Gen. Roger Atkinson Pryor
Col. John C. Hately (wounded 9/17)

14th Alabama, Maj. James Andrew Broome

2d Florida, Col. William Duncan Ballantine (wounded 9/17)
Lt. Geiger

5th Florida, Col. John C. Hately
Lt. Col. Thomas Bird Lamar (wounded 9/17)
Maj. Benjamin F. Davis

8th Florida, Lt. Col. Georges Auguste Gaston Coppens (Louisiana Zouave Battalion; killed 9/17)
Capt. Richard A. Waller (killed 9/17)
Capt. William Baya

3d Virginia, Col. Joseph Mayo, Jr. (wounded 9/17)
Lt. Col. Alexander Daniel Callcote

Featherston's Brigade

Brig. Gen. Winfield Scott Featherston
Col. Carnot Posey (16th Miss.)

12th Mississippi, Col. William H. Taylor

16th Mississippi, Capt. Abram Morrell Feltus

19th Mississippi, Col. Nathaniel Harrison Harris (wounded 9/17)

2d Mississippi Battalion (6 companies), Maj. William Sydney Wilson (mortally wounded 9/17)

Artillery

Maj. John Seldon Saunders
Dixie (Va.) Artillery, Capt. William Henry Chapman
Donaldsonville (La.) Artillery, Capt. Victor Maurin
Moorman's (Va.) battery, Capt. Marcellus Newton Moorman
Norfolk (Va.) Artillery, Capt. Frank Huger
Lt. C. R. Phelps
Portsmouth (Va.) Artillery, Capt. Cary F. Grimes (killed 9/17)
[Thomas (Va.) Artillery, Capt. Edwin J. Anderson]

D. H. HILL'S DIVISION

Maj. Gen. Daniel Harvey Hill

Rodes's Brigade

Brig. Gen. Robert Emmett Rodes (wounded 9/17)
3d Alabama, Col. Cullen Andrews Battle
5th Alabama, Maj. Edwin Lafayette Hobson
6th Alabama, Col. John Brown Gordon (wounded 9/17)
Lt. Col. James Newell Lightfoot (wounded 9/17)
12th Alabama, Col. Bristor B. Gayle (killed 9/14)
Lt. Col. Samuel Bonneau Pickens (wounded 9/14)
Capt. Tucker (killed 9/17)
Capt. Maroney (wounded 9/17)
Capt. Adolph Proskauer (wounded 9/17)
26th Alabama, Col. Edward Asbury O'Neal (wounded 9/17)

G. B. Anderson's Brigade

Brig. Gen. George Burgwyn Anderson (mortally wounded 9/17)
Col. Charles Courtenay Tew (killed 9/17)
Col. Risden Tyler Bennett (wounded 9/17)
2d North Carolina, Col. Charles Courtenay Tew (killed 9/17)
Maj. John Howard (wounded 9/17)
Capt. G. M. Roberts
4th North Carolina, Col. Bryan Grimes
Capt. W. T. Marsh (killed 9/17)
Capt. Edwin Augustus Osborne (wounded 9/17; POW)
Capt. D. P. Latham (killed 9/17)

14th North Carolina, Col. Risden Tyler Bennett
Lt. Col. William A. Johnston (wounded 9/17)
Maj. A. J. Griffith (not in Krick)
30th North Carolina, Col. Francis Marion Parker (wounded 9/17)
Maj. William Walter Sillers

Garland's Brigade

Brig. Gen. Samuel Garland, Jr. (killed 9/14)
Col. Duncan Kirkland McRae (wounded 9/17; Krick says wounded 9/14)
5th North Carolina, Col. Duncan Kirkland McRae
Capt. Thomas Miles Garrett (wounded 9/17)
12th North Carolina, Capt. S. Snow
13th North Carolina, Lt. Col. Thomas Ruffin, Jr. (wounded 9/14)
Capt. Joseph Henry Hyman
20th North Carolina, Col. Alfred Iverson
23d North Carolina, Col. Daniel Harvey Christie

Rains's Brigade

Col. Alfred Holt Colquitt (6th Ga.)
13th Alabama, Col. Birkett Davenport Fry (wounded 9/17)
Maj. A. S. Reaves (wounded 9/17; not in Krick)
6th Georgia, Lt. Col. James Mitchell Newton (killed 9/17)
Maj. Philemon Tracy (mortally wounded in thigh 9/17)
Lt. E. P. Bennett
23d Georgia, Col. William P. Barclay (killed 9/17)
Lt. Col. Emory Fiske Best (wounded 9/17)
Maj. James Howard Huggins (wounded 9/17; Krick says wounded in both legs at South Mountain)
27th Georgia, Col. Levi Beck Smith (killed 9/17)
Lt. Col. Charles Thorton Zachry (wounded 9/17)
Capt. William H. Rentfro
28th Georgia, Maj. Tully Graybill (wounded 9/17)
Capt. N. J. Garrison (wounded 9/17)
Capt. G. W. Warthen

Ripley's Brigade

Brig. Gen. Roswell Sabine Ripley (wounded 9/17)
Col. George Pierce Doles

4th Georgia, Col. George Pierce Doles
  Maj. Robert S. Smith (killed 9/17)
  Capt. William Henry Willis
44th Georgia, Capt. John Calhoun Key
1st North Carolina, Lt. Col. Hamilton Allen Brown
3d North Carolina, Col. William Lord DeRosset (wounded 9/17)
  Maj. Stephen Decater Thruston (wounded 9/17)

Artillery

Maj. Scipio Francis Pierson
Hardaway's (Ala.) battery, Capt. Robert Archelaus Hardaway
Lt. John W. Tullis
Jeff. Davis (Ala.) Artillery, Capt. James William Bondurant
King William (Va.) Artillery, Capt. Thomas Henry Carter
[Peninsula (Va.) Artillery, Capt. William B. Jones]

MCLAWS'S DIVISION

  Maj. Gen. LaFayette McLaws

Semmes's Brigade

  Brig. Gen. Paul Jones Semmes
10th Georgia, Maj. Willis Cox Holt (wounded in head 9/17)
  Capt. William Johnston (wounded 9/17)
  Capt. Philologus H. Loud (wounded in head 9/17)
53d Georgia, Lt. Col. Thomas Sloan (mortally wounded 9/17)
  Capt. S. W. Marshborne
15th Virginia, Capt. Emmett Masalon Morrison (wounded and POW 9/17)
  Capt. Edward J. Willis
32d Virginia, Col. Edgar Burwell Montague

Cobb's Brigade

  Brig. Gen. Howell Cobb
  Lt. Col. Christopher Columbus Sanders (24th Ga.)
  Lt. Col. William McRae
16th Georgia, Lt. Col. Henry Philip Thomas
24th Georgia, Maj. Robert Emmett McMillan (wounded in leg 9/17)
Cobb's (Ga.) Legion (7 companies), Lt. Col. Luther Judson Glenn
15th North Carolina, Lt. Col. William McRae

Barksdale's Brigade

Brig. Gen. William Barksdale
13th Mississippi, Lt. Col. Kennon McElroy (wounded 9/15)
17th Mississippi, Lt. Col. John Calvin Fizer
18th Mississippi, Maj. James Charles Campbell (wounded 9/17)
Lt. Col. William Henry Luse
21st Mississippi, Capt. John Sims
Col. Benjamin Grubb Humphreys

Kershaw's Brigade

Brig. Gen. Joseph Brevard Kershaw
2d South Carolina, Col. John Doby Kennedy (wounded 9/17)
Maj. Franklin Gaillard
3d South Carolina, Col. James Drayton Nance
7th South Carolina, Col. David Wyatt Aiken (wounded 9/17)
Capt. John Stewart Hard
8th South Carolina, Lt. Col. Axalla John Hoole

Artillery

Maj. Samuel Prioleau Hamilton
Col. Henry Coalter Cabell
A, 1st N.C. Artillery, Capt. Basil Charles Manly
Magruder (Va.) Artillery, Capt. Thomas Jefferson Page, Jr.
Pulaski (Ga.) Artillery, Capt. John Postell Williamson Read
Richmond (Fayette) Artillery, Capt. Miles C. Macon
Lt. William Izard Clopton
Richmond (Va.) Howitzers, 1st Co., Capt. Edward S. McCarthy
Troup (Ga.) Artillery, Capt. Henry H. Carlton

WALKER'S DIVISION

Brig. Gen. John George Walker

Walker's Brigade

Col. Vannoy Hartrog Manning (3d Ark.; wounded 9/17)
Col. Edward Dudley Hall
3d Arkansas, Capt. John W. Reedy
[2d Georgia Battalion]
27th North Carolina, Col. John Rogers Cooke

46th North Carolina, Col. Edward Dudley Hall
Lt. Col. William Alexander Jenkins
48th North Carolina, Col. Robert Clinton Hill
Lt. Col. Samuel Hoey Walkup
30th Virginia, Lt. Col. Robert Stannard Chew (wounded 9/17)
Stafford (Va.) Artillery, Capt. Thomas B. French

Ransom's Brigade

Brig. Gen. Robert Ransom, Jr.
24th North Carolina, Lt. Col. John L. Harris
25th North Carolina, Col. Henry Middleton Rutledge
35th North Carolina, Col. Matt Whitaker Ransom
49th North Carolina, Lt. Col. Leroy Mangum McAfee
Branch's (Va.) battery, Capt. James Read Branch
Lt. Richard Gregory Pegram
Lloyd's (N.C.) battery, Capt. Whitmel P. Lloyd

Reserve Artillery

Brig. Gen. William Nelson Pendleton, commanding

Brown's Battalion

Col. John Thompson Brown
Powhatan (Va.) Artillery, Capt. Willis Jefferson Dance
Richmond (Va.) Howitzers, 2d company, Capt. David Watson
Richmond (Va.) Howitzers, 3d company, Capt. Benjamin H. Smith, Jr.
Salem (Va.) Artillery, Capt. Abraham Hupp
Williamsburg (Va.) Artillery, Capt. John A. Coke

Cutts's Battalion

Lt. Col. Allen Sherrod Cutts
Blackshears's (Ga.) battery, Capt. James A. Blackshear
Irwin (Ga.) Artillery, Capt. John Lane
Patterson's (Ga.) battery, Capt. George M. Patterson
Ross's (Ga.) battery, Capt. Hugh M. Ross

Jones's Battalion

Maj. Hilary Pollard Jones
Long Island (Va.) Artillery, Capt. Abram Wimbish
Morris Louisa (Va.) Artillery, Capt. Richard Channing Moore Page
Orange (Va.) Artillery, Capt. Jefferson Peyton
Turner's (Va.) battery, Capt. William H. Turner

Nelson's Battalion

Maj. William Nelson
Amherst (Va.) Artillery, Capt. Thomas Jellis Kirkpatrick
Fluvanna (Va.) Artillery, Capt. John J. Ancell
[Hanover (Va.) Artillery, Capt. George Washington Nelson]
Huckstep's (Va.) battery, Capt. Charles T. Huckstep
Johnson's (Va.) battery, Capt. Marmaduke Johnson
Milledge (Ga.) Artillery, Capt. John Milledge

Lee's Battalion

Col. Stephen Dill Lee
Ashland (Va.) Artillery, Capt. Pichegru Woolfolk, Jr.
Bedford (Va.) Artillery, Capt. Tyler Calhoun Jordan
Brooks (S.C.) Artillery, Lt. William Elliot
Eubank's (Va.) battery, Capt. John L. Eubank
Madison (La.) Artillery, Capt. George V. Moody
Parker's (Va.) battery, Capt. William Watts Parker

[Richardson's Battalion]

[Miscellaneous Batteries]

Cavalry Division

Maj. Gen. James Ewell Brown Stuart, commanding

Lee's Brigade

Brig. Gen. Fitz Hugh Lee
1st Virginia, Lt. Col. Luke Tiernan Brien

3d Virginia, Lt. Col. John Thruston Thornton (killed 9/17)
Capt. Thomas H. Owens
4th Virginia, Col. William Carter Wickham
5th Virginia, Col. Thomas Lafayette Rosser
9th Virginia, Col William Henry Fitzhugh Lee (wounded 9/15)
Stuart's (Va.) Horse Artillery, Maj. John Pelham

Robertson's Brigade

Brig. Gen. Beverly Holcombe Robertson
Col. Thomas Taylor Munford
2d Virginia, Col. Thomas Taylor Munford
Lt. Col. Richard Horseley Burks (12th Va.)
[6th Virginia]
7th Virginia, Capt. Samuel B. Myers
12th Virginia, Col. Asher Waterman Harmon
[17th Virginia Battalion (7 companies)]
Chew's (Va.) horse battery, Capt. Roger Preston Chew

Hampton's Brigade

Brig. Gen. Wade Hampton
1st North Carolina, Col. Laurence Simmons Baker
2d South Carolina, Col. Matthew Calbraith Butler
[10th Virginia]
Cobb's (Ga.) Legion (5 or 11 companies), Lt. Col. Pierce Manning Butler Young
Maj. William Gaston Delony
Jeff. Davis (Miss.) Legion (6 companies), Lt. Col. William Thompson Martin
Hart's (S.C.) horse battery, Capt. James Franklin Hart

Comments on the Organization of the Army of Northern Virginia in the Maryland Campaign and Its Evolution

Army of Northern Virginia

At Second Manassas, Lee's army was organized as follows: Longstreet's command (divisions of Kemper, Wilcox, D. R. Jones, and Evans); Jackson's command (divisions of Jackson, Ewell, and A. P. Hill); infantry reserve (R. H. Anderson); artillery reserve (S. D. Lee's battalion); and cavalry division (brigades of F. Lee and Robertson).

From September 2 to 5, Lee was reenforced by the arrival from Richmond of the army's "third wing" (infantry divisions of D. H. Hill, McLaws, and Walker; Hampton's cavalry brigade; and five battalions of artillery under Pendleton). Lee did not incorporate the infantry divisions into the commands of Longstreet and Jackson. Hampton was, however, at once merged with Stuart; and Pendleton, after abolishing Richardson's battalion, assumed at least titular command of S. D. Lee. Hence, at the beginning of the Maryland campaign the army was composed of two commands, three independent divisions, a cavalry division of three brigades, and an Artillery Reserve of five battalions.

During the campaign the following major organizational changes occurred: (1) on September 4–5, Kemper's division was merged into D. R. Jones's division; (2) on September 10, Wilcox's division was merged into R. H. Anderson's division; (3) on September 14, Evans's division was broken up into Hood's division and Evans's independent brigade; and (4) during the withdrawal from Sharpsburg on the night of September 18, Lee began to treat the infantry as if it were divided into two commands or corps, with D. H. Hill going to Jackson while Anderson, McLaws, and Walker were added to Longstreet.

The restructuring sometimes (including herein) referred to as the October reorganization actually covered a seven-week period. The most dramatic change, the assignment of all of the infantry and its supporting artillery to either Longstreet or Jackson occurred on September 18; but other changes, such as the shifting of brigades and the balancing of divisions, took weeks to accomplish, and the results were not announced until the first week in November.

A partial chronology for the reorganization would include:

On September 18 the Confederate Congress passed a law authorizing the creation of corps of two or more divisions and the new rank of lieutenant general for the commander of the larger unit.[1] Coincidentally, Lee began to act as if his army were divided into two corps. While he could not have been aware of the passage of the law at this time, he may have known that it was under consideration.

On September 22 there appeared written evidence of the reorganization in an order Lee issued jointly to Longstreet and

Jackson and in Field Returns of the same date, which used the term "corps."[2]

On September 26 Lee's S.O. 201 referred to a right wing under Longstreet and a left wing under Jackson.[3]

On September 28 Davis wrote a letter informing Lee of the passage of the law and asking for recommendations for corps and lieutenant generals in the Army of Northern Virginia.[4]

On October 2, having received Davis's letter the previous day, Lee proposed a First and Second Corps for his army, with Longstreet to command the former and Jackson the latter.[5]

On October 27, with the reorganization virtually complete, Lee wrote to Secretary of War Randolph recommending promotions for commanders of divisions and brigades.[6]

On November 6 S.O. 234 announced the reorganization to the army.[7]

While it may seem that Lee was awaiting only legal authorization before creating corps, this is probably a misapprehension. Lee had not previously shied (nor had his predecessor Johnston) from creating multidivision commands. His hesitancy in the Maryland campaign probably arose from three other factors: his doubts concerning Jackson's qualifications; his uncertainty as to whether the army should be divided into halves or thirds; and his search for a commander for a third wing, including the testing of D.H. Hill and McLaws.[8] During the campaign, two developments settled the question in Lee's mind: first, his increased appreciation of Jackson; and, second, his disappointment in the manner in which both D.H. Hill and McLaws exercised independent command.

Indeed, when Lee wrote to Davis on October 2, he would not only aver that "at present I do not think that more than two commanders of corps are necessary for this army," he would declare that after Longstreet and Jackson, "I consider General A. P. Hill the best commander with me."[9] It is doubtful he would have been prepared to make such a statement just a month earlier.

Longstreet's Command

At the start of the Maryland campaign, Longstreet's command or wing of the army, was composed of four divisions (of three brigades each), a total of twelve brigades: D.R. Jones (Toombs, Drayton, G.T. Anderson); Kemper (Kemper, Pickett, Jenkins); Wilcox (Wilcox, Featherston, Pryor); Evans (Evans, Hood, Law).

On September 4–5 Kemper's division was merged into D.R. Jones's. On September 9 Longstreet, who believed the force being sent to capture Harpers Ferry was too weak, offered Wilcox's division. On September 10 Wilcox was merged into R.H. Anderson's division, where it remained for the rest of the campaign. On September 14, when Hood was released from arrest, Evans's division was dismantled into Hood's division (Hood, Law) and Evans's independent brigade.

Throughout the campaign the Washington (La.) Artillery battalion (four batteries) acted as reserve for the entire command.

Escort and scouts for Longstreet were provided by an independent company of South Carolina cavalry, commanded by Capt. James Doby. The company may have originated in the cavalry battalion of the Holcombe Legion; it would later become Company E, 7th South Carolina Cavalry.[10]

In the October reorganization, Longstreet was promoted to lieutenant general and given command of the First Corps, composed of five divisions of twenty brigades: McLaws (Kershaw, Barksdale, Cobb, Semmes); R.H. Anderson (Wilcox, Mahone, Featherston, Wright, Perry); Pickett (Garnett, Armistead, Kemper, Jenkins, Corse); Hood (Law, Robertson, G.T. Anderson, Toombs); Ransom (Ransom, Cooke). The corps artillery reserve would include the Washington (La.) Artillery and Alexander's battalion.

D. R. JONES'S DIVISION

During the Seven Days campaign David R. Jones commanded a small division of two brigades—Toombs's and his own old Georgia brigade then under G.T. Anderson. During July Drayton's brigade, newly arrived from the south Atlantic defenses, was added, and these three brigades formed Jones's division during Second Manassas.

At the start of the Maryland campaign, on September 4 or 5, Kemper's small division of three brigades (Kemper, Jenkins, and Pickett) were added.[11] Thus, in Maryland Jones commanded a division that was unusually large in terms of units: six brigades of twenty-seven regiments and two battalions (not counting Phillips's Legion). The division was, nevertheless, numerically weak, which was probably the cause of the consolidation.

After the Maryland campaign, Jones suffered a heart attack in mid-October and left the army, dying on January 15, 1863. His division was dismantled. Kemper, Jenkins, and Pickett formed the core of a new division under George Pickett; G. T. Anderson and Toombs were transferred to Hood's division; and Drayton was temporarily placed in McLaws's division.

Toombs's Brigade

After D. R. Jones assumed command of the expanded division, he asked Toombs to take charge of his three old brigades: Toombs, G. T. Anderson, and Drayton. This arrangement seems to have lasted only from September 5 to 13, and it may have been no more than an internal convenience for Jones with no authorization from above.[12]

Toombs's brigade (including Toombs himself) remained in Hagerstown on September 14, perhaps by accident, when the rest of Jones's division returned to Boonsboro to support D. H. Hill. In the evening it was ordered to Sharpsburg.

Col. Henry Benning commanded the brigade for virtually the entire campaign *vice* Toombs, as the latter, even after losing control of Drayton and G. T. Anderson, continued to act as a demi-division commander.[13]

In the October reorganization, the brigade was shifted—in tact—to Hood's expanded division. Toombs returned to Georgia to recover from an injury suffered on September 18. In March 1863 he resigned from the army.

G. T. Anderson's Brigade

For some reason George T. Anderson's brigade did considerable "floating" during the Maryland campaign. Starting directly under D. R. Jones, Anderson was put in Toombs's subcommand on September 5. Then, on the night of September 14, he was assigned to Hood to cover the withdrawal from Turner's Gap. This arrangement apparently ended upon the arrival at Sharpsburg on the 15th, when Anderson reverted directly under D. R. Jones. At approximately 7:30 on the morning of the 17th, Anderson was pulled from Jones's line on the Boonsboro Pike and sent to the support of Hood near the Dunkard Church. For the remainder of the battle Anderson seems to have acted virtually independently of higher command.[14]

When Jones's division left Hagerstown for Boonsboro on the morning of the 14th, the 11th Georgia was detached to accompany the wagon trains to Williamsport. The regiment divided into two wings to protect the van and rear of the column. The right wing, under Major Little, rejoined the army on the 17th in time to take part in the battle. The left wing, under Captain Stokes, continued on to Martinsburg.[15]

In the October reorganization, the brigade was shifted—in tact—to Hood's expanded division.

Drayton's Brigade

Drayton's brigade arrived in Richmond from the south Atlantic coast in July and was added to D. R. Jones's small division (Toombs and G. T. Anderson). It remained in Jones's division throughout the Second Manassas and Maryland campaigns. Drayton was evidently a poor administrator (and perhaps a poor commander all around), and the makeup of his brigade is uncertain from time to time.

The 3d South Carolina battalion is not listed in the *Official Records* organizational table. The unit definitely did participate in the Maryland campaign, however, losing its commander, Lt. Col. George James, at Turner's Gap, and its surgeon, Simon Baruch, who remained behind to treat the wounded at Sharpsburg.[16]

The presence of the Phillips's Legion in the Maryland campaign is slightly less certain. The unit is not listed in the tables of either the *Official Records* or Carman, and its Record of Events cards in the National Archives list its station as Fredericksburg. This latter is highly unlikely in September 1862, however. Moreover, individual soldiers are identified as fighting at Sharpsburg, and the Legion was part of Drayton's brigade at the Battles of Second Manassas and Fredericksburg.[17]

When Jones's division was broken up in mid-October, Drayton was temporarily placed in McLaws's division, but by Fredericksburg he had been relieved and his regiments distributed as follows: the 50th and 51st Georgia to Semmes's brigade; Phillips's Legion to Cobb's brigade; and the 15th and 3d South Carolina battalion to Kershaw's brigade.

Kemper's Brigade

The brigades of Kemper, Jenkins, and Pickett originally constituted one-half of the division commanded by James Longstreet in the Seven Days. During the Second Manassas campaign, Longstreet divided his division, giving these three to Kemper and the other three to Cadmus Wilcox. On September 4 or 5 Kemper's division was merged into D. R. Jones's division, with the latter in command.[18] It may be assumed that

Longstreet found Kemper wanting as a division commander, as he never again led more than a brigade.

This brigade traces its origins to the brigade commanded by Longstreet at First Bull Run and was later under A. P. Hill as part of Longstreet's division.

Upon the breakup of Jones's division in mid-October, these same three brigades would form the core of the new division commanded by George Pickett.

Jenkins's Brigade

This South Carolina brigade had formerly belonged to Richard H. Anderson, before his transfer to command Huger's division from Norfolk. Micah Jenkins was severely wounded at Second Manassas.

Upon the breakup of Jones's division in mid-October, the brigade would be transferred to the new division commanded by George Pickett.

Pickett's Brigade

George Pickett was wounded in the Seven Days, and he would not return to the army until October, thus creating a vacancy at the head of his brigade. Richard Garnett had been arrested by Jackson during the Valley campaign. He was released and ordered to Longstreet by S.O. 188, Headquarters Department of Northern Virginia, September 5, 1862.[19] Then, or shortly thereafter, Longstreet appointed him to the temporary command of Pickett's Brigade, *vice* its senior colonel, Eppa Hunton.

Additional information on the 56th Virginia is from McPhail's report.[20]

Upon the breakup of Jones's division in mid-October, the brigade would be transferred to the new division commanded by George Pickett.

D. R. Jones's Artillery Battalion

Only the Wise Artillery is listed in the table in the *Official Records*, and it is possible this battalion never existed: (1) there is no known commander for it; (2) at Second Manassas the Fauquier, Loudoun, and Goochland batteries (along with the Washington [La.] Artillery) formed a battalion commanded by Col. J. B. Walton that served as a reserve (along with R. H. Anderson's division) to the entire army; (3) the Fauquier, Loudoun, and Goochland Artillery were then adjudged unfit for duty and left behind at Leesburg;[21] (4) the Wise Artillery does not appear to have been at Second Manassas, and, as it was Company B of the 1st Virginia Artillery, it may have been part of the Reserve Artillery brought from Richmond by Pendleton; (5) the battalion does not exist in the October reorganization, as the Wise, Loudoun, and Goochland Artillery were abolished and the Fauquier assigned to Dearing's battalion of Pickett's division.

Whether or not this battalion ever existed, it is clear that a single battery (Wise) was attached to D. R. Jones's division during the Maryland campaign. Why this deficit should have existed is uncertain. At Sharpsburg, the Washington (La.) Artillery, technically a reserve for Longstreet's entire command, would support D. R. Jones's infantry line.

HOOD'S DIVISION

This small division is all that remained of the five brigades formerly commanded by G. W. Smith and subsequently by W. H. C. Whiting. Originally these were the brigades of Hood and Whiting. After the other three brigades were detached or abolished and Whiting went on leave after the Seven Days, John B. Hood succeeded to command as the senior brigadier. In early August Hood was ordered from Richmond to report to Longstreet at Gordonsville. Thereafter, this division, in some form or another, served with Longstreet's command or corps of the Army of Northern Virginia until the end of the war.

Longstreet apparently had a penchant for three-brigade divisions, and, at some point during the Second Manassas campaign, he assigned Evans's brigade, recently arrived from South Carolina, to this division. Whether he did so intentionally or not, he thereby succeeded Hood in command, because Evans's commission was of an earlier date. Hood and Evans apparently did not get along, and on August 31, over a question of captured wagons, Evans placed Hood under arrest, where he remained until September 14. Presumably, although evidence is lacking, Evans commanded the division in the intervening two weeks.

On the 14th, as the units went into battle at Turner's Gap, Robert E. Lee restored Hood to the command of the two brigades and sent Evans to a different part of the field.[22] Thereafter, Hood remained in command, and Evans seems to have reported directly to Lee as an independent brigade. Who, if anyone, commanded these two brigades as an entity in the interval of Hood's arrest is unknown.

On the night of the 14th, Lee added the brigade of G. T. Anderson to Hood's command to cover the withdrawal from Boonsboro. This arrangement seems to have lasted only until the army reached Sharpsburg on the 15th.[23] Hood was at first placed on the far right, near the lower bridge, and in contiguous line with D. R. Jones, Longstreet's other division. Later on the 15th, Hood was shifted to the far left and the vicinity of the Dunkard Church. This arrangement placed D.H. Hill's independent division in the middle of Longstreet's two divisions. On the 16th, Jackson took command of the left wing of the army, including Hood, and Hood fought under Jackson on the 17th.

After the Maryland campaign, Hood was promoted to major general, and the size of his division doubled by the addition of the brigades of Toombs (Benning) and G.T. Anderson.

Hood's Brigade

Known as the Texas brigade, this was originally Hood's command. Wofford commanded it for the entirety of the Maryland campaign, as Hood was either under arrest (while Evans commanded the division) or in command of the division.

Col. John Cotelett Garrett of the 4th Texas was present at Boonsboro and Sharpsburg but too ill to lead the regiment.[24] He is not listed in the table herein, which is reserved for those exercising command.

In the October reorganization, the 18th Georgia was transferred to Cobb's brigade and the Hampton Legion to Jenkins's brigade. The 3d Arkansas (from Walker's brigade) was added, thus creating an all Trans-Mississippi brigade under J. B. Robertson of the 5th Texas.

Law's Brigade

This is Whiting's old brigade. Evander Law took command as senior colonel upon Whiting's leave after Seven Days. Lt. Col. McLemore commanded the 4th Alabama *vice* Law.

In the October reorganization, the 2d and 11th Mississippi were transferred to Richmond.[25] They would return to the Army of Northern Virginia as part of Joseph R. Davis's brigade in time for Chancellorsville. The 44th Alabama from Wright's brigade and the 57th North Carolina, a new regiment, took their place.

Frobel's Artillery Battalion

Frobel's battalion remained unchanged from the Second Manassas campaign.[26] Nor would it change in the October reorganization.

Evans's Independent Brigade

See Hood's Division above. After Hood was restored to command of the two-brigade division, Evans seems to have commanded only his own brigade and reported directly to Lee. As in the case of Toombs, however (and on the Federal side, Burnside and Sumner), Evans refused to relinquish his promotion. He continued to command a division that did not exist and thereby added an unnecessary level to the hierarchy.[27] Considering the four cases just mentioned, it might be concluded that Civil War officers operated on the assumption that it was dishonorable to step down unless specifically ordered to do so.

It should be noted in passing that, although it appears in no organizational chart, there was an "Evans's Division" for two of the three weeks of the Maryland campaign.

In the October reorganization Evans's brigade would be placed temporarily in McLaws's division. By early November, however, it had been ordered back to North Carolina.[28] This brigade had shed stragglers like dandruff during the Second Manassas and Maryland campaigns; Evans finally reporting barely a hundred men in line of battle on the 17th at Sharpsburg.[29] Lee probably believed he could make a gesture by returning the brigade while virtually losing no real strength to his army.

Macbeth Artillery

The Macbeth (S.C.) Artillery was the lone battery attached to Kemper's demi-division during the Second Manassas campaign. How and when it was transferred to Evans's brigade. is unknown. As to why, it was probably to satisfy the urge of units from the same state to serve together. The battery appears to have returned to South Carolina with Evans's brigade in November.

Longstreet's Artillery Reserve

Traditional tables accord Longstreet two battalions (Walton and S. D. Lee) of artillery as reserve for his command. Evidence suggests, however, that during the campaign S. D. Lee served as a fifth battalion of the Army of Northern Virginia's Reserve Artillery (see below).

Walton's Artillery Battalion

During the Second Manassas campaign, Walton's battalion included six additional batteries. At some point, probably at Leesburg, three of these batteries (Norfolk, Donaldsonville, and Lynchburg) were transferred to R. H. Anderson's division, and three were adjudged unfit to leave Virginia (Goochland, Fauquier, and Loudoun). Although thus reduced in size to the Washington (La.) Artillery, Walton continued to serve as the general reserve for Longstreet's command. His command would remain unchanged in the October reorganization.

Jackson's Command

Jackson had been given command of the Valley District of the Department of Northern Virginia in October 1861. Around the Stonewall Brigade—which had fought under him at First Bull Run—he built a division of three brigades. Ewell's division was added in early May 1862 on the eve of the Valley campaign. During the Seven Days Jackson also temporarily commanded the divisions of Whiting and D. H. Hill. By the time Jackson was sent to Gordonsville in mid-July, he had reverted to the command of just two divisions, his own and Ewell's. In late July A. P. Hill's division was sent to Jackson and thereafter attached to him.

In the Maryland campaign Jackson's command consisted throughout of the same three divisions, although on several occasions he exercised authority over other units. On September 5 and part of the 6th, while he was ranking officer north of the Potomac, Jackson once again temporarily commanded D. H. Hill. There is evidence that both Jackson and D. H. Hill believed the former continued to command the latter until the army marched from Frederick on September 10. Lee believed, however, that, except for the 5th and 6th, Hill was reporting directly to army headquarters.

By provision of S.O. 191, Jackson had the discretion to split his command, but he chose to take all three divisions with him. On September 13, after the capture of Martinsburg, when it became apparent that a siege of Harpers Ferry would be necessary, Jackson used his seniority to extend his control over Walker and McLaws. With the fall of the garrison two days later, Jackson's enlarged command ended when he ordered Walker and McLaws to hurry to Sharpsburg and report to Lee.

During both the Second Manassas and Maryland campaigns, the Black Horse Troop of the 4th Virginia Cavalry served as Jackson's escort.[30] During the first week or so of the Maryland campaign, White's cavalry was also attached to his headquarters.

White's cavalry began the campaign as a single company and ended as three. One company was already in process of organization and the third was raised from Maryland volunteers. White seems to have acted as guide and his command as escort to Jackson until reaching Frederick. Sometime around September 7 White was ordered to report to Jeb Stuart. When the two clashed, Stuart ordered White to return to Virginia. White appealed to Lee, and the commander compromised by sending White on a special mission to Harpers Ferry. White spent only a brief time at Harpers Ferry, and by the time the siege had started he took his command eastward to Leesburg. Here he fought a skirmish on the 17th. This unit later became the 35th Virginia Battalion Cavalry.[31]

In the October reorganization, Jackson was promoted to lieutenant-general and given command of the Second Corps, Army of Northern Virginia, composed of four divisions of nineteen brigades: D. H. Hill (Rodes, Doles, Colquitt, Iverson, Grimes); A. P. Hill (Brockenbrough, Gregg, Thomas, Lane, Archer, Pender); Ewell (Lawton, Trimble, Early, Hays); and Jackson (Paxton, J. R. Jones, Warren, Pendleton). At this time Stonewall was given something he had not previously possessed when Brown's battalion was transferred from the army's Reserve Artillery to serve as reserve for his corps.

JACKSON'S (STONEWALL) DIVISION

This was the old division Jackson had formed in the Valley in 1861 and had first commanded. In spite of a succession of subsequent commanders, it would be known in the army as Jackson's division until his death after Chancellorsville. It was sometimes also called the Stonewall division. In the Battle of Antietam it is sometimes referred to as J.R. Jones's division.

After the October reorganization it would once again—as it had been at his wounding at Second Manassas—be commanded by William B. Taliaferro.

Stonewall (Winder's) Brigade

This was the famous Stonewall Brigade, the same five regiments Jackson commanded at First Bull Run. Led by Charles S. Winder through the Valley campaign and the Seven Days (he was mortally wounded at

Cedar Mountain while commanding the division), the brigade then fell to a succession of its senior regimental officers.

The 2d Virginia was composed mostly of men from the Martinsburg–Shepherdstown–Harpers Ferry area. On September 13 Jackson detached the unit to the garrison at Martinsburg, and it did not rejoin its brigade until after the army recrossed into Virginia.[32]

J. R. Jones's Brigade

Known as the Second Brigade throughout the Valley campaign, these regiments were given to Brig. Gen. John R. Jones in the Seven Days. When Jones was wounded in the last battle, Jackson brought in outsider Col. Bradley T. Johnson (unemployed after the disbanding of the Maryland Line) to command the brigade during Second Manassas and the early stages of the Maryland campaign. Because Johnson was a native of Frederick, he was made provost marshal and the brigade the provost guard of that town during the Confederate occupation.

Jones rejoined the army in Frederick and, since he immediately succeeded to the command of the division, should not have replaced Johnson. Nonetheless, Johnson disappears at this point; it is not even certain that he remained with the army for the remainder of the campaign. The brigade thus devolved upon Capt. John E. Penn (42d Va.), the senior officer present.

Taliaferro's Brigade

The three Virginia regiments were originally known as the Third Brigade. They were joined in July 1862 by two new regiments from Alabama. Taliaferro commanded the brigade during the Valley campaign, and subsequently it was lead by a succession of senior regimental officers.

With no explanation, Ezra Carman has drawn expunging lines through the 10th Virginia on his manuscript organizational chart for the battle, thus seeming to indicate the regiment was not present on September 17. There is no doubt the unit participated in the Maryland campaign, and it was the first of Jackson's men to cross the Potomac on September 5. The mystery was solved with the discovery that the 10th—as was the 2d Virginia of the Stonewall Brigade—was detached by Jackson on September 13 to the garrison at Martinsburg. It did not rejoin its own brigade until the army recrossed into Virginia.[33]

Starke's Brigade

Richard Taylor's brigade of Louisianians (6th, 7th, 8th, 9th, and Wheat's Battalion) joined Jackson for the Valley campaign and served in Ewell's division. In July the Louisiana regiments scattered throughout the Army of Northern Virginia (1st, 2d, 5th, 10th, and Coppens's Battalion), and a newly formed regiment (15th) was sent to Jackson. The regiments were merged and reorganized into two brigades: one (with the 1st from Wright, the 2d from Cobb, the 9th from Taylor, the 10th from Semmes, Coppens from Pryor, and the new 15th) was given to William E. Starke and assigned to Jackson's division; the other was assigned to Ewell (see below). In the October reorganization this became Nicholls's brigade.

Lt. Col. Georges A. G. Coppens was killed on September 17 while in temporary command of the 8th Florida.[34] It does not seem that this arrangement could have been made on the 17th, however, as the 8th Florida (Pryor's brigade, R. H. Anderson's division) did not arrive on the field until after sunrise, rested southwest of Sharpsburg, and then proceeded directly to the Sunken Road around 10.00 A.M. Moreover, Jackson's and Anderson's divisions had been operating at a distance from one another since September 10. In the lack of contrary evidence, therefore, it seems likely the loan of a field officer was made to the 8th Florida early in the campaign. Coppens had served under Pryor in the Seven Days.

There is some indication that at least a portion of Wheat's battalion had merged with Coppens's and fought with the Zouaves in Maryland.[35]

Shumaker's Artillery Battalion

Both the Eighth Star (Rice) and Winchester (Cutshaw) Artillery are listed by the *Official Records*, Carman, and Jennings Wise under "Miscellaneous Batteries" of the entire army.[36] Since both were part of Shumaker's battalion in the Second Manassas campaign and again as early after the return to Virginia as September 22, it seems likely that they were also part of the battalion while in Maryland.[37]

There is some evidence that the Winchester Artillery was on the field at Sharpsburg and that its commander, Capt. Wilfred Cutshaw, was wounded in the battle. In the October reorganization it was consolidated with the Allegheny (Carpenter) Artillery.[38]

The Eighth Star Artillery was probably not on the field at Sharpsburg but was likely guarding the fords at either Williamsport or Shepherdstown on the 17th. In October the unit was consolidated with the Danville (Wooding) Artillery.[39]

All of the remaining six batteries are listed in the *Official Records* as having been at Sharpsburg on September 17.[40] Stapleton Crutchfield attests to the presence of Brockenbrough's battery at Sharpsburg.[41]

Carman does not include the Hampden Artillery (Caskie) on his organizational chart, which may mean that he believed the battery was left at Harpers Ferry. If so, it was probably brought to Sharpsburg on the 18th by order of Jubal Early.[42] Curiously, Caskie was the only battery commander not to report to Shumaker by September 22; the battery would not be abolished in October.

On September 6 Capt. William Poague of the Rockbridge Artillery was placed under arrest by Jackson because Maj. Frank Paxton had seen the artillerist permit his men to ride the caissons across the Potomac River. Poague was released on approximately the 10th; in the interim Lt. Graham commanded the battery. Poague implies that a number of Shumaker's battery commanders were placed under arrest at the same time and for the same cause.[43]

In the October reorganization the battalion remained largely intact. Shumaker was replaced by Brockenbrough; Poague was transferred to Brown's battalion and Brockenbrough's to the Horse Artillery; and Lusk's 2d Rockbridge Artillery was added.

EWELL'S DIVISION

The origin of this unit is the old division (brigades of Elzey, Trimble, and Taylor) commanded by Kirby Smith at Centreville in 1861. After Smith was transferred west, the division was given to Richard S. Ewell, who commanded it until his wounding at Brawner Farm on August 28, 1862. In the meantime, the division had been left behind at Gordonsville by Johnston when the Army of Northern Virginia was transferred to the Peninsula. In May Ewell was added to Jackson's Valley army; and in June the division was enlarged by the addition of Lawton's brigade fresh from Georgia.

In the October reorganization the division remained substantially unchanged.

Early's Brigade

This brigade was under Arnold Elzey until his wounding at Gaines's Mill. Thereafter it was given to Jubal Early, who returned from a wound suffered at Williamsburg. At dawn on the morning of the 17th, Jackson sent the brigade on an independent mission to support the Horse Artillery on Nicodemus Hill. Several hours later, when Early returned to the vicinity of the Dunkard Church, he detached the 13th Virginia to remain with Stuart.[44] After the wounding of Lawton, Early succeeded to the division and Col. William "Extra Billy" Smith, former and future governor of Virginia, took charge of the brigade.

The 13th Virginia remained detached for the rest of the day. It participated in the pursuit of Sedgwick's routed division and may have cooperated with Stuart in the abortive turning movement late in the day.[45]

Trimble's Brigade

Isaac Trimble commanded this brigade until his wounding at Second Manassas. Col. James Walker was transferred (ca. September 1st) from the 13th Virginia (Early) to be temporary commander.

The 1st North Carolina Battalion was composed of two companies of sharpshooters formed from the twelve-company 21st North Carolina, which continued to operate with the regiment.[46]

Hays's Brigade

Essentially this was Richard Taylor's old brigade. The 9th Louisiana was transferred to Starke in Jackson's division; the 5th was added from Semmes's brigade; and after Cedar Mountain and the death of Roberdeau Wheat, his Special Battalion was disbanded.

Lawton's Brigade

Lawton brought his fresh brigade from Georgia in early June and was sent to bolster Jackson's force in the Valley, because at the time a further offensive was contemplated by Stonewall. Jackson assigned the brigade to Ewell. Lawton succeeded to division command upon the severe wounding of Ewell at Second Manassas, and the brigade was under Colonel Douglass until his own wounding on the 17th.

Courtney's Artillery Battalion

There is some controversy over the participation of the batteries in Courtney's battalion. It is agreed that Johnson and D'Aquin were with the division throughout the campaign, including the battle on the 17th.[47]

In late July Carrington was transferred from Nelson's Battalion of the Artillery Reserve to Jackson's command, but the battery did not join the army until September 21, after it had returned to Virginia. According to Jeb Stuart, Carrington was present at Antietam, but, as in the case of assigning Pegram's battery to the Confederate left, his memory is proved false.[48]

Brown's battery was left at Harpers Ferry on September 15 as disabled. Jubal Early ordered it to Sharpsburg on morning of the 18th.[49]

Latimer's battery was left at Harpers Ferry on September 15 as disabled. A portion was brought to Sharpsburg on the evening of the 17th by Crutchfield.[50]

The batteries of Dement and Balthis (Garbor) were left at Harpers Ferry on September 15 as disabled. Jubal Early ordered them to Sharpsburg on the morning of the 18th. Carman implies, however, that both were present for the fighting on the 17th.[51]

A. P. HILL'S (LIGHT) DIVISION

The term "Light" refers neither to less equipment or to numerical weakness but to the division's alleged ability to move quickly. It was never armed differently from the rest of the army, and from the first was one of the largest divisions.

The division was created on the eve of the Battle of Seven Pines, when the three brigades at Hanover Junction (Field, Gregg, and J. R. Anderson) were joined with the brigade at Gordonsville (Branch) that had replaced Ewell when he was sent to Jackson. A. P. Hill was taken from a brigade under Longstreet and promoted to major general to take command. In June the brigades of Hampton, Hutton, and Pettigrew of Whiting's division were merged into two new brigades (Archer and Pender) and given to Hill.

During the Maryland campaign, the structure of the division was stable, but its command was not.

On September 4 Jackson placed Hill under arrest for his alleged inability to march his men efficiently. For the next six days the senior brigadier, Lawrence Branch, was in command. Hill was restored on September 10 as the army left Frederick. When Hill left Harpers Ferry on the morning of the 17th, he detached Thomas's brigade to remain behind. Thomas never recrossed into Maryland and joined the division on the 20th in time for the fight at Shepherdstown.

According to S.O. 188, the company of Cobb's (Ga.) Legion that served as Hill's escort should have been returned to Stuart on or shortly after September 5. Hill in his report implies the possibility, however, that it continued to serve at his headquarters.[52]

The division remained essentially unchanged by the October reorganization.

Branch's Brigade

It is probable that Col. James Lane commanded the brigade from September 4 to 10, while Branch commanded the division in place of the arrested A. P. Hill. Hence, Lane would not be totally devoid of command experience at the brigade level, when Branch was killed on September 17.

Archer's Brigade

On September 14–15 this brigade was part of a demi-division commanded by Pender.

Archer first reported "being too unwell for duty" on the morning of September 16, and he turned the command over to Colonel Turney. On the 17th he followed behind the brigade in an ambulance and resumed command on the field just as his men went into action. On the morning of the 18th, around 9:00 A.M., he again relinquished command, only to resume it on the night of the 19th in time for the Battle of Shepherdstown.[53]

Presumably someone else commanded the 1st Tennessee (PAC) in the intervals when Turney commanded the brigade.

Archer reported that the 5th Alabama Battalion for some reason was left at Harpers Ferry on the 17th and that it did not participate—at least with its brigade—on September 20 at Shepherdstown. Yet at least one member of Company A is reported to have been at the Battle of Sharpsburg.[54]

Gregg's Brigade

Sometime after the army left Frederick, anywhere from the 10th to the 12th of September, Maj. Frank Paxton, Jackson's aide, arrested Col. Dixon Barnes under the incorrect assumption that members of the 12th South Carolina were plundering a nearby apple orchard. Either late on the 14th or early on the 15th A. P. Hill suspended the arrest and had Barnes sword returned to him.[55] Presumably, in the interval Lt. Col. Cadwallader Jones commanded the regiment.

Pender's Brigade

According to Pender, when his brigade worked its way forward on September 14 to confront the enemy on the flank of Bolivar Heights, "Colonel Brewer was in command of the brigade at this time, and did himself great credit in the manner in which he handled it."[56] The editors of the *Official Records* list Col. R. H. Brewer as having commanded the brigade at some point in the campaign; and A. P. Hill thanks a Colonel Brewer along with several other field officers of regiments in his division.[57] No "Colonel" Brewer could be found among the field officers in Pender's regiments, however, or from any North Carolina regiment. Eventually it was discovered that 1st Lt. Richard Henry Brewer was a volunteer aide on Pender's staff. Brewer, an 1853 graduate of West Point and a former lieutenant in the old 1st U.S. Dragoons, had somewhere picked up the honorary title of colonel.[58] On the 14th, Pender exercised command of three brigades (Pender, Archer, and Field) and for some reason remanded the command of his own brigade temporarily to his volunteer aid, rather than the senior regimental officer.[59] Hence, Lieutenant (not Colonel) Brewer does belong in the table of organization of the Army of Northern Virginia in the Maryland Campaign.

Field's Brigade

Brig. Gen. Charles William Field commanded this brigade until severely wounded at Second Manassas. It then reverted to its senior colonel, John Brockenbrough. On September 14–15 the brigade was part of a demi-division commanded by Pender.

Thomas's Brigade

Brig. Gen. Joseph Reid Anderson commanded this brigade until July, when he resigned to take charge of the Tredegar Iron Works in Richmond. The brigade was detached on September 17 and remained at Harpers Ferry until the morning of the 19th, when it moved up the Virginia side of the Potomac to rejoin the army. Col. Edward Thomas would be promoted and take permanent charge of the brigade in the October reorganization.

Walker's Artillery Battalion

The batteries of Latham and Fleet were left at Leesburg to recruit deficiencies.[60]

The batteries of Crenshaw, Braxton, and McIntosh participated in all the operations of the campaign.[61]

Davidson's battery participated with the battalion until it was left behind on September 17 with Thomas's brigade at Harpers Ferry.[62]

One section of Pegram's battery was left behind at Leesburg to recruit deficiencies; the other section participated in all of the operations of the campaign.[63]

Unattached Divisions

Beginning with the organizational table published in 1887 by the editors of the *Official Records*, it has been traditional to view the Army of Northern Virginia as divided into two commands, Longstreet and Jackson, in the Maryland campaign. This view does not reflect, however, the way the army actually operated during the period.

Anderson's division—in its original three-brigade form—was with the army in the Second Manassas campaign. It served as the general reserve and reported directly to Lee.

The infantry divisions of D. H. Hill, McLaws, and Walker; the cavalry brigade of Hampton; and the five battalions of the Artillery Reserve under Pendleton constituted what Lee referred to as the third "wing" of the Army of Northern Virginia. All of these units remained in the defenses of Richmond when Lee went north with Longstreet and Anderson to join Jackson and confront Pope. Lee called for them to join him, and Davis released them; but a threat from the Fredericksburg area held them at Hanover Junction until it was too late to be present at Second Manassas. Except for a vanguard of two brigades under Ripley, D. H. Hill commanded the remainder of his division, McLaws's division, and the Artillery Reserve in its march to join Lee.

Upon arrival in the vicinity of Chantilly on September 2, D. H. Hill reverted to divisional command, and for the remainder of the campaign (except for the two days when Jackson commanded everything north of the Potomac), the infantry divisions reported directly to Lee. Pendleton also reported to Lee, although from time to time various battalions were assigned to other commanders. Hampton was immediately incorporated into Stuart's cavalry division.

It seems that throughout this period Lee was leaning toward forming the Army of Northern Virginia into three parts. Perhaps the only factor restraining him was uncertainty over who should command at the same level as Longstreet and Jackson. He seems already to have become prejudiced against D. H. Hill, the senior and logical candidate. It is possible that the reason he assigned McLaws to command the central part of the Valley expedition was to test the abilities of the Georgian in independent command. McLaws failed in Lee's eyes, as did D. H. Hill in his stand at Turner's Gap. Hence, after Sharpsburg Lee turned to the concept of two corps only and reorganized the army accordingly in October.

R. H. ANDERSON'S DIVISION

This division originated in the three brigades (Armistead, Mahone, and Wright) that had constituted the Department of Norfolk under Benjamin Huger. After the fall of Norfolk, the division, under Huger, was incorporated into the Army of Northern Virginia on the eve of Seven Pines. After the Seven Days, Huger was reassigned to an administrative position, and R. H. Anderson was transferred from the South Carolina brigade (Jenkins) under Longstreet to command the division. This was the last unit shifted northward from Richmond to Gordonsville, and Lee retained it as general reserve for the army under his own direct command.[64]

On September 9, S.O. 191 assigned Anderson to McLaws for the Valley expedition. The following day, Longstreet persuaded Lee to strengthen the force by adding Wilcox's division (the brigades of Wilcox, Pryor, and Featherston) to Anderson. The merger would be permanent for the remainder of the campaign, with Longstreet thus losing direct control of one-half of his former division. Anderson would cease to be under McLaws upon the arrival at Sharpsburg around dawn of September 17.

In the October reorganization, Anderson would become part of Longstreet's First Corps. Pryor's and Armistead's brigades would be shifted to Pickett's new division and replaced by Barksdale's from McLaws.

Armistead's Brigade

Armistead was named provost marshal of the Army of Northern Virginia on September 6, but he had already been named to direct the provost guard on September 4.[65] As no revocation of the orders has been found, it is uncertain how long Armistead served in this capacity. Nor is it known what troops he used to carry out his duties or whether he turned over the brigade to Col. James Hodges. In the absence of evidence, the most plausible theory is that Armistead did relinquish command of his own brigade and stationed himself with some force in the rear of the army on the march.

Once the army settled into camp around Frederick, Armistead likely returned to his own command, even if he retained the responsibility of provost marshal. It is also likely that he ceased functioning as provost on September 10, when the army split into five columns with different destinations. In any case, he was in command of his own brigade at the start of September 17, before being wounded in the foot. On the 17th the brigade was detached from the division and sent to the support of McLaws in the vicinity of the Dunkard Church.[66]

On September 6 the 5th Virginia Battalion was merged into the 53d Virginia.

Mahone's Brigade

Brig. Gen. William Mahone was wounded at Second Manassas. The brigade, already weakened by heavy straggling, suffered severely at Crampton's Gap. It was so small at Sharpsburg (numbering less than a hundred) that it was consolidated into a regiment and temporarily attached to Pryor's brigade.[67]

Although the 61st Virginia is listed by the editors of the *Official Records,* it is correctly omitted by Carman. The regiment, newly formed from expansion of the 7th Battalion Heavy Artillery, got no farther north than the Rappahannock.[68] It would be added to Mahone's brigade in October.

Wright's Brigade

Very little is known about Wright's brigade, but apparently its commander and regiments participated in all of the operations of its division through September 17. At Sharpsburg Wright was severely wounded but refused to relinquish command until after the fighting had closed.[69]

Wilcox's Brigade

The brigades of Wilcox, Featherston, and Pryor constituted one-half of Longstreet's division during the Seven Days. Then, in the Second Manassas campaign, the three brigades formed a small division under Wilcox.

Although one source implies Wilcox participated in the Maryland campaign, yet another states that he was too ill to command and that Col. Alfred Cumming—who was returning to his 10th Georgia—was given temporary charge of the brigade.[70] It is possible that Wilcox was present, although too ill to exercise command, in a situation similar to that of Archer and Key. It is also possible that the incapacity of Wilcox, along with Longstreet's distrust of the abilities of Featherston and Pryor, played a role in Longstreet's recommendation that the small division be merged with R. H. Anderson.

Pryor's Brigade

Pryor was the senior brigadier of the division and would assume command with the wounding of Anderson early on September 17. Correctly perceived as a political general lacking military abilities, Pryor would be transferred from the army in November. The Florida regiments would form a separate brigade for the remainder of the war.

Although the 5th Florida is not listed by the editors of the *Official Records*, there can be no doubt it was present on the September 17. Carman includes the regiment, and its battleflag was captured in the Sunken Road.[71]

Lt. Col. Coppens was on loan from the 1st Louisiana Zouave Battalion because of the lack of field officers in the 8th Florida.[72]

Featherston's Brigade

Featherston is listed by the editors of the *Official Records*. He is not listed by Carman, however, and one biographer says he "missed the Maryland campaign." Yet another source suggests that Featherston was at least present on September 15 and commanded the brigade briefly.[73]

Saunders's Artillery Battalion

The Dixie (Chapman) and Thomas (Anderson) Artillery are listed by the Official Records, Carman, and Jennings Wise under the "Miscellaneous Batteries" of the entire army.[74] Yet, both were attached to Wilcox's demi-division in the Second Manassas campaign and likely came to Leesburg on September 5 in that capacity.[75]

At Leesburg the Thomas Artillery was adjudged deficient and ordered to remain behind in Virginia. In October it was consolidated with the Hampden Artillery (Caskie) and attached to the Stonewall division.[76]

The Dixie Artillery, which evidence suggests both before and after the Maryland campaign had a special affiliation with Featherston's brigade, probably continued with Wilcox until that small division merged with R.H. Anderson on the 10th. There is also indication that for a time in September it operated with Kershaw of McLaws. While there is but slight evidence of its being on the field at Sharpsburg, it was at Shepherdstown on the 19th and 20th. In October it was disbanded.[77]

The four remaining batteries (Donaldsonville, Norfolk, Moorman's, and Portsmouth) were probably assigned to Anderson's division at Leesburg (September 5–7). They came from Walton's Battalion of Longstreet's reserve and took the place of S. D. Lee's Battalion, which in turn came under Pendleton and served as part of a reserve for the entire army. See note on S.D. Lee below under Artillery Reserve.

In the October reorganization the Portsmouth Artillery would be disbanded. The Donaldsonville and Norfolk Artillery would continue to serve in the divisional artillery, while eventually Moorman's battery would be transferred to the Horse Artillery.[78]

The table submitted by Pendleton in November seems to imply that the batteries of Lewis and Grandy also served in Saunder's battalion at Sharpsburg.[79] Pendleton's list includes batteries known to have missed the Maryland campaign, such as Carpenter's. Moreover, Lewis and Grandy are not listed by the editors of the *Official Records* or by Carman;[80] and Pendleton's report, dated October 2, refers only to the batteries of Moorman, Huger, and Maurin as being with Anderson.

It is not likely, therefore, that Lewis and Grandy were with the battalion in Maryland. Indeed, where they came from is unknown, as they appear not to have taken part in Second Manassas. They would be in Anderson's divisional battalion by late October, however, and perhaps that is why they appear in Pendleton's November table.

D. H. HILL'S DIVISION

This was one of the most stable divisions in Lee's army. It reached its present form on the eve of Seven Days with the addition of Ripley's brigade, and it would remain largely unchanged until the reorganization after Chancellorsville. D. H. Hill commanded the core of the division as early as Yorktown. After the Seven Days, when Theophilus Holmes was transferred to the Trans-Mississippi and the Department of North Carolina was downgraded to a district under Lee's immediate command, Hill was removed from the division and sent to North Carolina. It did not take long for Hill as a semi-independent commander to disappoint Lee; and, after the dismal failure of the attempt to threaten McClellan at Harrison's Landing from Coggins Point in early August, Hill was returned to the command of his division. In the interim it had been under Roswell Ripley, its senior brigadier. Hill then commanded the bulk of the reenforcements that marched from Richmond and joined Lee on September 2.

Except for a very brief period, Lee viewed this division as independent of the Longstreet/Jackson command structure. On September 5 Lee named Jackson to command all of the forces north of the Potomac, which at that time included D.H. Hill. As far as Lee was concerned this arrangement ended when he personally crossed the river on September 6. Jackson and Hill, however, apparently believed the arrangement continued at least another four days. It was this misunderstanding that led to duplicate copies of S.O. 191 being written for Hill, one of which would go astray and become the infamous lost orders. Hill continued to operate independently until the 18th and the recrossing of the Potomac.

In the October reorganization, the division would be made part of Jackson's Second Corps.

Rodes's Brigade

The 5th, 6th, and 12th Alabama formed the core of this brigade as early as Seven Pines. By the Seven Days the 3d and 26th had been added to make it an all-Alabama brigade.

G. B. Anderson's Brigade

Commanded by W. S. Featherston at Seven Pines, only G. B. Anderson's 4th North Carolina was original to the brigade. By the Seven Days the 2d, 14th, and 30th had been added to make it an all–North Carolina brigade.

The campaign so wore down this brigade in both men and officers that on September 18 Hill merged it with Garland's brigade and gave the command to Maj. J. W. Ratchford, divisional adjutant.[81]

Garland's Brigade

Only the 5th and 23d North Carolina were part of the brigade at Seven Pines. By the Seven Days, the 12th, 13th, and 20th had been added to make it an all–North Carolina brigade.

The campaign so wore down this brigade in both men and officers that on September 18 Hill merged it with G. B. Anderson's brigade and gave the command to Maj. J. W. Ratchford, divisional adjutant.

Rains's Brigade

The 13th Alabama and 6th and 23d Georgia formed the core of this brigade under Gabriel J. Rains at Seven Pines. By the Seven Days, Rains had been transferred out of the army, and the 27th and 28th Georgia added to the brigade. Still known in the army as Rains's brigade, Colquitt would be promoted and given its permanent command after the Maryland campaign. Along with Ripley, this brigade reached Lee late on August 30.

Ripley's Brigade

This was the last brigade added to the division, arriving from Georgia just before the Seven Days; but Ripley held the senior commission among the brigadiers. Hence, during D. H. Hill's absence in July and early August, he commanded the division. Also, he was in charge of the two brigades (Ripley's and Colquitt's) that were started as the van of the reenforcements from Richmond. Ripley reached Manassas on the 30th—too late to participate in the battle.

Ripley did not perform well at Turner's Gap, marching his men down the mountain and away from the battle. He would be wounded almost at the start of the fighting on the 17th. D. H. Hill considered Ripley a "coward."[82]

In the October reorganization Ripley would be transferred to South Carolina, and Col. George Doles would succeed to command of the brigade.

Pierson's Artillery Battalion

The Hardaway, Bondurant, and Carter batteries fought at Sharpsburg and would remain with the division after the reorganization. Briefly, on September 14 at the Battle of South Mountain, Bondurant was attached to Cutts's Battalion of the Reserve Artillery.

William Jones's battery, also called the Peninsula Artillery, is reported by both Carman and the editors of the *Official Records* to have fought at Sharpsburg. Yet it is also said to have been disbanded in June 1862.[83]

MCLAWS'S DIVISION

During the Seven Days John Magruder commanded three small divisions, D. R. Jones (Toombs and G. T. Anderson), McLaws (Kershaw and

Semmes), and Magruder (Cobb and Barksdale). Immediately thereafter Magruder was transferred to the Trans-Mississippi, and two of his divisions were consolidated into a single division under McLaws.

The new division remained in the defenses of Richmond until ordered north to join Lee in early August. It became part of, and shared in, the vicissitudes of the reenforcing column under D. H. Hill, not reaching the Army of Northern Virginia until September 2 near Chantilly.

It is interesting that the newly arrived McLaws was selected by Lee for the most important mission in the Valley expedition: the capture of Maryland Heights and Harpers Ferry. In addition to his own, McLaws commanded the expanded division of R. H. Anderson from September 10 until early on the morning of the 17th, a total of ten brigades, or one-quarter of the army. It is possible that Lee was testing McLaws for the command of the third wing of the army. Lee was clearly disappointed in McLaws's performance, especially the late arrival of his division on the field at Sharpsburg.

In the October reorganization McLaws would temporarily acquire the brigades of Drayton and Evans and lose Barksdale. Before long, however, Barksdale would be returned, Evans transferred to North Carolina, and Drayton dismantled. The brigades of the division are listed in the table as they were numbered (1st–4th) when under Magruder's command in the Seven Days.

Semmes's Brigade

Originally this was McLaws's brigade in John Magruder's Army of the Peninsula. It was incorporated into Joe Johnston's army in April 1862 as part of Magruder's division. During the Seven Days this large division was denominated a command and split into three demi-divisions of two brigades each. One of these (McLaws and Kershaw) was given to McLaws, and Paul Semmes took over the brigade. After Magruder was transferred to the West, Cobb and Barksdale were added to the division.

On September 13 Semmes was detached to guard the Brownsville Gap through South Mountain. On the following day, only the 10th Georgia, which had been sent to watch the road to Boonsboro, would participate in the Battle of Crampton's Gap.

In the October reorganization the 15th and 32d Virginia would be sent to Corse's brigade (Pickett's division), and Semmes would command an all-Georgia brigade with the addition of the 50th and 51st regiments from Drayton (D. R. Jones).

Cobb's Brigade

Originally Cobb was in John Magruder's Army of the Peninsula. He was incorporated into Joe Johnston's army in April 1862 as part of Magruder's division. During the Seven Days this large division was denominated a command and split into three demi-divisions of two brigades each. One of these (Cobb and Griffith) Magruder retained under his personal command. After Magruder was transferred to the West, Cobb and Barksdale (formerly Griffiths) were added to McLaws's division.

During the Valley expedition, Cobb was given the semi-independent mission of guarding the eastern end of the Sandy Hook road at the base of Maryland Heights. On September 14 he was ordered back to defend the South Mountain passes, and he would be in command of his own, Mahone's, and Munford's brigades after his arrival at Crampton's Gap. Rightly or not, Cobb would receive most of the blame for the debacle at that battle. It is not clear if he was present at Sharpsburg, but he would not command his much-reduced brigade on the 17th, and soon after he would request transfer and leave the army.

In the October reorganization Cobb's brigade, now commanded by Howell's brother Thomas, would lose the 15th North Carolina to Cooke (Ransom) and receive the 18th Georgia. from the Texas brigade (Hood) and Phillips's Legion from Drayton (D.R. Jones).

Barksdale's Brigade

Originally this was Richard Griffith's brigade in John Magruder's Army of the Peninsula. It was incorporated into Joe Johnston's army in April 1862 as part of Magruder's division. During the Seven Days this large division was denominated a command and split into three demi-divisions of two brigades each. One of these (Cobb and Griffith) Magruder retained under his personal command. Griffith was killed in the Seven Days, and William Barksdale succeeded to command. After Magruder was transferred to the West, Barksdale and Cobb were added to McLaws's division.

In the Maryland campaign, Barksdale's brigade came under the command of Joseph Kershaw for the three days (September 12–14) of the operations to take Maryland Heights.

In the October reorganization the brigade would remain unchanged, although it would be temporarily transferred out of the division.

Kershaw's Brigade

Originally Kershaw was in John Magruder's Army of the Peninsula. He was incorporated into Joe Johnston's army in April 1862 as part of Magruder's division. During the Seven Days this large division was denominated a command and split into three demi-divisions of two brigades each. One of these (McLaws and Kershaw) was given to McLaws. After Magruder was transferred to the West, Cobb and Barksdale were added to the division.

In the Maryland campaign, Kershaw commanded his own and Barksdale's brigade for the three days (September 12–14) of the operations to take Maryland Heights.

The 3d South Carolina left a "large detail" at Harpers Ferry "to bring up rations" that did not rejoin its regiment in time to participate in Antietam.[84]

In the October reorganization Kershaw would be increased by the addition of the 15th South Carolina and the 3d South Carolina battalions from Drayton's brigade (D.R. Jones).

Cabell's Artillery Battalion

All of the batteries are confirmed by the *Official Records*, Carman, and Jennings Wise, except the Magruder Artillery, which is listed by all three under "Miscellaneous Batteries" for the entire army.[85]

Guns from three of the batteries (two from Manly, two from Macon, and one from Page) were present at Brownsville Gap on September 14.[86]

Only four guns, two from Read and two from Carlton, were carried to the top of Maryland Heights.[87]

Ezra Carman concluded that Cabell had nineteen guns on the field at Sharpsburg, but only nine were engaged: four of the Read's, three of Carlton's, and two of McCarthy's.[88]

In the October reorganization, Macon would be transferred to the artillery battalion attached to Pickett's division; Page disbanded and distributed through S. D. Lee's battalion; and the remaining four batteries would continue to constitute the battalion attached to McLaws's division.[89]

WALKER'S DIVISION

This was two-thirds of the division Lee had shifted from the Department of North Carolina for the Seven Days campaign. At that time the three brigades (Walker, Daniel, and Ransom) had been led by Theophilus Holmes, who also commanded the department. For the brief period in July and August, when D. H. Hill headed the District of North Carolina, this was called D. H. Hill's division. Upon Hill's return to his old division, no one was named to command these three brigades. When President Davis decided to reenforce Lee as fully as possible, he sent Walker north with two of the brigades (Walker, now under Manning, and Ransom) from the defense of Petersburg.

Walker traveled northward separately from the reenforcing column and thus never came under the command of D. H. Hill. The division was the last to enter Maryland, not crossing the Potomac until September 7, and Walker probably did not report to Lee at Frederick until late in the morning of the 9th. Although this division is usually listed under Longstreet's command in the campaign, Walker seems to have reported directly to Lee except for two occasions (September 13–15 and the afternoon of September 17), and in these cases he came under Jackson's authority. Since Walker was given a minor independent command shortly after his arrival, it is possible that Lee was also testing him, although on a smaller scale than McLaws. If so, the results were apparently inconclusive.

At the time that Walker's division was created and ordered north, it was assigned three batteries (French, Branch, and Lloyd) from Deshler's battalion at Petersburg. These batteries never formed a battalion of their own but were officially attached to separate brigades: French to Walker (Manning) and Branch and Lloyd to Ransom.[90]

In the October reorganization, the small division was added to Longstreet's First Corps, and, when Walker was ordered to the Trans-Mississippi Department, Robert Ransom took its command.[91] It is interesting to note that Lee had the opportunity to stop Walker's transfer but took no action.[92]

Walker's Brigade

The core of this unit traces back to the brigade commanded by Walker in the Aquia District (Holmes) of the Department of Northern Virginia in the winter of 1861–62. Holmes and most of his troops, including Walker, were transferred to North Carolina in the spring of 1862 to counter the threat by Burnside's invasion. Here the brigade underwent many internal changes, but it emerged in the form given in the table to join the Army of Northern Virginia and participate in the Seven Days as part of Holmes's division.[93]

After Holmes had been transferred to the West and Walker given command of his own and Ransom's brigades, Col. Van Manning of the 3d Arkansas succeeded to command.

From September 13 to 15 Col. John R. Cooke commanded the detachment consisting of his own regiment (27th N.C.) and the 30th Virginia, which occupied Loudoun Heights during the siege of Harpers Ferry.[94]

About 9:30 A.M. on the morning of September 17, the 3d Arkansas and 27th North Carolina were detached under the command of Col. John Cooke to fill a gap in the Confederate line west of the Sunken Road. Cooke operated independently for the remainder of the battle. Later in the day, the 48th North Carolina and French's battery were given to Stuart as part of the unsuccessful attempt to turn the Federal flank.

The 2d Georgia Battalion was attached to this brigade during the Seven Days but seems to disappear until the Battle of Fredericksburg in December. According to the Record of Events cards in the National Archives, the unit was stationed at Fredericksburg from August through December. This is highly unlikely for September, at least, and the battalion may have been at Antietam, although so reduced in numbers as not to have been reported.[95]

The Stafford Artillery (French) may have been assigned to Walker, because of its previous association with the brigade the winter before in the Fredericksburg area.[96] Capt. Thomas B. French, with three guns from his own battery and two from Branch's, occupied Loudoun Heights on September 14–15.[97] Late on the afternoon of the 17th, French (along with Branch) briefly reoccupied Nicodemus Hill during Stuart's abortive attempt to turn the Federal flank.[98]

In the October reorganization, Cooke was promoted to command the brigade; the 2d Georgia was transferred to Wright's brigade (R. H. Anderson); the 3d Arkansas was transferred to Robertson (Hood); the 30th Virginia transferred to Corse (Pickett); and the 15th North Carolina was added from Cobb (McLaws); making it an all–North Carolina brigade, except for the Virginia battery, which was still attached.

Ransom's Brigade

The core of this brigade coalesced in North Carolina in the winter of 1861–62, with Ransom being assigned to command in the spring. By the Seven Days, when it joined the Army of Northern Virginia, its constituent units were substantially intact.[99]

During the Battle of Antietam, the 24th North Carolina accidentally became detached in the pursuit of Sedgwick's division. Later it may have participated in Stuart's unsuccessful attempt to turn the Federal flank.

Branch's battery served throughout the campaign with Ransom's brigade. On September 14–15 two of its guns occupied Loudoun Heights. Late on the afternoon of the 17th, along with French, it briefly reoccupied Nicodemus Hill as part of Stuart's abortive movement to turn the Federal flank.[100]

Lloyd's battery is quite a different story. Formed in the winter of 1862 by Capt. Whitmel P. Lloyd, a former company officer of the disbanded 1st North Carolina Infantry (the short-term unit known as the Bethel Regiment), the battery was part of Deshler's battalion at Petersburg when it was ordered to report to Ransom's brigade.[101] It was utterly green, never having been under fire and having poor discipline.[102] Indeed, it would not fire a shot in the Maryland campaign, and it may never have actually served with Ransom. Falling seriously behind Walker's trains and artillery in the march from Petersburg, the battery arrived late at Leesburg, struggled to cross the Potomac, and arrived in the Frederick area after its division had already departed on its mission to Harpers Ferry. For five days (September 10–14), the battery may have been an orphan, with no superior commander and no one even aware of its presence. About sunrise of the 15th, Lt. Col. A. S. Cutts awoke in the midst of his reserve battalion just west of Boonsboro to find that the main Confederate army had moved on without anyone telling him. Ordering his men to break camp and fall into column, Cutts rode back to town to see how close the enemy was. In the outskirts, in the near presence of the advancing Federals, he found Lloyd's battery at the side of the road, "men asleep, horses unharnessed." Cutts managed to extricate the battery and, following a circuitous route, reached Sharpsburg latter in the day.[103] Although ordered to rejoin its proper command, Lloyd apparently never did. After the campaign a disgusted Ransom wrote that Lloyd's battery "did not fire a gun and was not exposed to fire, but succeeded in losing one gun and two caissons." He urged that it be disbanded.[104] In October the battery was abolished, and its remaining three guns (one 6-pounder and two 12-pounder howitzers), men, and horses were distributed to the North Carolina batteries of Manly and Reilly.[105] Captain Lloyd would reappear at the end of the war as lieutenant colonel in the North Carolina Home Guards.[106] Previously, Lloyd's battery has been mistakenly attributed to Cutts's battalion in organizational charts.[107]

In the October reorganization the brigade infantry remained unchanged.

RESERVE ARTILLERY

After its poor performance in the Seven Days, the Reserve Artillery of the army was withdrawn to Richmond for reorganization, refitting, and training. By late July Pendleton had organized his force of twenty-seven batteries into one regiment and four battalions: the 1st Virginia Light Artillery Regiment, under Col. J. Thompson Brown (eleven batteries); the First, or Sumter, Battalion, under Lt. Col. A. S. Cutts (five batteries); the Second Battalion, under Maj. Charles Richardson (three batteries); the Third Battalion, under Maj. William Nelson (four batteries); and the Fourth Battalion, under Maj. H. P. Jones (four batteries).[108]

When Pendleton left Richmond on August 19 to join the army in the field, he took with him all five units, but each in an altered form: Brown's regiment was reduced to a battalion of five batteries (Coke, Dance, Hupp, Smith, and Watson); Cutts's battalion was reduced to four batteries (Blackshear, Lane, Ross, and Patterson); Richardson's was reduced to two (Ancell and Milledge), with Woolfolk having left earlier to serve with S. D. Lee. Nelson remained at four by taking two old batteries (Huckstep and Kirkpatrick), leaving Carrington in Richmond and losing Page to Jones, but adding M. Johnson and the Hanover Artillery. Jones also remained at four by taking three batteries (Peyton, Turner, and Wimbish), with Rhett having left earlier to serve with S. D. Lee but being replaced by Page from Nelson. Hence, the Reserve Artillery brought to the army nineteen batteries in five battalions.

After reaching Leesburg, Pendleton was assigned the task of weeding out the deficient batteries. He established an artillery depot at Winchester under Maj. Charles Richardson and transferred the two batteries of Richardson (Ancell and Milledge) to Nelson's battalion.[109] Pendleton's command would again be increased to five battalions after he reached Frederick, when S. D. Lee came under his authority.

During the campaign, the Artillery Reserve operated as a loose formation, with battalions constantly being detached from Pendleton to serve elsewhere. Pendleton functioned mostly as a chief of artillery for the entire army in terms of inspection and administration. Cutts, from his entry into Maryland, served with D. H. Hill. From September 10 on Jones may have been with D. H. Hill. On the 14th Brown was detached at Williamsport to guard Light's Ford. S. D. Lee acted independently throughout. And Pendleton was finally reduced to the direct control of Nelson's battalion.

At the Battle of Antietam three of the battalions were engaged. Cutts and Jones supported D. H. Hill, and S. D. Lee supported Jackson and Hill. On the 17th Brown remained at or near Williamsport, and Pendleton, with Nelson, guarded Boteler's Ford below Shepherdstown. Not until the rearguard action at the latter place on the 19th and 20th did Pendleton personally become involved in the fighting.

In the October reorganization, with many internal changes, Brown's Battalion became the reserve for Jackson's Second Corps; S. D. Lee's Battalion (under E. P. Alexander) became the second reserve battalion of Longstreet's First Corps; Jones was transferred to D. H. Hill's division; and only Cutts and Nelson remained as reserve for the entire army.

Brown's Battalion

This five-battery remnant of the 1st Virginia Artillery Regiment served with the main body of the reserve until detached on September 14 at Williamsport to guard Light's Ford. There—or nearby—it remained until the 19th, when it participated in Jeb Stuart's brief reentry into Maryland before rejoining the army at Martinsburg.

In the October reorganization Brown's battalion became the reserve for Jackson's Second Corps, retaining four batteries (Dance, Watson, Smith, and Hupp), losing one battery (Coke) to consolidation, and gaining two batteries (Poague from Jackson's division, and Brooke from Richmond).

Cutts's Battalion

Cutts was detached from the reserve on September 8, and from that point on he served with D. H. Hill's division.[110] On the 14th he was also assigned Bondurant's battery (D. H. Hill), and in the retreat from Boonsboro—separated from the army and almost captured—he also briefly commanded Lloyd's battery (Ransom).[111]

In the October reorganization Cutts's Battalion became the First Battalion of the army reserve, retaining three batteries (Lane, Patterson, and Ross) and losing one (Blackshear) to consolidation.

H. P. Jones's Battalion

The artillery battalion of Hilary P. Jones is something of a ghost unit in the Maryland campaign. The editors of the *Official Records* list it as containing four Virginia batteries in the Artillery Reserve.[112] At no point in the campaign does Pendleton acknowledge the existence of this battalion. It would be reasonable to assume the editors erred and that these batteries (three of which were weak) had been left behind in Virginia—except for one piece of evidence: Antietam Battlefield Plaque No. 316 states that Jones's Battalion fought on September 17 on the ridge north of the Boonsboro Pike, and presumably this information was supplied by veterans to Ezra Carman, who wrote the text for the plaques.

The location named by the plaque, plus a footnote in the *Official Records*, indicates that Jones was attached to D.H. Hill during the Battle of Antietam. It is possible to speculate that Jones was given to Hill on September 10 and left behind at Boonsboro, when the remainder of the army departed on the Valley expedition. Jones likely then remained with D.H. Hill for the rest of the campaign, although there is no indication that it was in any way connected with Cutts's Battalion.

In the October reorganization Jones became the battalion chief for D. H. Hill's division, taking with him two batteries (Page and Peyton) and receiving three batteries (Hardaway, Bondurant, and Carter). Two batteries (Turner and Wimbish) of his old battalion were abolished.

Nelson's Battalion

Increased by two batteries (Ancell and Milledge) from Richardson and losing one (G.W. Nelson) due to deficiencies at Leesburg, Maj. William Nelson's battalion remained with the main body of the army until ordered to recross the Potomac by way of Williamsport on the night of September 14. Nelson then marched south to take up position to guard Boteler's Ford, where it remained until it formed the core of the Confederate defense on the 19th and 20th in the Battle of Shepherdstown. Throughout, the battalion operated under the direct supervision of Pendleton.[113] The Hanover Artillery (G.W. Nelson) was attached to D.H. Hill's division until August 15. On that date it was ordered to Hanover Junction, and, because its horses were "in very bad condition" and it could not move, it was transferred to Nelson's battalion of the Reserve Artillery. Although the battery finally reached Leesburg, it was in such poor shape that it was left behind and ordered to Winchester.[114]

In the October reorganization Nelson's Battalion became the Second Battalion of the army reserve, retaining three batteries (Kirkpatrick, Ancell, and Milledge) and losing one battery (M. Johnson) by transfer to D.H. Hill and two (Huckstep and G.W. Nelson) by consolidation.

S. D. Lee's Battalion

Traditionally, S. D. Lee has been listed as the 2d Reserve Battalion to Longstreet's command in the Maryland campaign. The reasons for so doing are probably among the following: (1) upon the arrival of the battalion on the Antietam on September 15, Longstreet would order it into position; (2) when S. D. Lee wrote his report of Sharpsburg on October 11, he would address it to Longstreet's adjutant; (3) as early as September 22 the battalion is reported on returns as part of Longstreet's corps; (4) both Carman and Wise, authorities on the subject, accept the artillery organization given in the *Official Records.*[115]

There are better reasons, however, for believing S. D. Lee's battalion ought more properly be considered as the 5th Battalion of the army's Artillery Reserve than Longstreet's Second Battalion. (1) In the Second Manassas campaign, with essentially the same batteries, S. D. Lee, along with R. H. Anderson, served as general reserve to the entire Army of Northern Virginia. S. D. Lee seems not to have served under R. H. Anderson—or any other infantry officer—but to have reported directly to R. E. Lee. Indeed, his report of Second Manassas, written on October 2, was directed to Col. R. H. Chilton. (2) After Second Manassas, S. D. Lee lost the Portsmouth Artillery (to the newly formed battalion attached to R. H. Anderson), and it was replaced by the Madison Artillery. It is not clear where the latter came from, as it seems not to have been in the Second Manassas campaign. In any case, there is no evidence that at this time, or at any time through September 17, S. D. Lee was transferred to Longstreet's command. (3) On the contrary, Colonel Lee reported to Pendleton after the arrival of the latter from Richmond. The exact date is unknown, but it was sometime between September 4 and 9. It is clear that Pendleton considered Lee's battalion under his command when the army left Frederick on September 10. (4) On the 14th Pendleton marched with the Artillery Reserve from Hagerstown to Boonsboro. At midnight General Lee ordered Pendleton to proceed with the Artillery Reserve (certainly the batteries of Brown and Nelson, and possibly also that of H. P. Jones) to Williamsport to guard the fords of the Potomac. At the same time S. D. Lee's Battalion (along with Cutts and probably H. P. Jones) was to remain with the army. It is possible that at this time Longstreet took general charge of S. D. Lee's battalion, although there is no proof beyond Longstreet's positioning its guns at Sharpsburg on the 15th. (5) Nevertheless, during the battle on the 17th, S. D. Lee acted generally in support of Jackson, Hood, and D. H. Hill and not Longstreet. (6) According to S. D. Lee, on the morning of the 18th he would be involved with Jackson in an unsuccessful plan to attack the Federal right flank.[116]

It is likely, therefore, that S. D. Lee, although he floated somewhat, was officially part of the Artillery Reserve throughout the Maryland campaign—at least until the withdrawal began on the evening of the 18th.

These batteries would become the 2d Reserve Battalion of Longstreet's corps in the October reorganization, and perhaps the anticipation of that fact has caused the earlier misassignment.

[Richardson's Battalion]

Maj. Charles Richardson came to Leesburg as part of the Reserve Artillery with a battalion reduced to two batteries (Ancell and Milledge). Here he was named to command the artillery depot established at Winchester and all the army's batteries ordered there because they were deemed unfit to enter Maryland. Richardson's two batteries were assigned to Nelson's Battalion.[117]

Miscellaneous Batteries

The *Official Records* and Jennings Wise list five batteries (Cutshaw, Chapman, T. J. Page, Jr., Rice, and E. J. Anderson) and Carman lists four (omitting Anderson) under the heading "Miscellaneous," as not attached to any infantry or cavalry unit or as part of the Reserve Artillery.[118]

There should have been no "miscellaneous" batteries, however, which would imply that each reported directly either to Pendleton or Lee. Herein, they have been assigned, based on such evidence as exists, as follows: Cutshaw and Rice to Shumaker's battalion, Stonewall division; Chapman and Anderson to Saunders's battalion, R. H. Anderson's division; and Page to Cabell's battalion, McLaws's division.

In the October reorganization all of these batteries were either abolished or consolidated.

CAVALRY DIVISION

By the end of the Seven Days, Stuart commanded a single, large brigade of seven regiments (six Virginia units and 1st N.C.), one battalion (15th Va.), and three legions (Cobb, J. Davis, and Hampton). When Stuart was sent north toward Hanover Junction on July 23, he took with him five of the Virginia regiments (1st, 3d, 4th, 5th, and 9th).

Two days later Stuart was promoted to major general, and his command denominated a division. The Virginia regiments with Stuart were formed into a brigade and given to Fitzhugh Lee, while the units remaining in Richmond (1st N.C.; 2d S.C., including the Hampton Legion; 10th Va.; Cobb Legion; and Jeff. Davis Legion) were formed into another brigade and given to Wade Hampton. Stuart would not exert effective control over Hampton for over a month, but at this same time he gained a third brigade from the cavalry that had been operating with Jackson in the Valley (2d, 6th, 7th, and 12th and 17th Va. Battalions) and was now under Beverly Robertson.

It was with the brigades of F. Lee and Robertson that Stuart participated in the Second Manassas campaign. He would be joined by Hampton on September 2, just before crossing the Potomac. Thus, the Maryland campaign was the first time Stuart commanded three brigades in the field.

By the nature of cavalry service, the command was widely scattered and subject to frequent detachments during the campaign.

In the October reorganization the division would retain its higher structure, although there would be various internal transfers.

F. Lee's Brigade

The 1st Va. was detached on September 10 to accompany Longstreet's command to Hagerstown. It then accompanied the trains to Williamsport on the 14th. Exactly how and when it returned to its bridgade is not certain, but at least a portion of the regiment supported Pelham's battery on September 17.[119]

The remainder of the brigade was detached on September 11 on a raid to Westminster, Maryland, and did not rejoin the army at Boonsboro until late on the 13th.

The 5th Virginia was detached on the morning of the 14th to remain at Fox's Gap, where it participated in the fighting that morning. It covered Lee's rear in the retreat from Boonsboro that night and until the afternoon of the 15th was the only cavalry with the main body.

The 3d, 4th, and 9th Virginia fought the Battle of Boonsboro on the 15th to delay the Federal advance from Turner's Gap. They then retreated toward Hagerstown and did not join the main body until late in the afternoon, when they took up position on the left flank. The 9th Virginia was used as skirmishers along the Antietam.

The 3d, 4th, 5th, and 9th (and possibly the 1st) were part of Stuart's unsuccessful attempt to turn the Federal flank late on the afternoon of the 17th. The brigade then covered the retreat across the Potomac at Boteler's Ford on the night of the 18th and the morning of the 19th.

Pelham's eight-gun battery seems to have served exclusively with this brigade until the 18th, when it was detached to join Stuart in his expedition to Williamsport.

In the October reorganization the brigade was named the 2d and retained its structure, except gaining the 2d Virginia and losing the 9th.

Robertson's Brigade

This unit, also known as the Laurel Brigade, had served with Jackson in the Valley. Beverly Robertson, who apparently could get along with neither Jackson nor Stuart, was relieved on September 3 and replaced by Col. Thomas Munford, the senior regimental commander present.

The 6th Virginia was detached at Centreville to collect arms from the Manassas battlefield, to cover the withdrawal of the wounded, and to take care of unfit horses. It did not rejoin the brigade until after the campaign.[120]

The 17th Virginia Battalion was detached before the campaign began to recruit and organize in the Shenandoah Valley. It did not rejoin its brigade until after the army had returned to Virginia.[121]

The 7th Virginia was detached on September 10 to accompany Jackson's command to Martinsburg. When it reached the field of Antietam late on the night of the 16th, it mistakenly went to the left flank. The next afternoon it would participate in Stuart's unsuccessful attempt to turn the Federal flank.

The 2d and 12th Virginia fought with Munford at Crampton's Gap on the 14th. They then took position on the right of the army at Sharpsburg. On the 18th, Stuart took the 12th Virginia with him on his expedition to Williamsport.

Chew's battery seems to have served exclusively with the brigade during the campaign.

In the October reorganization, the brigade was named the 3d; the command was given to Rooney Lee; and the 2d Virginia lost and the 9th gained.

Hampton's Brigade

This brigade joined the army on September 2 as part of the reenforcing column from Richmond and at once reported to Stuart.

Hampton alone skirmished with the van of the Federals at Frederick, Middletown, and near Burkittsville on September 12–13. The brigade was then detached to guard the water gap at Weverton and did not rejoin the army until it arrived on the field of Sharpsburg around noon on the 17th.[122] It then participated in Stuart's unsuccessful attempt to turn the Federal flank. The next night it formed the core of Stuart's expedition to Williamsport.

The Jeff. Davis Legion was detached to guard Solomon's Gap in Elk Ridge on the 14th, and it joined the army on the 16th and rejoined its brigade on the following afternoon.

The 10th Virginia—for reasons that have not been discovered—remained near Leesburg until at least September 11. By the 14th it had moved to the Winchester area. Late on the 17th or early on the 18th it crossed the Potomac and joined its brigade. It then went with Hampton on the expedition to Williamsport. Carman does not list the 10th Virginia, but there is some slight evidence that at least a portion of the regiment was under fire on the field of Antietam.[123]

Hart's battery seems to have served exclusively with the brigade during the campaign.

In the October reorganization, the brigade would be named the 1st and retain its units, except for losing the 10th Virginia and adding the Phillips's Legion Cavalry.

Pelham's Artillery Battalion

It has been traditional to depict the three batteries of the Horse Artillery as constituting a battalion under John Pelham. The following would be the reasons for doing so: (1) both Carman and the editors of the *Official Records* show the batteries comprising a battalion under Capt. John Pelham;[124] (2) apparently Pelham was promoted to major on August 9, which means he would have ranked Chew and Hart, who were both captains.[125]

There are better reasons, however, for believing that the battalion, if it existed at all, was purely administrative and for depicting the batteries as each directly attached to one of the three cavalry brigades, as they are in the table above: (1) there is no evidence that the batteries ever served together at any point in the campaign; or (2) that Pelham ever exercised authority over them as battalion commander. (3) Even if he was promoted on August 9, however, the rank may have been used to command only his own double battery of eight guns. (4) Part of the confusion stems from the double meaning of the term "Stuart Horse Artillery." There is no doubt that Pelham commanded it from its creation until his death. It seems to have referred only to Pelham's battery, however, until after the Maryland campaign, whereupon it came to mean all of the artillery attached to Stuart's command.

Pelham's battery served exclusively with F. Lee's brigade, first at New Market and then in the mission to Westminster; with the rearguard at Turner's Gap; and on Nicodemus Hill. Likewise, Chew served with Munford and Hart with Hampton.

In the October reorganization the battalion would be formalized and Pelham's battery would be split into two.

CHAPTER THREE

Survey of Confederate Units in the Maryland Campaign and Their Combat Experience

Introduction

The five tables that follow provide convenient reference for research on Confederate units in the Maryland campaign. The first is an index by state of the Confederate regiments, battalions, and companies of infantry, artillery, and cavalry that participated in the campaign. It can be used as a quick checklist for bibliographical, genealogical, and other purposes. The second identifies those units that were in the campaign but not (or possibly not) at the Battle of Antietam. Any unit listed in the first but not the second can be assumed to have been at the battle.

The remaining three tables summarize the combat experience of the infantry units of Lee's army. Although confined to a single service branch, they include brigades and divisions as well as regiments and battalions. They provide the basis for the conclusions drawn in chapter 1 of *Taken at the Flood* regarding the degree to which the Confederate army was a veteran, cohesive, battle-tested force.

TABLE 1
Index of Confederate Units in the Maryland Campaign (by State)

Unit	*Branch*	*Brigade*	*Division*
ALABAMA			
3d	infantry	Rodes	D. H. Hill
4th	infantry	Law	Hood
5th	infantry	Rodes	D. H. Hill
6th	infantry	Rodes	D. H. Hill
8th	infantry	Wilcox	R. H. Anderson
9th	infantry	Wilcox	R. H. Anderson
10th	infantry	Wilcox	R. H. Anderson
11th	infantry	Wilcox	R. H. Anderson
12th	infantry	Rodes	D. H. Hill
13th	infantry	Rains	D. H. Hill
14th	infantry	Pryor	R. H. Anderson
15th	infantry	Trimble	Ewell
26th	infantry	Rodes	D. H. Hill
44th	infantry	Wright	R. H. Anderson
47th	infantry	Taliaferro	Jackson
48th	infantry	Taliaferro	Jackson
5th bttn.	infantry	Archer	A. P. Hill
Bondurant	battery	Pierson	D. H. Hill
Hardaway	artillery	Pierson	D. H. Hill
ARKANSAS			
3d	infantry	Manning	Walker
FLORIDA			
2d	infantry	Pryor	R. H. Anderson
5th	infantry	Pryor	R. H. Anderson
8th	infantry	Pryor	R. H. Anderson
GEORGIA			
1st (Regs.)	infantry	G. T. Anderson	D. R. Jones
2d	infantry	Toombs	D. R. Jones
3d	infantry	Wright	R. H. Anderson
4th	infantry	Ripley	D. H. Hill
6th	infantry	Rains	D. H. Hill
7th	infantry	G. T. Anderson	D. R. Jones
8th	infantry	G. T. Anderson	D. R. Jones
9th	infantry	G. T. Anderson	D. R. Jones

Unit	*Branch*	*Brigade*	*Division*
10th	infantry	Semmes	McLaws
11th	infantry	G. T. Anderson	D. R. Jones
12th	infantry	Trimble	Ewell
13th	infantry	Lawton	Ewell
14th	infantry	Thomas	A. P. Hill
15th	infantry	Toombs	D. R. Jones
16th	infantry	Cobb	McLaws
17th	infantry	Toombs	D. R. Jones
18th	infantry	Wofford	Hood
19th	infantry	Archer	A. P. Hill
20th	infantry	Toombs	D. R. Jones
21st	infantry	Trimble	Ewell
22d	infantry	Wright	R. H. Anderson
23d	infantry	Rains	D. H. Hill
24th	infantry	Cobb	McLaws
26th	infantry	Lawton	Ewell
27th	infantry	Rains	D. H. Hill
28th	infantry	Rains	D. H. Hill
31st	infantry	Lawton	Ewell
35th	infantry	Thomas	A. P. Hill
38th	infantry	Lawton	Ewell
44th	infantry	Ripley	D. H. Hill
45th	infantry	Thomas	A. P. Hill
48th	infantry	Wright	R. H. Anderson
49th	infantry	Thomas	A. P. Hill
50th	infantry	Drayton	D. R. Jones
51st	infantry	Drayton	D. R. Jones
53d	infantry	Semmes	McLaws
60th	infantry	Lawton	Ewell
61st	infantry	Lawton	Ewell
[2d bttn.	infantry	Manning	Walker]
Cobb's Leg.	infantry	Cobb	McLaws
[Phillips Leg.	infantry	Drayton	D. R. Jones]
Blackshear	artillery	Cutts	Pendleton
Carlton	artillery	Cabell	McLaws
Lane	artillery	Cutts	Pendleton
Milledge	artillery	Nelson	Pendleton

Unit	*Branch*	*Brigade*	*Division*
Patterson	artillery	Cutts	Pendleton
Read	artillery	Cabell	McLaws
Ross	artillery	Cutts	Pendleton
Cobb's Leg.	cavalry	Hampton	Stuart
LOUISIANA			
1st	infantry	Starke	Jackson
2d	infantry	Starke	Jackson
5th	infantry	Hays	Ewell
6th	infantry	Hays	Ewell
7th	infantry	Hays	Ewell
8th	infantry	Hays	Ewell
9th	infantry	Starke	Jackson
10th	infantry	Starke	Jackson
14th	infantry	Hays	Ewell
15th	infantry	Starke	Jackson
Coppens bttn.	infantry	Starke	Jackson
D'Aquin	artillery	Courtney	Ewell
Eshleman	artillery	Walton	Longstreet
Maurin	artillery	Saunders	R. H. Anderson
Miller	artillery	Walton	Longstreet
Moody	artillery	S. D. Lee	Pendleton
Richardson	artillery	Walton	Longstreet
Squires	artillery	Walton	Longstreet
MARYLAND			
Brockenbrough	artillery	Shumaker	Jackson
Brown	artillery	Courtney	Ewell
Dement	artillery	Courtney	Ewell
MISSISSIPPI			
2d	infantry	Law	Hood
11th	infantry	Law	Hood
12th	infantry	Featherston	R. H. Anderson
13th	infantry	Barksdale	McLaws
16th	infantry	Featherston	R. H. Anderson
17th	infantry	Barksdale	McLaws
18th	infantry	Barksdale	McLaws
19th	infantry	Featherston	R. H. Anderson
21st	infantry	Barksdale	McLaws

Unit	Branch	Brigade	Division
2d bttn.	infantry	Featherston	R. H. Anderson
J. Davis Leg.	cavalry	Hampton	Stuart
NORTH CAROLINA			
1st	infantry	Ripley	D. H. Hill
2d	infantry	G. B. Anderson	D. H. Hill
3d	infantry	Ripley	D. H. Hill
4th	infantry	G. B. Anderson	D. H. Hill
5th	infantry	Garland	D. H. Hill
6th	infantry	Law	Hood
7th	infantry	Branch	A. P. Hill
12th	infantry	Garland	D. H. Hill
13th	infantry	Garland	D. H. Hill
14th	infantry	G. B. Anderson	D. H. Hill
15th	infantry	Cobb	McLaws
16th	infantry	Pender	A. P. Hill
18th	infantry	Branch	A. P. Hill
20th	infantry	Garland	D. H. Hill
21st	infantry	Trimble	Ewell
22d	infantry	Pender	A. P. Hill
23d	infantry	Garland	D. H. Hill
24th	infantry	Ransom	Walker
25th	infantry	Ransom	Walker
27th	infantry	Manning	Walker
28th	infantry	Branch	A. P. Hill
30th	infantry	G. B. Anderson	D. H. Hill
33d	infantry	Branch	A. P. Hill
34th	infantry	Pender	A. P. Hill
35th	infantry	Ransom	Walker
37th	infantry	Branch	A. P. Hill
38th	infantry	Pender	A. P. Hill
46th	infantry	Manning	Walker
48th	infantry	Manning	Walker
49th	infantry	Ransom	Walker
1st bttn.	infantry	Trimble	Ewell
Manly	artillery	Cabell	McLaws
[Latham	artillery	R. L. Walker	A. P. Hill]
Lloyd	artillery	Ransom	Walker

Unit	*Branch*	*Brigade*	*Division*
Reilly	artillery	Frobel	Hood
1st	cavalry	Hampton	Stuart
SOUTH CAROLINA			
1st (Vols.)	infantry	Jenkins	D. R. Jones
1st (Prov.)	infantry	Gregg	A. P. Hill
1st Rifles	infantry	Gregg	A. P. Hill
2d (Vols.)	infantry	Kershaw	McLaws
2d Rifles	infantry	Jenkins	D. R. Jones
3d	infantry	Kershaw	McLaws
5th	infantry	Jenkins	D. R. Jones
6th	infantry	Jenkins	D. R. Jones
7th	infantry	Kershaw	McLaws
8th	infantry	Kershaw	McLaws
12th	infantry	Gregg	A. P. Hill
13th	infantry	Gregg	A. P. Hill
14th	infantry	Gregg	A. P. Hill
15th	infantry	Drayton	D. R. Jones
17th	infantry	Evans's Independent Brig.	–
18th	infantry	Evans's Independent Brig.	–
22d	infantry	Evans's Independent Brig.	–
23d	infantry	Evans's Independent Brig.	–
Hampton Leg.	infantry	Wofford	Hood
Holcombe Leg.	infantry	Evans's Independent Brig.	–
[3d bttn.	infantry	Drayton	D. R. Jones]
4th bttn.	infantry	Jenkins	D. R. Jones
Palmetto Rgt.	infantry	Jenkins	D. R. Jones
Bachman	artillery	Frobel	Hood
Boyce	artillery	Evans's Independent Brig.	–
Garden	artillery	Frobel	Hood
Elliott	artillery	S. D. Lee	Pendleton
Hart (Horse)	artillery	Hampton	Stuart
McIntosh	artillery	R. L. Walker	A. P. Hill
2d	cavalry	Hampton	Stuart
Doby's Co.	cavalry	–	Longstreet's Headquarters
TENNESSEE			
1st (Prov.)	infantry	Archer	A. P. Hill
7th	infantry	Archer	A. P. Hill
14th	infantry	Archer	A. P. Hill

Unit	Branch	Brigade	Division
TEXAS			
1st	infantry	Wofford	Hood
4th	infantry	Wofford	Hood
5th	infantry	Wofford	Hood
VIRGINIA			
1st	infantry	Kemper	D. R. Jones
2d	infantry	Stonewall	Jackson
3d	infantry	Pryor	R. H. Anderson
4th	infantry	Stonewall	Jackson
5th	infantry	Stonewall	Jackson
6th	infantry	Mahone	R. H. Anderson
7th	infantry	Kemper	D. R. Jones
8th	infantry	Pickett	D. R. Jones
9th	infantry	Armistead	R. H. Anderson
10th	infantry	Taliaferro	Jackson
11th	infantry	Kemper	D. R. Jones
12th	infantry	Mahone	R. H. Anderson
13th	infantry	Early	Ewell
14th	infantry	Armistead	R. H. Anderson
15th	infantry	Semmes	McLaws
16th	infantry	Mahone	R. H. Anderson
17th	infantry	Kemper	D. R. Jones
18th	infantry	Pickett	D. R. Jones
19th	infantry	Pickett	D. R. Jones
21st	infantry	J. R. Jones	Jackson
23d	infantry	Taliaferro	Jackson
24th	infantry	Kemper	D. R. Jones
25th	infantry	Early	Ewell
27th	infantry	Stonewall	Jackson
28th	infantry	Pickett	D. R. Jones
30th	infantry	Manning	Walker
31st	infantry	Early	Ewell
32d	infantry	Semmes	McLaws
33d	infantry	Stonewall	Jackson
37th	infantry	Taliaferro	Jackson
38th	infantry	Armistead	R. H. Anderson
40th	infantry	Field	A. P. Hill
41st	infantry	Mahone	R. H. Anderson
42d	infantry	J. R. Jones	Jackson

Unit	*Branch*	*Brigade*	*Division*
44th	infantry	Early	Ewell
47th	infantry	Field	A. P. Hill
48th	infantry	J. R. Jones	Jackson
49th	infantry	Early	Ewell
52d	infantry	Early	Ewell
53d	infantry	Armistead	R. H. Anderson
55th	infantry	Field	A. P. Hill
56th	infantry	Pickett	D. R. Jones
57th	infantry	Armistead	R. H. Anderson
58th	infantry	Early	Ewell
[61st	infantry	Mahone	R. H. Anderson]
1st bttn.	infantry	J. R. Jones	Jackson
[5th bttn.	infantry	Armistead	R. H. Anderson]
22d bttn.	infantry	Field	A. P. Hill
Ancell	artillery	Nelson	Pendleton
[Anderson	artillery	Saunders	R. H. Anderson]
Balthis	artillery	Courtney	Ewell
Branch	artillery	Ransom	Walker
Braxton	artillery	R. L. Walker	A. P. Hill
Carpenter	artillery	Shumaker	Jackson
[Carrington	artillery	Courtney	Ewell]
Carter	artillery	Pierson	D. H. Hill
Caskie	artillery	Shumaker	Jackson
Chapman	artillery	Saunders	R. H. Anderson
Chew (Horse)	artillery	Robertson	Stuart
Coke	artillery	Brown	Pendleton
Crenshaw	artillery	R. L. Walker	A. P. Hill
Cutshaw	artillery	Shumaker	Jackson
Dance	artillery	Brown	Pendleton
Davidson	artillery	R. L. Walker	A. P. Hill
Eubank	artillery	S. D. Lee	Pendleton
[Fleet	artillery	R. L. Walker	A. P. Hill]
French	artillery	Manning	Walker
Grimes	artillery	Saunders	R. H. Anderson
Huckstep	artillery	Nelson	Pendleton
Huger	artillery	Saunders	R. H. Anderson
Hupp	artillery	Brown	Pendleton

Unit	*Branch*	*Brigade*	*Division*
J. R. Johnson	artillery	Courtney	Ewell
M. Johnson	artillery	Nelson	Pendleton
W. B. Jones	artillery	Pierson	D. H. Hill
Jordan	artillery	S. D. Lee	Pendleton
Kirkpatrick	artillery	Nelson	Pendleton
Latimer	artillery	Courtney	Ewell
[Leake	artillery	–	D. R. Jones]
McCarthy	artillery	Cabell	McLaws
Macon	artillery	Cabell	McLaws
Moorman	artillery	Saunders	R. H. Anderson
[Nelson	artillery	Nelson	Pendleton]
Parker	artillery	S. D. Lee	Pendleton
R. C. M. Page	artillery	H. P. Jones	Pendleton
T. J. Page	artillery	Cabell	McLaws
Pegram	artillery	R. L. Walker	A. P. Hill
Pelham (Horse)	artillery	F. Lee	Stuart
Peyton	artillery	H. P. Jones	Pendleton
Poague	artillery	Shumaker	Jackson
Raine	artillery	Shumaker	Jackson
Rice	artillery	Shumaker	Jackson
[Rogers	artillery	–	D. R. Jones]
Smith	artillery	Brown	Pendleton
[Stribling	artillery	–	D. R. Jones]
Turner	artillery	H. P. Jones	Pendleton
Watson	artillery	Brown	Pendleton
Wimbish	artillery	H. P. Jones	Pendleton
Wise	artillery	–	D. R. Jones
Wooding	artillery	Shumaker	Jackson
Woolfolk	artillery	S. D. Lee	Pendleton
1st	cavalry	F. Lee	Stuart
2d	cavalry	Robertson	Stuart
3d	cavalry	F. Lee	Stuart
4th	cavalry	F. Lee	Stuart
5th	cavalry	F. Lee	Stuart
[6th	cavalry	Robertson	Stuart]
7th	cavalry	Robertson	Stuart
9th	cavalry	F. Lee	Stuart

Unit	*Branch*	*Brigade*	*Division*
10th	cavalry	Hampton	Stuart
12th	cavalry	Robertson	Stuart
[17th bttn.	cavalry	Robertson	Stuart]
White's bttn.	cavalry	–	Jackson's Headquarters

Sources: The information in this table is drawn entirely from the Organization of the Army of Northern Virginia given in chapter 2.

Comments: It should be emphasized that this list includes units with that were with the army at some point (no matter how brief) during the campaign. Where there is any doubt of its presence, the unit has been given in brackets. Several units in the campaign but not at the Battle of Antietam (e.g., 2d Virginia Infantry) are included without comment. A list of such units is given in the Table 2.

Table 2
Units Not (or Possibly Not) Present at the Battle of Antietam

Unit	*Comment*
ALABAMA	
5th inf. bttn.	possibly left at Harpers Ferry
GEORGIA	
11th inf.	left wing under Capt. Stokes at Martinsburg
14th inf.	Thomas's brigade, left at Harpers Ferry
35th inf.	
45th inf.	
49th inf.	
2d inf. bttn.	not in *OR* or Carman
Phillips Legion	not in *OR* or Carman
Milledge batt.	stationed at Shepherdstown Ford
MARYLAND	
Dement batt.	possibly left at Harpers Ferry
Brown batt.	left at Harpers Ferry
NORTH CAROLINA	
Latham batt.	left at Leesburg
SOUTH CAROLINA	
3d inf.	left large detachment at Harpers Ferry
3d inf. bttn.	not in *OR* but in Carman

Unit	Comment
VIRGINIA	
2d inf.	detached at Martinsburg
10th inf.	detached at Martinsburg
61st inf.	left on Rappahannock
5th inf. bttn.	merged into 53d Va.
Ancell batt.	stationed at Shepherdstown Ford
Anderson batt.	left at Leesburg
Balthis batt.	possibly left at Harpers Ferry
Carrington batt.	joined army after campaign
Caskie batt.	probably left at Harpers Ferry
Chapman batt.	no evidence on field of Sharpsburg
Coke batt.	stationed at Williamsport
Dance batt.	stationed at Williamsport
Davidson batt.	left at Harpers Ferry
Fleet batt.	left at Leesburg
Huckstep batt.	stationed at Shepherdstown Ford
Hupp batt.	stationed at Williamsport
M. Johnson batt.	stationed at Shepherdstown Ford
Kirkpatrick batt.	stationed at Shepherdstown Ford
Latimer batt.	left at Harpers Ferry
Leake batt.	left at Leesburg
Nelson batt.	left at Leesburg
T. J. Page batt.	no evidence on field of Sharpsburg
Rice batt.	probably guarding Potomac fords
Rogers batt.	left at Leesburg
Smith batt.	stationed at Williamsport
Stribling batt.	left at Leesburg
Watson batt.	stationed at Williamsport
1st cav.	may have been at Williamsport
6th cav.	detached at Centreville
10th cav.	possibly arrived on 18th
17th cav. bttn.	organizing in Shenandoah Valley
White's cav. bttn.	sent back to Virginia

Sources: The information in this table is drawn entirely from the Organization of the Army of Northern Virginia given in chapter 2.

Comments: For a discussion of each unit listed above, see that unit in the Organization of the Army of Northern Virginia chapter 2. Note that seven batteries have been identified as having been left behind at Leesburg: Anderson, Fleet, Latham, Leake, Nelson, Rogers, and Stribling.

TABLE 3
Combat Experience of Infantry Regiments and Battalions

State	*Number of Major Battles*					*State Unit Totals*
	1	*2*	*3*	*4*	*5*	
ALABAMA						
		3, 44, 47, 48	11, 12, 13, 26, 5 bttn (6)	4, 5, 6, 8, 9, 10, 14, 15		16.6
ARKANSAS						
	3					1.0
FLORIDA						
	5, 8			2		3.0
GEORGIA						
	10, 16, 24, 44, 50, 51, 53, Cobb (6), 2 bt (4), Phillips (9)	1, 2, 4, 11, 13, 15, 17, 20, 26, 31, 38, 48, 60, 61	3, 6, 7, 8, 9, 18, 22, 23, 27, 28, 45, 49	12, 14, 19, 21, 35		39.9
LOUISIANA						
		10, Coppens (6)	1, 2, 5	9, 15	6, 7, 8, 14	10.6
MISSISSIPPI						
	21	13, 17, 18	11, 16	2, 12, 19, 2 bttn (6)		9.6
NORTH CAROLINA						
	1, 2, 3, 12, 15, 20, 24, 25, 30, 35, 46, 48, 49	27, 1 bttn (2)	4, 6, 7, 13, 14, 18, 22, 23, 28, 33, 34, 37, 38	5, 16, 21		30.2
SOUTH CAROLINA						
	1 (Vols), 15, 17, 18, 22, 23, Holcombe (10), 3 bttn (7)	1 (Prov), 1 Rifles, 2 (Vols), 2 Rifles, 3, 7, 8, 12, 13, 14	4 bttn (5)	6, Hampton (10), Palmetto SS (10)	5	22.2
TENNESSEE						
			7, 14		1 (Prov)	3.0
TEXAS						
			1, 4, 5			3.0
VIRGINIA						
	15, 30	6, 16, 32, 57, 5 bttn (5), 22 bttn (6)	9, 12, 14, 21, 23, 31, 40, 41, 47, 53, 55, 56, 58	11, 13, 25, 37, 38, 42, 44, 48, 52, 1st bttn (5)	1, 2, 3, 4, 5, 7, 8, 10, 17, 18, 19, 24, 27, 28, 33, 49	45.6
UNIT TOTALS						
	35.6 (19.3%)	38.9 (21.1%)	51.1 (27.7%)	37.1 (20.1%)	22 (11.9%)	184.7

Comments: Infantry only was used for this table because of the relative difficulty of evaluating the degree of participation in battle of artillery and cavalry and the further difficulty of tracing the evolution of the units of both arms. In the case of battalions the number of companies is given in parentheses. In reckoning totals, companies have been consolidate into ten company regiments, and the remainder are expressed as decimals.

As stated in chapter 2, note 75, of *Taken at the Flood,* the battles/campaigns considered as major are: First Bull Run, Shenandoah Valley, Williamsburg, Seven Pines, Seven Days, Cedar Mountain, and Second Manassas.

It will be seen from the table that all of the Confederate infantry in the Maryland campaign had participated in at least one of these battles. Only 35.6 (19.3 percent) regiments had participated in just one battle; 110.2 (59.7 percent) were in three or more; and 149.1 (80.7 percent) were in two or more.

The table should be seen as a minimal reflection of the combat history of the regiments. A variety of things could have been done to make their experience seem more impressive: counting minor battles that were important to some regiments (Eltham's Landing); or breaking apart some of the campaigns into constituent major battles, such as the Valley campaign (McDowell, Front Royal, Cross Keyes, etc.) and Seven Days (Gaines' Mill, Malvern Hill, etc.)

The table reveals that the relative contributions of the states to Lee's army in terms of infantry regiments was as follows:

24.7%	Virginia
21.6%	Georgia
16.4%	North Carolina
12.0%	South Carolina
9.0%	Alabama
5.7%	Louisiana
5.2%	Mississippi
1.6%	Florida
1.6%	Tennessee
1.6%	Texas
0.5%	Arkansas

When it is remembered that Virginia contributed 64 percent of the artillery and 76 percent of the cavalry, it will be seen that units from the Old Dominion represented a much higher proportion of Lee's entire army than when infantry alone is considered.

The table also affords an interesting glimpse into the Confederate distribution of manpower resources. The states in the Eastern theater (Virginia, North Carolina) or in the tier immediately to the south (South Carolina, Georgia, Florida) contributed 76.3 percent of the infantry units in Lee's army. The Western states (Alabama, Louisiana, Mississippi, Tennessee, Texas, Arkansas) contributed 23.6 percent. Whether or not this represented an overemphasis on the East by the Davis administration must remain a matter of interpretation. In any final judgment, however, account must be taken of the significant number of regiments from Florida, South Carolina, and Georgia (plus a handful from North Carolina and Virginia) that served in Western armies.

On the other hand, it must be emphasized that numbers of units are a weak indicator of strength in terms of headcount. When it is recalled that many of North Carolina's regiments were swollen with conscripts and many of Virginia's were worn very thin, it is at least possible that the Tar Heel State had more soldiers on the field at Antietam than did the Old Dominion.

TABLE 4
Combat Experience of Infantry Brigades

	Battles						
Brigades	*1st Bull Run*	*Williams-burg*	*Shenanan-doah Valley*	*Seven Pines*	*Seven Days*	*Cedar Mount*	*2d Manassas*
Kemper	+	+	–	+	+	–	+
Stonewall	+	–	+	–	+	+	+
Pickett	+	+	–	+	+	–	+
Kershaw	+	–	–	–	+	–	–
G. T. Anderson	+	–	–	–	+	–	+
Hays	–	–	+	–	+	+	+
Texas	–	–	–	+	+	–	+
Barksdale	–	–	–	–	+	–	–
Cobb	–	–	–	–	+	–	–
Law	–	–	–	+	+	–	+
J. R. Jones	–	–	+	–	+	+	+
Trimble	–	–	+	–	+	+	+
Lawton	–	–	–	–	+	+	+
Early	–	–	–	–	+	+	+
Rodes	–	–	–	–	+	–	–
G. B. Anderson	–	–	–	–	+	–	–
Garland	–	–	–	–	+	–	–
Rains	–	–	–	–	+	–	–
Ripley	–	–	–	–	+	–	–
Semmes	–	–	–	–	+	–	–
Toombs	–	–	–	–	+	–	+
Jenkins	–	–	–	–	+	–	+
Wilcox	–	–	–	–	+	–	+
Featherston	–	–	–	–	+	–	+
Mahone	–	–	–	–	+	–	+
Wright	–	–	–	–	+	–	+
Armistead	–	–	–	–	+	–	+

	Battles						
Brigades	*1st Bull Run*	*Williams-burg*	*Shenanan-doah Valley*	*Seven Pines*	*Seven Days*	*Cedar Mount*	*2d Manassas*
Walker	–	–	–	–	+	–	–
Ransom	–	–	–	–	+	–	–
Gregg	–	–	–	–	+	–	+
Field	–	–	–	–	+	+	+
Branch	–	–	–	–	+	+	+
Archer	–	–	–	–	+	+	+
Thomas	–	–	–	–	+	+	+
Pender	–	–	–	–	+	+	+
Taliaferro	–	–	–	–	–	+	+
Starke	–	–	–	–	–	+	+
Pryor	–	–	–	–	–	–	+
Drayton	–	–	–	–	–	–	+
Evans	–	–	–	–	–	–	+

Summary of Brigades

In 1 campaign (13, 32.5%): Barksdale, Cobb, Rodes, G. B. Anderson, Garland, Rains, Ripley, Semmes, Walker, Ransom, Pryor, Drayton, Evans

In 2 campaigns (11, 27.5%): Kershaw, Toombs, Jenkins, Wilcox, Featherston, Mahone, Wright, Armistead, Gregg, Taliaferro, Starke

In 3 campaigns (10, 25.0%): G. T. Anderson, Texas, Law, Early, Lawton, Field, Branch, Archer, Thomas, Pender

In 4 campaigns (3, 7.5%): J. R. Jones, Trimble, Hays

In 5 campaigns (3, 7.5%): Kemper, Stonewall, Pickett

Sources: The constituent regiments for each brigade were determined from the Organization of the Army of Northern Virginia in chapter 2. The combat experience of each brigade was derived from research in the *Official Records;* Crute, *Units of the Confederate Army;* and the tables in Johnson and Buel, eds., *Battles and Leaders.*

Comments: The name used for each brigade is the one believed to be most common in the Maryland campaign. Many of the brigades were known by other names earlier in their existence (e.g., Kemper's was Longstreet's).

Some brigades contained individual regiments with long experience serving together but did not assume brigade form until later (e.g., Taliaferro and Starke).

Table 5
Combat Experience of Infantry Divisions

	Battles						
Divisions	*1st Bull Run*	*Williams-burg*	*Shenanan-doah Valley*	*Seven Pines*	*Seven Days*	*Cedar Mount*	*2d Manassas*
Kemper	-	+	-	+	+	-	+
Wilcox	-	+	-	+	+	-	+
Jackson	-	-	+	-	+	+	+
Ewell	-	-	+	-	+	+	+
R. H. Anderson	-	-	-	+	+	-	+
Hood	-	-	-	+	+	-	+
A. P. Hill	-	-	-	-	+	+	+
D. R. Jones	-	-	-	-	+	-	+
D. H. Hill	-	-	-	-	+	-	-
McLaws	-	-	-	-	+	-	-
Walker	-	-	-	-	+	-	-

Summary of Divisions

In 1 campaign (3, 27.3%): D. H. Hill, McLaws, Walker

In 2 campaigns (1, 9.1%): D. R. Jones

In 3 campaigns (3, 27.3%): R. H. Anderson, Hood, A. P. Hill

In 4 campaigns (4, 36.7%): Kemper, Wilcox, Jackson, Ewell

Sources: The formation of the divisions is taken from the organization in chapter 2. The combat experience of each division is derived from research in the *Official Records;* Crute, *Units of the Confederate Army*; and the tables in Johnson and Buel, eds., *Battles and Leaders.*

Comments: Lee began the Maryland campaign on September 2 with the eleven divisions listed above. By the Battle at Sharpsburg the number would be reduced to nine, with Kemper consolidated into D. R. Jones and Wilcox into R. H. Anderson. The early form is used here because it reflects the organization at the time Lee decided to enter Maryland.

The three brigades under Kemper and the three under Wilcox formed a single division of six brigades under Longstreet from Williamsburg through the Seven Days. They were split into two demi-divisions for Second Manassas but still operated under Longstreet's supervision.

Three of Jackson's brigades (Stonewall, J. R. Jones, and Taliaferro) formed a division before the Valley campaign; Starke was added in time for Cedar Mountain.

Three of Ewell's brigades (Trimble, Early, Hays) formed a division before the Valley campaign; Lawton added in time for Seven Days.

R. H. Anderson's division was Huger's through the Seven Days. It was assigned the flank assault at Seven Pines but did virtually no fighting. Its size was doubled by the addition of Wilcox's three brigades in Maryland.

As two-thirds of Smith/Whiting, Hood's division had fought together since Seven Pines.

Gregg's brigade of A. P. Hill's division missed Cedar Mountain.

Two-thirds of D. R. Jones's division fought together as a demi-division in Magruder's command; with Drayton added in time for Second Manassas. Its size was doubled with the addition of Kemper's three brigades for the Maryland campaign.

Harvey Hill commanded a division at Yorktown, but his units shifted too much to be counted for experience purposes until the Seven Days.

McLaws's four brigades fought as two demi-divisions (one under McLaws) in Magruder's command in the Seven Days. Afterward they were joined into a single division. Walker's brigades formed two-thirds of Holmes's division in the Seven Days. Daniel was left behind at Richmond.

CHAPTER FOUR

Gazetteer for the Maryland Campaign of 1862

Introduction

The following tables were compiled to reveal similarities and differences among Virginia, Maryland, and Pennsylvania and in particular among the counties of these states that either were or could have been the scene of operations of the Army of Northern Virginia.

It bears repeating that none of the refined statistics from the Eighth Census—not published until 1864–66—could have been available to Lee. The figures do confirm, however, Confederate impressions gained by experience and observation.

Most of the statistics in the tables that follow are drawn from the printed volumes of the Eighth Census (U.S. Bureau of the Census, 1860): *Agriculture of the United States in 1860: Compiled from the Original Returns of the Eighth Census* (Washington, D.C.: GPO, 1864), hereafter cited as 8th Census, *Agriculture; Manufactures of the United States in 1860: Compiled from the Original Returns of the Eighth Census* (Washington, D.C.: GPO, 1865), hereafter cited as 8th Census, *Manufactures; Population of the United States in 1860: Compiled from the Original Returns of the Eighth Census* (Washington, D.C.: GPO, 1864), hereafter cited as 8th Census, *Population; Statistics of the United States (Including Mortality, Property, &c.) in 1860* (Washington, D.C.: GPO, 1866), hereafter cited as 8th Census, *Mortality.*

TABLE 6
Tri-State Area and Population in 1860

	Area (sq. mi.)	*Population*	*Per sq. mi.*	*Slaves (%)*	*Free Blacks (%)*
Pennsylvania	46,000	2,906,215	63.0	–	2.0
Maryland	11,124	687,049	61.0	12.7	12.2
Virginia (1860)	61,352	1,596,318	26.0	30.7	3.6
Virginia (1863)	38,352	1,219,631	31.8	38.7	4.5

Sources: Pennsylvania, Maryland, and Virginia areas and densities are from 8th Census, *Mortality,* 339.

Populations, including slave and free blacks, from 8th Census, *Population,* 214 (Md.), 412 (Pa.), 518 (Va.). Percentages of slaves and free blacks have been calculated from the raw totals provided by the census.

Virginia (1860) represents the figures from the 8th Census. Virginia (1863) reflects the remainder after deductions for West Virginia. Estimates of square miles for West Virginia are from *Tribune Almanac for 1866* (New York: Tribune Association, 1865), 71. Population figures for West Virginia are from totals of the individual counties in 8th Census, *Population,* 516–18.

Comments: Graphically demonstrated here are the differences among a free state (Pennsylvania), a border state (Maryland), and a slave state (Virginia).

Note that slaves—entirely absent from Pennsylvania—make up nearly one-third of the population of Virginia, which is almost three times the percentage of Maryland. Also, Maryland has almost as many free blacks as slaves, while slaves are ten times more numerous than free blacks in Virginia.

In head count free blacks numbered as follows: 83,942 in Maryland; 59,042 in Virginia; and 56,949 in Pennsylvania. Hence, not only were there two-thirds more free blacks in Maryland than in either its neighboring slave state or free state, but there were 2,000 more free blacks in Virginia, where free blacks were (supposedly) unwelcome, than in Pennsylvania, where they were (supposedly) welcome.

Note also that the population is over twice as dense (persons per square mile) in Pennsylvania and Maryland as in Virginia. However, the figures given for Virginia in the 1860 census include the fifty counties that would be split off to form West Virginia. To adjust the Virginia total, deduct 23,000 square miles; 376,687 total population; 18,371 slaves; and 2,771 free blacks.

In the adjusted line for Virginia, the deduction of West Virginia raises the percentage of slaves by 8, the percentage of free blacks by 0.9, and the density per square mile by 5.8 persons.

Likewise, if the City of Baltimore is deducted from the population of Maryland, the state's density drops to 42.7 persons per square mile. Hence, even with Baltimore and West Virginia deducted, Maryland still has 10.9 more persons per square mile than Virginia.

TABLE 7
Tri-State Slaveholders

Slaveholders in State Owning	*Number of slaves owned* 1	2	3	4	5	6	7
Pennsylvania	–	–	–	–	–	–	–
Maryland	4,119	1,952	1,279	1,023	815	666	523
Virginia	11,085	5,989	4,474	3,807	3,233	2,824	2,393

Slaveholders in State Owning	*Number of slaves owned* 8	9	10–14	15–19	20–29	30–39	40–49
Pennsylvania	–	–	–	–	–	–	–
Maryland	446	380	1,173	545	487	179	81
Virginia	1,984	1,788	5,686	3,088	3,017	1,291	609

Slaveholders in State Owning	*Number of slaves owned* 50–69	70–99	100–199	300–299	300–499	500–999	1,000+
Pennsylvania	–	–	–	–	–	–	–
Maryland	75	24	15	–	1	–	–
Virginia	503	243	105	8	1	–	–

State	*Number of slaveholders*	*Average number of slaves owned*	*Percentage of slave-holders in Population*
Pennsylvania	–	–	–
Maryland	13,783	6.33	2.30
Virginia (1860)	52,128	9.42	4.72
Virginia (1863)	48,222	9.68	6.53

Sources: The number of slaveholders in each category is from 8th Census, *Agriculture,* 231 (Md.), 245 (Va.).

The average number of slaves owned (not provided by the census) was calculated by dividing the number of slaves by the number of owners. To adjust for West Virginia, 3,306 slaveholders and 18,371 slaves were deducted from the 1860 total for Virginia

The percentage of slaveholders in the total population (not provided by the census) was calculated by dividing the number of slaveholders by the free population. The free population of Maryland was 599,860 and Virginia 1,105,453 (8th Census, *Population,* 214, 518).

To adjust for West Virginia, 358,316 was deducted from the 1860 free population of Virginia.

Comments: The category Virginia (1863) represents Virginia after the separation of West Virginia. The deduction of the western Virginia counties only slightly raises the average number of slaves owned in the state, but it increases by half the percentage of slaveholders in the total population.

Using the 1863 figures for Virginia, it will be seen that in the Old Dominion the percentage of slaveholders in the entire population was nearly three times greater than in Maryland. Also, the average Virginia slaveholder owned half again as many slaves as his Maryland counterpart.

It should be noted that only heads of household were listed by the census as slaveholders. This relatively small figure does not represent the true number of persons with a pecuniary interest in or dependence upon slavery. This latter figure can probably never be calculated with precision. As a start, however, the number of slaveholders should be multiplied by 5+ to represent the average-sized family in 1860; also to be included should be overseers and their families, slave dealers and their families, and the farmer and his family who hired slaves on a regular basis.

TABLE 8
Tri-State Banking

	Capital ($)	*Loans ($)*	*Deposits ($)*	*Savings per person ($)*
Pennsylvania	25,565,582	50,327,157	26,167,843	9.00
Maryland	12,568,962	20,898,762	8,874,180	14.79
Virginia	16,005,156	24,975,792	7,729,652	6.99

Sources: Capital, loans, and deposits statistics are from 8th Census, *Mortality,* 292.

Per person savings is calculated from free populations figures found in 8th Census, *Population,* 412 (Pa.), 214 (Md.), and 518 (Va.).

Comments: The savings per person is calculated by dividing the bank deposits by the total free population of the state. The census does not give the actual number of depositors. Banking statistics are not broken down by county in the census.

TABLE 9
Select Tri-State Counties: Population

County	*White*	*Free black*	*%*	*Slave*	*%*	*Aggregate*
PENNSYLVANIA						
Adams	27,532	474	1.7	–	–	28,006
Franklin	40,327	1,799	4.3	–	–	42,126
MARYLAND						
Montgomery	11,349	1,552	8.5	5,421	29.6	18,322
Frederick	38,391	4,957	10.6	3,243	7.0	46,591
Washington	28,305	1,677	5.3	1,435	4.6	31,417
VIRGINIA						
Culpeper	4,959	429	3.6	6,675	55.3	12,063
Faquier	10,430	487	2.2	10,455	48.2	21,706
Prince William	5,690	519	6.1	2,356	27.5	8,565
Fairfax	8,046	672	5.7	3,116	26.3	11,834
Loudoun	15,021	1,252	5.7	5,501	25.3	21,774
Frederick	13,079	1,208	7.3	2,259	13.7	16,546
Rockingham	20,489	532	2.3	2,387	10.2	23,408
Rockbridge	12,841	422	2.4	3,985	23.1	17,248

Sources: Population statistics are from 8th Census, *Population,* 214 (Md.), 412 (Pa.), 516–18 (Va.).

Comments: The first two counties are in Pennsylvania, the following three in Maryland, and the final eight in Virginia. The Maryland counties were chosen because they constituted the scene of the operations of the Maryland campaign. The Pennsylvania counties border Maryland and would have been the scene of operations if Lee had shifted his campaign slightly northward. Lee marched through five of the Virginia counties (Culpeper, Faquier, Prince William, Fairfax, and Loudoun) on his way to Maryland, and, therefore, they provide an immediate frame of reference for comparison. The other three (Frederick, Rockingham, and Rockbridge) are typical counties from the Valley of Virginia, commonly considered to be the agricultural heartland of Virginia.

Note that in this and subsequent tables the county statistics bear out the same differences shown among free, border, and slaves states demonstrated by the state statistics. The Pennsylvania counties have no slaves and few free blacks.

The Maryland counties illustrate a striking difference from east to west. Montgomery, the easternmost county of the three, is the most like a typical county from a slave state: lower population and a higher percentage of slaves. The only abnormal statistic is the unusually high percentage of free blacks. The percentage of slaves drops drastically as one moves west in Maryland. Both Frederick and Washington Counties have large total populations and few slaves.

The Virginia counties present a less clear pattern. However, the northern counties, nearer the Potomac, tend to be below the state percentage for slaves and above it for free blacks. Two of the central counties (Culpeper and Faquier) exhibit statistics similar to Virginia's tidewater counties, or counties in newly developing states such as Alabama and Mississippi. In any case, the Virginia counties present a striking contrast in the percentages of slaves and a somewhat less dramatic difference in percentage of free blacks.

TABLE 10
Select Tri-State Counties: Slaveholders

Slaveholders in County Owning	*Number of slaves owned*								
	1	*2*	*3*	*4*	*5*	*6*	*7*	*8*	*9*
MARYLAND									
Montgomery	173	107	55	44	52	44	44	32	35
Frederick	257	144	93	62	58	39	25	20	18
Washington	143	67	47	31	29	20	13	12	14
VIRGINIA									
Culpeper	73	46	57	42	34	31	38	32	28
Faquier	116	84	66	64	63	71	57	43	43
Prince William	44	35	31	25	15	19	12	11	13
Fairfax	151	59	60	38	37	37	19	26	11
Loudoun	124	84	61	83	46	39	35	27	22
Frederick	105	56	53	32	20	23	17	19	12
Rockingham	104	63	49	40	26	22	16	17	13
Rockbridge	96	72	58	44	44	47	32	31	28

Slaveholders in County Owning	*Number of slaves owned*							
	10–14	*15–19*	*20–29*	*30–39*	*40–49*	*50–69*	*70–99*	*100–199*
MARYLAND								
Montgomery	88	47	32	9	3	4	–	1
Frederick	60	10	5	2	1	–	–	–
Washington	16	4	2	–	–	–	–	–
VIRGINIA								
Culpeper	95	52	52	16	8	3	4	–
Faquier	137	61	71	29	13	11	3	1
Prince William	35	11	13	5	1	2	1	–
Fairfax	51	20	15	3	2	–	–	–
Loudoun	80	36	23	4	4	1	–	1
Frederick	33	21	14	1	–	–	–	-
Rockingham	44	13	9	2	1	–	1	–
Rockbridge	65	24	16	3	2	6	1	–

County	*Number of slaveholders*	*Average number of slaves owned*	*Percent of Slave-holders in population*
MARYLAND			
Montgomery	770	7.04	5.97
Frederick	794	4.08	1.83
Washington	398	3.61	1.33
VIRGINIA			
Culpeper	611	10.92	11.34
Faquier	933	11.21	8.54
Prince William	273	8.63	4.40
Fairfax	529	5.89	6.07
Loudoun	670	8.21	4.12
Frederick	406	5.56	2.84
Rockingham	420	5.68	2.00
Rockbridge	569	7.00	4.29

Source: Categories of slaves owned and number of slaveholders are from 8th Census, *Agriculture,* 231 (Md.), 243–44 (Va.). Other information is the result of calculations.

Comments: Regarding the numbers of slaves owned by slaveholders, generally there were more small slaveholders in Maryland and fewer in Virginia; and there were more large slaveholders in Virginia and fewer in Maryland.

The average number of slaves owned was calculated by dividing the number of slaveholders into the number of slaves in each county. Both Frederick and Washington Counties fell well below the state average of 6.33. The Virginia counties, excepting only Culpeper and Faquier, fell below their state average of 9.42 (or 9.68 without West Virginia).

The percentage of slaveholders in the population was calculated by dividing the free population (white and black) into the number of slaveholders in each county. Both Frederick and Washington Counties fell well below the state average of 2.30 percent. The Virginia counties, excepting Culpeper, Faquier, and Fairfax, also fell below their state average of 4.72 percent. Fairfax fell below the 1863 Virginia average, which becomes 6.53 percent when West Virginia is deducted.

TABLE 11

Select Tri-State Counties: Area, Density, and County Seats

County	*Square Miles*	*Density*	*County seat*
PENNSYLVANIA			
Adams	526	53.2	Gettysburg
Franklin	754	55.9	Chambersburg
MARYLAND			
Montgomery	496	36.9	Rockville
Frederick	665	70.1	Frederick
Washington	459	68.4	Hagerstown
VIRGINIA			
Culpeper	389	31.0	Culpeper Court House
Faquier	660	32.9	Warrenton
Prince William	345	24.8	Brentsville
Fairfax	399	29.7	Fairfax Court House
Loudoun	517	42.1	Leesburg
Frederick	433	38.2	Winchester
Rockingham	868	27.0	Harrisonburg
Rockbridge	604	28.6	Lexington

Sources: The 8th Census does not give county area in square miles. It has been necessary, therefore, to use the contemporary *Webster's New Geographical Dictionary* (1984).

The density (persons per square miles) has been calculated by dividing the modern area into the 1860 population.

Comments: The density figures are approximate only, as they do not allow for changes in size in the area of the counties in the past one hundred years or for the inclusion of water surfaces in the modern figures. It is known, for example, that Fairfax County was larger in 1860 than 399 square miles, because at that time it included Arlington County, which has since been detached, and an area west of Alexandria that has been subsequently annexed by that city. Thus, Fairfax was even slightly less dense than the 29.7 figure given above.

It will be noted that the Pennsylvania counties are below that state's average in density (63.0).

In Maryland Montgomery County is barely half the state average density (61.0) and, in fact, is similar in this respect to a Virginia county. Frederick and Washington Counties, however, are above the state average. When it is remembered that the state average after Baltimore has been deducted is only 42.7, it will appear that the counties were indeed unusually densely populated for rural counties. Lee and his men would have encountered a density twice that they had recently been accustomed to in Virginia.

All of the Virginia counties hover around the 31.8 average for the state after the deduction of the western counties. Most have less than half the persons per square mile of the two western Maryland counties.

Table 12
Select Tri-State Counties: Value of Farms and Farm Machinery

County	*Acres Cultivated*	*Rank (Md./Va.)*	*Farms Acres*	*Percent Cultivated*	*Value of Farms ($)*	*Rank (Md./Va.)*	*Value of Machinery ($)*	*Rank (Md./Va.)*
PENNSYLVANIA								
Adams	192,996	–	256,674	75.2	9,339,119	–	394,523	–
Franklin	261,390	–	401,315	65.1	16,265,894	–	448,716	–
MARYLAND								
Montgomery	176,790	–	291,604	60.6	5,920,318	–	314,708	–
Frederick	271,998	1/2	339,343	80.2	14,127,925	2/1	441,814	2/1
Washington	196,503	3/8	240,140	81.8	11,954,803	3/2	354,938	3/2
VIRGINIA								
Culpeper	153,291	–	238,858	64.2	4,985,786	–	110,061	–
Faquier	268,431	–	383,479	70.0	10,062,472	–	241,740	–
Prince William	97,353	–	174,099	55.9	2,373,100	–	63,366	–
Fairfax	84,690	–	200,606	42.2	3,866,075	–	111,097	–
Loudoun	220,266	–	296,142	74.4	10,508,211	–	238,264	–
Frederick	116,117	–	190,473	61.0	3,987,945	–	148,515	–
Rockingham	200,803	–	345,968	58.0	9,718,613	–	262,506	–
Rockbridge	139,236	–	340,122	40.9	5,785,123	–	109,223	–

Source: Statistics are from 8th Census, *Agriculture,* 122 (Pa.), 72 (Md.), 154, 158 (Va.).

Comments: For acres cultivated the census seems to include only land under cultivation for growing crops. Thus, although the census definition is not entirely clear, it would seem to include orchards but exclude meadows used for grazing livestock. The Virginia county with the largest acreage in cultivation was Halifax, with 277,913 acres.

Rank is applied only to the Maryland counties of Frederick and Washington and shows the actual ranking of the counties in Maryland and what their ranking would have been if included among Virginia counties. In this case, the two counties drop slightly in comparison to Virginia.

Farm acres were calculated by adding acres cultivated to acres uncultivated in the census. With the exception of three Virginia counties (Prince William, Fairfax, and Frederick), all of the other counties are in the same general range.

The percentages of acres cultivated were calculated by dividing farm acres into acres cultivated. Two important points need to be noted. First, in the tables cited the editors of the census use the terms "improved" and "unimproved," rather than "cultivated" and "uncultivated." The latter terms are used herein because they are more descriptive and are employed in the introductory essay of the census (8th Census, *Agriculture,* viii). Secondly, the category of "uncultivated" does not mean all the land in the county other than the acres cultivated but, instead, all of the farm acres in the county that are uncultivated. In other words, a one-hundred-acre farm with fifty acres cultivated would be considered 50 percent cultivated. In the above column, Frederick and Washington Counties (Md.) exceed 80 percent in cultivation of farm lands, and they compare favorably with the Pennsylvania counties and very favorably with the Virginia counties.

In regards to cash value, note that, in general terms, the farther north the farm, the greater its cash value. Undoubtedly, this higher value is a reflection of greater productivity, more improvements, and inflation. Note also Montgomery county—in both acres cultivated (including percentage) and farm value—resembles a Virginia county rather than its western neighbors in Maryland. The two western Maryland counties, although only second and third among the twenty-one counties of their own state, would top the 148 counties of Virginia as first and second. The Virginia county with the highest cash value for its farms was Augusta with $10,997,286.

In determining the cash value of machinery, the census includes not only advanced machinery—such as mowers, reapers, and cotton gins—but also the more primitive tools, such as axes, shovels, hoes, and the like. Not surprisingly, there is a correlation between the presence of slavery and investment in farm machinery. The only exception is Montgomery County, which in this instance appears to be more of a Northern than a Southern county. Once again, the two western Maryland counties, although only second and third among the twenty-one counties of their own state, would top the 148 counties of Virginia as first and second. The Virginia county with the highest cash value of farm machinery was Augusta, with $296,390.

TABLE 13
Select Tri-State Counties: Size of Farms

	Numbers of acres							*Total number of farms*	*Average farm acreage*
	3–9	*10–19*	*20–49*	*50–99*	*100–499*	*500–999*	*1000+*		
PENNSYLVANIA									
Adams	18	140	379	684	942	–	–	2,163	118.67
Franklin	23	90	324	676	1,379	2	–	2,494	160.91
MARYLAND									
Montgomery	24	36	212	331	658	33	5	1,299	224.48
Frederick	20	129	351	540	1,309	15	1	2,365	143.49
Washington	7	60	131	245	591	4	1	1,039	231.13
VIRGINIA									
Culpeper	12	17	48	61	346	77	15	576	414.68
Faquier	22	27	94	108	565	117	33	966	396.98
Prince William	3	21	98	136	291	26	6	581	299.65
Fairfax	50	53	166	249	322	12	–	852	235.45
Loudoun	5	16	94	221	826	36	9	1,207	245.35
Frederick	6	10	57	163	495	20	–	751	253.63
Rockingham	5	72	448	447	855	13	3	1,843	187.72
Rockbridge	15	17	98	189	493	35	4	851	399.67

Source: Sizes of farms by categories are from 8th Census, *Agriculture*, 213 (Pa.), 203 (Md.), 218 (Va.). Farm totals were calculated from raw data. Average sizes of farms were calculated by dividing the number of farms into the total farm acreage.

Comments: Both Adams and Franklin Counties were significantly above the 65-acre Pennsylvania state average. The Maryland state average was 190 acres; surprisingly, Frederick was below but Washington above this. The Virginia counties have larger but fewer farms. The Virginia state average was 340 acres; only Culpeper, Faquier, and Rockbridge were above this average. The general trend was for farms to grow smaller, moving from south to north.

TABLE 14
Select Tri-State Counties: Livestock

	Horses	Rank (Md./Va.)	Milch cows	Rank (Md./Va.)	Cattle	Rank (Md./Va.)	Sheep	Rank (Md./Va.)
PENNSYLVANIA								
Adams	7,927	–	10,502	–	7,433	–	5,965	–
Franklin	11,104	–	11,333	–	15,862	–	9,921	–
MARYLAND								
Montgomery	5,587	–	5,202	–	5,761	–	10,487	–
Frederick	11,287	1/1	11,180	1/1	10,237	2/8	10,389	5/27
Washington	8,027	3/8	6,841	4/2	11,424	1/5	10,460	3/25
VIRGINIA								
Culpeper	3,136	–	3,200	–	8,098	–	15,303	–
Faquier	6,721	–	5,489	–	23,192	–	24,754	–
Prince William	2,190	–	2,259	–	3,596	–	7,001	–
Fairfax	2,725	–	3,709	–	3,919	–	6,093	–
Loudoun	7,503	–	5,809	–	14,504	–	10,625	–
Frederick	4,084	–	2,926	–	5,420	–	9,892	–
Rockingham	7,874	–	6,011	–	13,299	–	13,364	–
Rockbridge	4,381	–	4,046	–	9,227	–	10,298	–

Source: The statistics are from 8th Census, *Agriculture*, 122 (Pa.), 72 (Md.), 154, and 158 (Va.).

Comments: The horses category includes all varieties—draft, carriage, and riding. Even in 1860, when counted by the census, the Pennsylvania and Maryland counties (except Montgomery) owned more horses than the Virginia counties. The difference was probably even more striking after two years of war, which almost certainly reduced the number of horses in Virginia. Lee's army was especially short of horses to pull wagons, ambulances, and artillery. The Virginia county with the most horses in 1860 was Augusta, with 8,852.

Milch cows, or dairy cattle, are an important indicator of the richness of a farming area, and it will be noted that Frederick and Washington had more than any Virginia counties. Militarily, however, dairy cattle were of limited importance. Milk, a highly perishable commodity, could not be carried with the army. The Virginia county with the most milch cows was Halifax, with 8,609.

The "other cattle" category is, for the most part, comprised of cattle raised to provide beef. Here Frederick and Washington Counties, although not at the top, compare favorably with their Virginia counterparts. Fresh beef, known in army parlance as "green beef," was viewed by military leaders as less desirable than beef that had been preserved in some manner such as salting or pickling. The difficulty in cooking fresh beef thoroughly, combined with its short life before spoilage, resulted in severe digestive problems for the soldiers. The Virginia county with most "other cattle" was Faquier.

In terms of sheep, the Maryland counties (and even less so the Pennsylvania counties) do not compare favorably with Culpeper, Faquier, or Loudoun. The only immediate importance of sheep to an army, however, was to provide fresh lambchops. The Virginia county with most sheep was Brunswick, with 40,620.

TABLE 15

Select Tri-State Counties: Livestock (continued)

	Swine	*Rank (Md./Va.)*	*Value of livestock ($)*	*Rank (Md./Va.)*	*Value of livestock slaughtered ($)*	*Rank (Md./Va.)*
PENNSYLVANIA						
Adams	18,864	–	100,499	–	199,649	–
Franklin	33,281	–	1,440,197	–	268,402	–
MARYLAND						
Montgomery	22,823	–	852,767	–	194,186	–
Frederick	40,548	1/1	1,534,048	1/1	281,467	1/1
Washington	29,425	2/5	1,056,125	3/5	207,034	2/8
VIRGINIA						
Culpeper	13,532	–	540.572	–	114,849	–
Faquier	26,912	–	1,494,504	–	230,192	–
Prince William	7,937	–	318,445	–	62,089	
Fairfax	11,660	–	371,443	–	68,491	–
Loudoun	23,153	–	1,182,355	–	202,746	–
Frederick	12,939	–	519,296	–	96,524	–
Rockingham	37,307	–	1,139,690	–	260,691	–
Rockbridge	18,762	–	652,399	–	168,764	–

Source: Statistics are from 8th Census, *Agriculture*, 123, 125 (Pa.), 73 (Md.), 155, 157, 159, 161 (Va.).

Comments: In numbers of swine, Frederick and Washington Counties compare most favorably with the Virginia counties. Fresh pork, like fresh beef, was believed to be inferior to the preserved kind. In particular, Lee searched for bacon in Maryland. The Virginia county with the most swine was Rockingham.

In the value of livestock, Frederick and Washington Counties also compare most favorably with the Virginia counties. The entry for Adams County is almost certainly either a typographical error or is based on incomplete returns. In the two years of warfare after the census was taken, it is likely that the Virginia counties had suffered a greater loss of livestock than the Maryland counties. The Virginia county with the highest value of livestock was Faquier.

In the value of livestock slaughtered, Frederick and Washington Counties again compare most favorably with the Virginia counties. The Virginia county with the highest value of livestock slaughtered was Albemarle with $267,222.

TABLE 16
Select Tri-State Counties: Grain (by bushels)

	Wheat (bu.)	*Rank (Md./Va.)*	*Rye (bu.)*	*Rank (Md./Va.)*	*Corn (bu.)*	*Rank (Md./Va.)*	*Oats (bu.)*	*Rank (Md./Va.)*
PENNSYLVANIA								
Adams	401,885	–	53,408	–	551,110	–	461,850	–
Franklin	714,857	–	113,840	–	645,580	–	437,898	–
MARYLAND								
Montgomery	341,087	–	27,036	–	686,843	–	222,674	–
Frederick	976,143	1/1	94,251	1/1	1,082,903	1/1	272,082	5/3
Washington	882,814	2/2	77,993	2/2	669,322	11/5	175,445	7/7
VIRGINIA								
Culpeper	191,358	–	9,938	–	442,191	–	60,074	–
Faquier	280,279	–	43,513	–	717,450	–	178,906	–
Prince William	54,069	–	11,403	–	188,270	–	96,489	–
Fairfax	49,318	–	15,156	–	263,225	–	155,409	–
Loudoun	396,297	–	28,946	–	931,465	–	188,717	–
Frederick	224,471	–	27,677	–	285,770	–	85,241	–
Rockingham	358,653	–	45,362	–	684,239	–	128,010	–
Rockbridge	193,338	–	18,889	–	423,952	–	138,298	–

Source: Statistics are from 8th Census, *Agriculture*, 123 (Pa.), 73 (Md.), 155, 159 (Va.).

Comments: In wheat, Frederick and Washington Counties greatly outproduced the counties in Pennsylvania and Virginia. The Virginia county producing the most wheat was Jefferson, with 422,514 bushels.

In rye, Frederick and Washington Counties also outproduced the counties in Pennsylvania and Virginia. The Virginia county producing the most rye was Hampshire, with 75,257 bushels.

In Indian corn, Frederick and Washington Counties again outproduced the Virginia counties but not the Pennsylvania counties. The Virginia county producing the most Indian corn was Loudoun.

Oats were more important for fodder than for human consumption. While not at the very top, Frederick and Washington Counties were rich in this staple that was so important to Lee's army. The Virginia county producing the most oats was Accomack, with 366,200 bushels.

TABLE 17
Select Tri-State Counties: Miscellaneous Produce

	Orchard products ($)	*Rank (Md./Va.)*	*Butter (lbs.)*	*Rank (Md./Va.)*	*Honey (lbs.)*	*Rank (Md./Va.)*	*Hay (tons)*	*Rank (Md./Va.)*
PENNSYLVANIA								
Adams	18,031	–	863,572	–	9,680	–	49,621	–
Franklin	32,819	–	784,639	–	6,714	–	45,776	–
MARYLAND								
Montgomery	3,227	–	278,141	–	53,003	1/4	13,167	–
Frederick	11,064	7/22	969,797	1/1	4,568	12/	32,078	1/1
Washington	20,656	4/3	550,898	2/2	11,510	5/34	21,352	4/3
VIRGINIA								
Culpeper	575	–	107,270	–	8,545	–	4,765	–
Faquier	2,287	–	284,005	–	42,193	–	11,756	–
Prince William	1,493	–	96,535	–	13,052	–	4,239	–
Fairfax	6,715	–	163,166	–	2,557	–	8,088	–
Loudoun	3,823	–	425,117	–	26,993	–	12,835	–
Frederick	7,518	–	215,758	–	22,012	–	7,777	–
Rockingham	16,351	–	427,593	–	9,827	–	19,174	–
Rockbridge	13,782	–	199,756	–	10,092	–	9,638	–

Source: Statistics are from 8th Census, *Agriculture,* 124, 125 (Pa.), 72, 73 (Md.), 156, 157, 160, 161 (Va.).

Comments: "Orchard products" is a confusing but important category. Not only is it unclear what fruits are included, but no explanation is given of how the valuation is made. It cannot be considered, therefore, more than a relative guide to the fruit available. Within these restraints, it will be seen that Frederick and Washington compare very favorably to the Virginia counties. The Virginia county producing the most orchard products was Southampton, with $61,642.

Frederick and Washington Counties produced more butter than any of the Virginia counties. The Virginia county producing the most butter was Augusta, with 451,305 pounds. Butter was highly perishable and could not be conveniently be carried with the army.

For honey, Frederick and Washington do not compare as well with the Virginia counties. Honey was the army's favorite sweetener but not an essential for everyday eating. The Virginia county producing the most honey was Pittsylvania, with 78,844 lbs.

Frederick and Washington produced more hay than their Virginia counterparts. Hay was the prime fodder for the animals of the army. The Virginia county producing the most hay was Augusta, with 21,687 tons.

TABLE 18
Select Tri-State Counties: Miscellaneous Produce (continued)

	Wool (bu.)	*Rank (Md./Va.)*	*Potatoes (bu.)*	*Rank (Md./Va.)*	*Tobacco (lbs.)*
PENNSYLVANIA					
Adams	20,998	–	58,401	–	300
Franklin	40,031	–	101,148	–	–
MARYLAND					
Montgomery	38,674	–	109,745	–	843,300
Frederick	31,650	4/14	94,043	5/2	387,100
Washington	47,133	1/6	68,816	7/3	50
VIRGINIA					
Culpeper	54,992	–	19,215	–	179,805
Faquier	102,257	–	38,746	–	271,232
Prince William	24,327	–	14,445	–	12,921
Fairfax	14,391	–	54,383	–	29,100
Loudoun	42,580	–	43,953	–	–
Frederick	37,936	–	29,890	–	832
Rockingham	36,294	–	39,269	–	153,304
Rockbridge	19,431	–	26,441	–	456,556

Sources: Statistics are from 8th Census, *Agriculture*, 123 (Pa.), 73 (Md.), 155, 159 (Va.).

Comments: Although not at the top, Frederick and Washington compare favorably in wool production with the Virginia counties. Although wool was essential to the production of cloth for uniforms, it was not of immediate importance to Lee's army. The Virginia county producing the most wool was Brooke, with 112,774 pounds.

Frederick and Washington Counties produced significantly more Irish potatoes than the Virginia counties did. Irish potatoes seem not to have been popular with the Confederate army. The Virginia county producing the most Irish potatoes was Norfolk, with 102,605 pounds.

Surprisingly, Frederick produced more tobacco than any of the Virginia counties listed except Rockbridge, and Montgomery produced more than twice as much as Frederick. Lee's soldiers always seemed to have enough tobacco, and they did not need to go to Maryland to replenish their supply. It becomes obvious that none of the above counties were heavily into tobacco, when it is considered that the Virginia county producing the most tobacco was Halifax, with 8,544,532 lbs.

TABLE 19
Select Tri-State Counties: Manufacturing

	Boots and shoes		*Flour and meal*		*All manufacturing*	
	Number of establishments	*Annual value*	*Number of establishments*	*Annual value*	*Number of establishments*	*Annual value*
PENNSYLVANNIA						
Adams	–	–	40	356,758	159	683,925
Franklin	30	51,610	60	659,519	317	1,722,626
MARYLAND						
Montgomery	–	–	34	318,657	44	380,267
Frederick	73	112,707	79	1,286,171	501	2,894,169
Washington	18	37,625	–	–	–	–
VIRGINIA						
Culpeper	–	–	–	–	7	159,175
Faquier	5	12,465	26	109,819	110	337,848
Prince William	2	3,400	17	153,729	47	235,927
Fairfax	–	–	–	–	–	–
Loudoun	11	18,732	26	566,741	83	750,178
Frederick	5	21,119	37	397,009	127	729,051
Rockingham	18	18,445	24	224,680	122	422,588
Rockbridge	8	17,810	52	406,609	220	958,743

Sources: The figures for boots and shoes/flour and meal are from 8th Census, *Manufactures*, 493, 509 (Pa.); 224–27 (Md.); 611–12, 613, 620, 627, 629 (Va.) The "all manufacturing" numbers are from ibid., 537 (Pa.), 228 (Md.), 635–36 (Va.).

Comments: Frederick and Washington Counties should have been able to provide Lee with a stock of footwear to shod his army. He would in fact report acquiring 1,000 pairs in Frederick, 400 in Hagerstown, and 250 in Williamsport.[1] Unfortunately, the macadamized roads in Maryland were especially hard on Confederate shoes.

The editor's introductory essay (8th Census, *Manufacture*, lxviii) implies that, as a rule of thumb, the average cost of a pair of boots or shoes in 1860 was $1.25; therefore, it is possible to translate roughly the quantity of footwear as 80 percent of the annual value. The Virginia county leading in the production of boots and shoes was Henrico, with twenty establishments producing an annual value of $173,450.

Flour is meal that has been finely ground and bolted (sifted). Meal is grain that has been coarsely ground and unbolted (unsifted). Flour and meal were second in importance only to meat in the feeding of Lee's army. Lee reported acquiring about 1,500 barrels of flour by the time he had reached Hagerstown on September 12.[2] Maj. John F. Edwards, chief commissary for McLaws's division, remembered getting only about twenty barrels of flour in Pleasant Valley. The grain he acquired could not be ground in the mills because the water had been let out of the canal.[3] In Virginia, Rockbridge County had the most mills, but Henrico, with only twelve mills, produced flour and meal annually worth $3,063,050.

The "all manufacturing" category is not nearly as helpful as it appears to be, or ought to be. The major problem is the broad definition employed by the census. For example, a single smithy operating his own blacksmith shop was included as a manufacturing establishment. Within these constraints, and with particular reference to the annual value of products, it is evident that Frederick and Washington dwarfed the manufacturing in the Virginia counties. Henrico County led Virginia with 320 manufacturing establishments, producing goods worth $12,926,949 annually.

TABLE 20
Select Tri-State Counties: Real and Personal Estate Valuations

	Real	*Personal*	*Aggregate*	*Worth of average family*
PENNSYLVANIA				
Adams	12,339,770	4,416,152	16,755,922	3,183.12
Franklin	20,079,556	6,586,922	26,666,478	3,459.14
MARYLAND				
Montgomery	6,923,493	6,400,750	13,324,243	5,660.26
Frederick	16,290,757	11,677,941	27,968,698	3,603.75
Washington	13,832,836	4,555,392	18,388,228	3,260.32
VIRGINIA				
Culpeper	5,541,402	6,425,009	11,966,411	11,374.92
Faquier	13,308,772	14,052,831	27,361,603	12,961.44
Prince William	2,483,400	2,822,626	5,306,026	4,977.51
Fairfax	4,071,722	3,285,394	7,357,166	4,527.49
Loudoun	12,545,236	8,626,701	21,171,937	7,211.15
Frederick	6,711,276	5,168,807	11,880,083	4,586.90
Rockingham	10,359,061	6,726,645	17,085,706	4,665.68
Rockbridge	8,290,943	6,170,188	14,461,131	6,078.66

Sources: Real and personal estate values are from 8th Census, *Mortality*, 311 (Pa.); 304 (Md.); 315 (Va.).

The worth of average families was calculated by dividing the total real and personal estate values by the number of families in the county. Family numbers, including only free population, may be found in 8th Census, *Mortality*, 347 (Pa.); 344 (Md.); 349–350 (Va.).

Comments: Frederick and Washington Counties exceed all of the Virginia counties in real estate values.

Slaves were included in personal estate values. Note that in Culpeper and Faquier Counties, both with large slave populations, the personal property values exceed those of real estate values. Washington Countians have less valuable personal property than do residents of any of the Virginia counties, except Prince William and Fairfax.

The Virginia counties compare favorably with both the Pennsylvania and Maryland counties in total money invested in real and personal property (aggregate values). The foregoing tables clearly indicate, however, that the Virginia counties were receiving less return from their investment.

The Pennsylvania state average family worth was $3,163.06: Franklin County was above and Adams almost exactly on this average. The Maryland average was $3,783.91: Montgomery County was much above, Frederick slightly below, and Washington significantly below that of the state. The Virginia average was $5,374.99: Culpeper and Faquier more than doubled the average; Loudoun and Rockbridge were significantly above; and all of the other counties were below the state average.

Unfortunately, the census gives no statistics on income. It must remain speculation that Maryland and Pennsylvania families, even with lesser estates, earned more annually than their Virginia counterparts. In this regard, see Table 8 on banking, which suggests that Maryland families may have had $39 and Pennsylvania families $10 more each year to save than Virginia families. Banking statistics are not broken down by county in the census.

Table 21
Select Tri-State Counties: Towns and Village Populations

State/County/City	*Population*
DISTRICT OF COLUMBIA (TOTAL: 75,080)	
Washington	61,122
Georgetown	8,733
MARYLAND	
Baltimore	212,418
Frederick County	
Frederick	8,142
Washington County	
Boonsboro	864*
Cavetown	ca. 175*†

State/County/City	*Population*
Clear Spring	ca. 680*†
Funkstown	647*
Hagerstown	4,132*
Hancock	ca. 850*†
Keedysville	ca. 380*†
Leitersburg	ca.300*†
Sharpsburg	ca.900*†
Smithsburg	475*
Williamsport	1,016*
Other Maryland towns (for context)	
Annapolis	4,529
PENNSYLVANIA	
Adams County	
Gettysburg	2,390
Franklin County	
Chambersburg	5,255
Greencastle	1,399
Waynesboro	1,233
Other Pennsylvania towns (for context)	
Harrisburg	13,405
Philadelphia	565,529
Pittsburgh	49,217
VIRGINIA	
Alexandria	12,654
Fairfax County	
Fairfax Court House	ca.250†
Centreville	ca.200†
Pleasant Valley	ca. 40†
Loudoun County	
Leesburg	1,130
Waterford	429
Faquier County	
Warrenton	604
Culpeper County	
Culpeper Court House	1,056
Frederick County	
Winchester	4,392

State/County/City	*Population*
Other Virginia towns (for context)	
Charleston	1,520
Farmville	1,536
Fredericksburg	5,023
Front Royal	412
Hampton	1,848
Harrisonburg	1,023
Jeffersonton	162
Lexington	2,135
Lynchburg	6,853
New Market	1,422
Norfolk	14,620
Petersburg	18,266
Portsmouth	9,496
Richmond	37,910
Staunton	3,875
Strasburg	1,583
Suffolk	1,395
Wheeling	14,083
Wytheville	1,111
[WEST VIRGINIA]	
Jefferson County	
Charlestown	1,376
Harpers Ferry	1,339
Bolivar	1,130
Shepherdstown	1,219
Berkeley County	
Martinsburg	3,364

Sources: Populations, unless otherwise noted, are from 8th Census, *Population,* 588 (D.C.); 214 (Md.); 413–37 (Pa.); 518–20 (Va. and W.Va.).

Populations marked with an asterisk (*) were provided by John Frye, curator of the Western Maryland Room, Washington County Public Library.

Populations marked with a dagger (†) were estimated by the author based on earlier and/or later census information.

Comments: In the 1860 census, Pennsylvania towns and villages were regularly reported, Virginia towns were regularly reported (but villages only sporadically so), and Maryland towns and villages were reported sporadically and randomly.

Frederick was the second largest town in Maryland. It was much larger than Virginia towns such as Fredericksburg, Winchester, and Leesburg and was, by a considerable margin, the biggest urban area visited by the Army of Northern Virginia since leaving Richmond. It was, indeed, the third largest town (after Richmond and Petersburg) Lee ever occupied.

It has been estimated that Richmond's wartime population would grow to 150,000, and, doubtless, it was much greater than 37,910 by September 1862.

Table 22
Railroads

A. Railroads Important to the Maryland Campaign

Railroad	*Mileage*	*Cost (in millions)*
MARYLAND		
Baltimore & Ohio	416.8 (incl. 30 Wash. Branch and 241 in Va.)	$25.0
North Central	142.0 (incl. 102 in Pa.)	$8.2
Cumberland & Pennsylvania	27.5	$1.3
Western Maryland	18.0	$0.3
VIRGINIA		
Alexandria, Loudoun & Hampshire	41.5	$1.5
Manassas Gap	86.7	$3.2
Orange & Alexandria	156.8	$6.4
Winchester & Potomac	32.0	$0.5

B. Railroads Having More Than 200 Miles of Track

Rank	*Railroad*	*Mileage*	*Cost (in millions)*
1	Illinois Central	738.3	$27.2
2	New York Central	555.9	$30.8
3	Michigan Southern & Northern Indiana	484.6	$15.6
4	Mobile & Ohio	482.8	$14.5

Rank	*Railroad*	*Mileage*	*Cost (in millions)*
5	Pittsburgh, Ft. Wayne & Chicago	467.5	$17.5
6	New York & Erie	465.0	$35.3
7	Baltimore & Ohio	416.8	$25.0
8	Pennsylvania	359.2	$26.6
9	Memphis & Charleston	290.1	$6.7
10	Louisville, New Albany & Chicago	288.0	$7.0
11	Michigan Central	284.8	$13.2
12	Galena & Chicago Union	261.3	$9.4
13	Louisville & Nashville	253.2	$8.5
14	Toledo, Wabash & Western	243.0	$8.0
15	South Carolina	242.0	$6.5
16	Milwaukee & Prairie du Chein	234.4	$7.5
17	Georgia	232.0	$4.2
18	North Carolina	223.0	$4.2
19	Chicago, Alton & St. Louis	220.0	$10.0
20	Virginia & Tennessee	214.9	$7.4
21	Chicago & Northwestern	213.0	$10.7
22	Southwestern Georgia	209.1	$4.2
23	Terre Haute, Alton & St. Louis	208.3	$8.9
24	Hannibal & St. Joseph	206.8	$12.4
25	New Orleans, Opelousas & Great Western	206.0	$6.6
26	Cleveland & Pittsburgh	203.5	$9.3
TOTAL FOR U.S. (402 miles of city passenger lines not included)		30,793.7	$1,151,561

Source: 8th Census, *Mortality*, 325–32.

Comments: Note that the Baltimore & Ohio clearly dominated the railroad in the area of operations for the Maryland campaign. Although only ranked seventh, it was one of the largest lines in the United States.

Interestingly, of the top twenty-six railroads, twelve were either entirely within slave states or had an extensive part of their trackage there.

Damage to the Baltimore & Ohio (including the destruction of the iron bridge at Monocacy Junction, southeast of Frederick) by the Confederates and the time and cost of repair are discussed in several studies.[4]

Table 23
The Top Seven Canals in 1862

Rank	*Name*	*Navigable miles*	*Connecting*	*Width x depth (ft.)*	*Number of locks*	*Cost (in millions)*
1	Wabash & Erie	379.0	Evansville to Ohio border	–	–	–
2	Erie	350.6	Albany to Buffalo	70 x 7	71	$40.0
3	Ohio & Erie	307.0	Portsmouth to Cleveland	40 x 4	152	–
4	Chesapeake & Ohio	184.5	Georgetown, D.C., to Cumberland, Md.	50 x 6	74	$10.5
5	Miami & Erie	178.0	Cincinnati to Defiance, Oh.	–	–	–
6	Pennsylvania	156.0	Columbia to Hollidaysburg, Pa.	40 x 4	76	$1.0
7	James River & Kanawha	147.8	Richmond to Buchanan, Va.	–	–	$6.1

Source: 8th Census, *Mortality*, 335–36.

Comments: It is evident from the table that the C&O was one of the nation's major canals. The C&O built aqueducts over the Conocheague at Williamsport, over the Monocacy above Poolesville, and over the Antietam near its juncture with the Potomac. There is no evidence that, after their failed attempt to destroy the Monocacy aqueduct, the Confederates wasted their time on the others.

The Confederates damaged the canal itself by cutting its banks to let out the water and by rolling large stones into the dry bed. This proved counterproductive on at least one occasion, when mills operating on the canal were thereafter unable to grind Confederate grain into flour. In the end, Confederates inflicted minimal damage on the canal.[5]

CHAPTER FIVE

Research Appendixes on Lee's Decision to Enter Maryland

A. Lee's View That Action Was Imperative in Early September

Lee's belief that he must act after Second Manassas was a variation on his more basic view that the Confederates' situation—especially their inferiority in human and material resources—demanded that he must continue to hold and press the initiative. Nowhere did he state this more succinctly than in the letter in which he proposed the Maryland campaign: "Still, we cannot afford to be idle, and though weaker than our opponents in men and military equipments, must endeavor to harass if we cannot destroy them."[1] In his final report of the operations in Maryland, Lee referred briefly of his desire "not to permit the season for active operations to pass without endeavoring to inflict further injury upon the enemy."[2]

That such views were not a passing notion but came from his long-range thinking about the war was evidenced by Lee rephrasing his axiom nine months later: "There is always hazard in military movements, but we must decide between the positive loss of inactivity and the risk of action."[3]

Finally, Lee would give an uncharacteristically detailed explanation on why the Confederates could not afford to be idle later as he sat at Williamsport, Maryland, this time on his way to Pennsylvania:[4]

> So strong is my conviction of the necessity of activity on our part in military affairs, that you will excuse my adverting to the subject again, notwithstanding what I have said in my previous letter of today.
>
> It seems to me that we cannot afford to keep our troops awaiting possible movements of the enemy, but that our true policy is,

as far as we can, so to employ our own forces as to give occupation to his at points of our selection. . . .

[Lee goes on to suggest that Generals Simon Buckner and Samuel Jones move into Kentucky.]

They could render valuable service by collecting and bringing out supplies, if they do no more, and would embarrass the enemy and prevent troops now there from being sent to other points. If they are too weak to attempt this object, they need not be idle. . . . They might be sent with benefit to reinforce Genl Johnston or Genl Bragg, or to constitute a part of the proposed army of Genl Beauregard at Culpeper Court House, or they might accomplish good results by going into northwestern Virginia. It should never be forgotten that our concentration at any point compels that of the enemy, and his numbers being limited, tends to relieve all other threatened localities.

In this dispatch Lee not only justifies his move then under way into Pennsylvania, but he also explains his expedition into Maryland of the previous autumn. He uses "activity" as synonymous with pressing the initiative. Note here also a rare acknowledgment by Lee that the numbers of the enemy are "limited."

Charles Marshall of Lee's personal staff gave a succinct and powerful summary of the reasons Lee believed he must press forward after Second Manassas, and in the process he restated Lee's strategy for winning the war. This passage is so critical that it deserves to be quoted in full:[5]

I must say again that General Lee's policy was not to capture any portion of Federal territory, but to protract the war by breaking up the enemy's campaigns and so bringing about the pecuniary exhaustion of the North. At the same time he desired to increase the power of resistance of the South by keeping the enemy out of the Confederate territory.

If he had retired after the second Manassas, none of these results would have been obtained from the campaign of 1862. That campaign would have opened with the Federal army around Richmond; bloody and successful battles would have been fought; the Confederate by putting forth their whole strength would have succeeded in raising the siege of Richmond for a time, and in forcing the enemy back to the Potomac River. Then, had General Lee been unable for any reason to follow up the advantage of the victory he had gained, the campaign would have ended with the Federal army

> once again besieging Richmond and the Confederate once more defending it.
>
> There can be no doubt as to which side would have appeared to have the substantial advantages of a campaign ending in the way supposed. The great fact would have remained that all the efforts of the Confederates had failed to loosen the hold the enemy had on Richmond, the key to the possession of the great State of Virginia. What effect would such a result have had on the credit of the North? The credit of the Federal Government did not depend upon its actual resources more than it depended upon moral causes, that is, upon the prospect of ultimate success and especially upon the prospect of speedy success.
>
> It can scarcely be doubted that had the second battle of Manassas been followed by the retirement of General Lee's army to the line of the Rapidan, or that of the lower Rappahannock, the Northern people would have seen in such a result solid reasons for expecting ultimate and not very remote success, and so far as the pecuniary conditions of Mr. Lincoln's government depended upon popular belief that the war would end soon and successfully, that belief must have received substantial encouragement.

Lee was not alone in his view of the path to Confederate victory. Six weeks earlier the *Richmond Examiner* stated its belief there was "but one method of putting an end to the war, and that is by destroying Federal credit."[6]

General agreement by Confederate veterans that the moment was ripe for action is provided by James Longstreet, Moxley Sorrel, and William Allan. Two recent historians, Robert Krick and Scott Hartwig, have agreed.[7]

B. Lee on Attacking Washington

Lee's six comments on the inadvisability of attacking Washington—both at the time and later—were consistent and unambiguous. In addition to his remark to his cousin quoted in the text of *Taken at the Flood*, Lee also said or wrote:

> (2) "I did not think it would be advantageous to follow him farther. I had no intention of attacking him in his fortifications, and am not prepared to invest them."[8]

(3) "the enemy had conducted his retreat so rapidly that the attempt to intercept him was abandoned. The proximity of the fortifications around Alexandria and Washington rendered further pursuit useless."[9]

(4) "He [Lee] said that after Chantilly (about Sept. 1) he found he could do nothing more against the Yankees, unless he attacked them in their fortifications around Washington, which he did not want to do."[10]

(5) "It was, in the first place, to get the enemy away from the works in front of Washington, which he thought it folly to attack from the Manassas side." And, "He could not go straight forward, for he thought it injudicious to attack the fortifications."[11]

(6) "I considered it useless to attack the fortifications around Alexandria and Washington."[12]

C. Lee's Comments on Supply Problems

In the April 15, 1868, letter to William McDonald quoted in *Taken at the Flood*, Lee seemed to lay equal stress on the barrenness of Fairfax and the deficiencies of his commissary trains. Earlier on the same day he had made a similar comment to William Allan: "He could not stay where he was at Manassas from want of supplies and adequate transportation."[13]

In other statements, however, Lee seemed more concerned about his army's transportation weaknesses. On September 2, 1862, he wrote to Secretary of War Randolph of "the heavy stress upon the commissary department in its efforts to supply this army with subsistence."[14] On September 3, 1862, he wrote to Davis, "If I possessed the munitions [to attack Washington], I should be unable to supply provisions for the troops."[15] And in a second dispatch to Davis of the same date, he confessed that "the progress & protection of our trains have caused the greatest difficulties."[16]

Lee's concern over food and its transportation would continue throughout the war. In 1864 he commented that "food for this army gives me more trouble and uneasiness than every thing else combined."[17] And after the war he would detail "numerous instances" of the "mismanagement of the Confederate Commissary Department" and "his embarrassments in consequence."[18]

D. Strategic Reasons for Lee Not Remaining in Fairfax County

Lee did not comment in writing on the strategic unsoundness of remaining in Fairfax. According to Charles Marshall, however, it was part of the Confederate commander's analysis that "there was nothing to prevent the enemy as soon as he should recover from the recent disasters from repeating General McClellan's plan and sending such a force by water to Richmond as must have taken General Lee back immediately to the place from which he set out on his Northern campaign."[19] Based on what the Confederates could have known at the time this is a reasonable evaluation. It is wrong, of course, because it fails to account for Lincoln's unwillingness to permit a repetition of an operation that had, in his view, so imperiled the capital. While Lee perceived and exploited Lincoln's "anxiety," he apparently did not comprehend its depth.[20]

William Allan and Bradley Johnson also mention the strategic weakness of remaining in Fairfax, but it is not clear that either was privy to special information on Lee's thinking on this point at the time.[21]

E. Lee's Views on Invading the North in September 1862

On September 3 Lee would write to Davis, "The army is not properly equipped for an invasion of an enemy's territory."[22] And in his report on the Maryland campaign he would repeat that his force was "not properly equipped for an invasion."[23]

After the war, William Allan recorded a conversation in which "General Lee said he had never invaded the north with an eye to holding permanently the hostile portions of it. He said that especially in 1862 his object was not primarily to take Baltimore, or to undertake any very decided offensive movement."[24]

It should be noted that Lee singled out Baltimore only because William M. McDonald, who proposed to write a history textbook, had written expressly asking Lee why he had not taken Baltimore when everyone had expected he would. In his reply to McDonald, written on the same day as the conversation with Allan, Lee explained flatly: "In relation to your first question, I will state that in crossing the Potomac I did not propose to invade the North, for I did not believe that the Army of Northern Virginia was strong enough for the purpose, nor was I in any degree influenced by popular expectation."[25]

Hence, during the war Lee mentioned only lack of supplies as a deterrent and said nothing about the size of his force. After the war, however, and perhaps after the recurring theme of Confederate inferiority in numbers had begun to take hold in Southern thinking, Lee wrote to McDonald that his force was not "strong enough for the purpose." Of course, "strong" is ambiguous. While Lee may still be referring only to his army's condition, he seems to be implying size as well.

After the war, Henry Heth claimed to have had an interview with Lee "a short time before . . . the spring of 1864" in which the Confederate commander seemed to express a philosophy almost the direct opposite, extolling the benefits of invasion and averring the capture of Philadelphia "would have given us peace" in the Gettysburg campaign.[26] This is so much at variance with everything else Lee wrote and said on the subject as to raise doubts about the accuracy of Heth's memory.

F. Lee's Views on a Westward Movement in September 1862

Lee's views on moving westward with his army after Second Manassas were made in two separate conversations with William Allan after the war, and, although jumbled a bit by Allan's imperfect understanding, are clear enough when set in the context of Lee's known thinking at the time. According to the memoranda made by Allan, on February 15, 1868, Lee remembered having "talked to Gen. Jackson, who advised him to go up into the Valley. . . . He (Lee) opposed this, because it took him too far from McClellan, and might not induce the latter to cross over, which was his main object."[27] And on April 15 of the same year, Lee said, "To have retired into Loudoun was to give the enemy possession of Fairfax, etc. and to invite him to flank towards Richmond."[28]

Two observations are in order. First, Lee's postwar reference to McClellan is misleading, since at the time his correspondence was still referring to Pope as his opponent. Second, the suggestion that a Confederate position in Loudoun might invite the Federals to flank toward Richmond only makes sense if Lee is referring to a flanking movement by water down the Chesapeake.

G. The Fallacy of Coincidence: The Absence of Foreign Affairs Considerations in Lee's Decision to enter Maryland

The fallacy of assuming—without direct evidence—that events occurring simultaneously in Europe influenced Lee's decision to enter Maryland is an ancient error in Antietam historiography. It seems to have originated with the Comte de Paris, Louis Philippe Albert d'Orleans. The count served for less than a year on the staff of McClellan and then returned to Europe to write a four-volume history of the American Civil War. As Orleanist pretender to the French throne, Louis was a natural opponent of all Bonapartists. In his second volume (which appeared in a translated American edition in 1876), in discussing the Maryland campaign, he wrote at some length about the mistakenly pro-Confederate policy of Napoleon III and asserted that only the wisdom of the British kept the two powers from acting in some fashion in the fall of 1862. Furthermore, he seems to imply that Lee understood the importance of striking "a blow which should resound on the other side of the Atlantic."[29]

In 1884 the fallacy appeared to be validated by a veteran of the campaign who would have been in a position to know something about Lee's thinking. Bradley T. Johnson, a brigade commander in Jackson's division, was summoned to headquarters on the night of September 4 to discuss aspects of the pending operations. (See chapter 2 of *Taken at the Flood* for a discussion of this meeting.) In an address to survivors of the Army of Northern Virginia, Johnson alluded to the possibility that foreign intervention might have resulted from the Maryland campaign. A close reading of Johnson's speech, however, reveals that he makes no claim that Lee intended to influence France or Great Britain. Indeed, Johnson's words are a suspiciously close paraphrase of the Comte de Paris and add nothing new to the discussion.[30]

The fallacious connection reached the status of historical certainty when James Murfin asserted it as the fifth of eight reasons Lee crossed the Potomac. According to Murfin, "Europe's eyes were on Lee's progress, and he knew what was at stake."[31]

H. The Strength of the Army of Northern Virginia on September 2, 1862

John Allen's master's thesis, "Strength of the Union and Confederate Forces at Second Manassas," was based on the muster rolls and regimental returns in RG 109, Confederate Records, in the National Archives, Washington, D.C. Allen includes twenty-two tables showing the size of the armies at various times and places. The table below is from his figures for the Confederates on September 2. In the case of forty-seven regiments (about one-quarter of the total) Allen found reports for September 1; elsewhere he estimated regimental strength based on the last available figures from July or August. In one of his most interesting discoveries, he found that straggling in July–August was slightly more than offset by the return of convalescents. All figures below are present for duty.[32]

TABLE 24

Army of Northern Virginia, September 2, 1862

Unit	*Number present for duty*
Army headquarters	8
LONGSTREET'S COMMAND	
Headquarters	7
D. R. Jones's division	3,728
Wilcox's division	5,582
Kemper's division	4,887
Evans's division	4,834
Artillery	590
Subtotal	19,628
JACKSON'S COMMAND	
Headquarters	9
Stonewall division	5,650
Ewell's division	6,383
A. P. Hill's division	8,570
Subtotal	20,612
R. H. Anderson's division	5,712
Stuart's cavalry	4,155
REINFORCING COLUMN	
McLaws's division	7,652
D. H. Hill's division	9,794
Walker's division	5,159
Hampton's brigade	1,509
Artillery Reserve	1,299
Subtotal	25,413
TOTAL	75,528

Walter Herron Taylor, one of the most avid statisticians of the Lost Cause, gave Lee 49,077 men at Second Manassas and 35,255 at Sharpsburg.[33] In neither of his books does Taylor estimate the size of the Confederate army at the time of crossing the Potomac, nor does he assign a figure to the reenforcements from Richmond.

William Allan puts Lee at 50,000 on September 2 by taking Taylor's figure for Second Manassas and then assuming the reinforcements "fully made up for his losses in battle, but it is not so certain that they covered the additional losses from sickness and straggling."[34] A. L. Long wrote the army "did not exceed 45,000 effective men."[35]

Bradley Johnson went to the extreme of giving Lee only 35,000 men present for duty on entering Maryland, but he apparently made the error of using Taylor's figures for September 17 without accounting for either battle or straggling losses between the 2d and the 17th.[36]

Contemporary historian Stephen Sears concluded, "Reinforcements from Richmond . . . were at hand or on the way, but they barely made good the 9,000 men lost at Bull Run and Chantilly. On this date [September 3] Lee could count perhaps 50,000 troops with which to undertake his expedition beyond the Confederacy's northern frontier."[37] Sears offers no source for his figures, but the echo is so strong as to suggest he adopted Allan's views.

On the other side, several authors have suggested Lee had a somewhat larger army at the time. Without specifying a number, Longstreet's chief of staff, Moxley Sorrell, noted: "The enemy had suffered a serious defeat and was driven into his capital, his numbers again very great, but of demoralized and raw-recruited men. On the other hand, Lee also had a strong army (for Confederate numbers—we had been accustomed to be outnumbered.)"[38]

Historian James Murfin decided: "The most men he counted on taking into Maryland was 70,000, and this number would probably be depleted even more by the time he crossed the Potomac."[39] Murfin cites no source for his conclusion, nor does he explain why serious depletion was expected between Chantilly and the crossing of the Potomac. He perhaps alludes to the drop-outs who objected to leaving the Confederacy.

I. Corps Structure of the Army of Northern Virginia in September 1862

It has traditionally been assumed that Lee's army had firmly jelled into two corps by the time it crossed the Potomac. This is not quite the case, however. The error probably derived from the fact that the October reorganization of the army is read backward one month. Even some Confederates confused this point after the war. It is clear, however, that neither McLaws nor Walker operated under Longstreet until the evening of September 18, and R.H. Anderson may not have until the morning of 17th. Indeed, after the war Anderson claimed he had reported directly to Lee until the official reorganization in October.[40] D.H. Hill was under Jackson—at least in Lee's mind—only for the two days that both crossed the Potomac in advance of the remainder of the army.

This less structured view of the Army of Northern Virginia helps to clear up two otherwise puzzling points. (1) Why did Lee abandon his corps organization in issuing S.O. 191? Answer: He could not abandon what he did not yet have. And (2) why did Lee send a copy of those orders directly to D.H. Hill? Answer: Because Hill was not assigned to Jackson.

E. Porter Alexander wrote that "Confederate organization into corps was slowly developing," and he admitted that in the earlier stages of the Maryland campaign "there was much independence of action by some divisions."[41]

Postwar Lee would remember "that Genrl. Hill had moved up from Richmond, and not then being regularly incorporated in a corps," and he had himself ordered Hill to cross the Potomac in advance of the army.[42] The remark is neutral and does not settle whether there simply was not time; Lee was unsure about making the corps structure permanent; or even that he might have been considering the creation of a third corps.

J. Officer Cadre of the Army of Northern Virginia in September 1862

Historian Robert Krick gives the impression of a shaky officer corps for the Army of Northern Virginia with his observation that thirteen of its officers at the brigade and division level "washed out" in the Maryland campaign "or soon thereafter" and by concluding that "none of the army's other campaigns equaled that purgative record."[43] Krick's list seems to include the following (the last two names are uncertain): D. H. Hill, Howell Cobb, Robert Toombs, Roger Pryor, Roswell Ripley, Nathan Evans, Winfield Featherston, Thomas Drayton, John R. Jones, David R. Jones, Alexander Grigsby, and possibly John G. Walker and Alfred Colquitt.

First, it might be noted that thirteen bad apples out of fifty-five (Krick includes cavalry) is not at all a bad proportion for a Civil War army, particularly in the first two years of the war. Secondly, while all of the officers named did leave the Army of Northern Virginia (although Colquitt and J. R. Jones did not leave until after Chancellorsville), "washed out" is too severe a term for most of them. By Krick's own account five of the officers (Toombs, D. R. Jones, Grigsby, Walker, and Colquitt) would perform well in the campaign. A sixth (Featherston) was absent for most, if not all, of it. And a seventh (D. H. Hill) arguably performed better than any other division commander on either side. Only six generals (Ripley, Evans, Cobb, Pryor, Drayton, and J. R. Jones) were clearly wanting in ability.

K. Condition of the Reenforcing Column from Richmond

Although the reinforcing column was fresh compared to the men who had been with Lee through the Second Manassas campaign, there can be no doubt that various of its units were subjected to severe marching conditions.

The rotund politician-turned-general Howell Cobb thought the pace "inhuman" and wrote to his wife, "Men absolutely fell and died on the side of the road from the heat—one case I know of and I have heard of others."[44] Walter Lee (4th N.C. of G. B. Anderson) wrote home of two men dying in one day from "sun stroke."[45]

The heavy straggling in the divisions of McLaws and D. H. Hill reflected the inevitable losses of a shakedown march in which the physically unfit were weeded out. Civil War soldiers submitted to only the crudest medical examination—if any at all—at enlistment, and it is not surprising that many were accepted who were physically or mentally unfit for the rigors of campaigning. In this case those rigors seem to have been exacerbated by the failure of officers to provide adequate water.[46]

LaFayette McLaws wrote to his wife of the "very fatiguing marching," and told her of the stragglers who "say they intend to join their regiments as soon as they become rested a little."[47] In at least one battery in the Artillery Reserve the horses "gave entirely out," and the company was ordered to rest before following on.[48]

Curiously, Emmett Morrison, who commanded the 15th Virginia as its senior captain, did not recall any special problem with straggling in his regiment in either August or September. As part of Semmes's brigade, his experiences should have been much the same as Cobb's, except for not having to deal with the addition of conscripts.[49]

In the rear, the men of John G. Walker traveled by train for about one-third of the distance and thereafter marched at a slower pace. They suffered less than either the vanguard or the main body. For comments on the miles marched by the main body of the reinforcements, see *Taken at the Flood* (chap. 1, note 65).

L. Condition of the Army of Northern Virginia in September 1862

The condition of the Army of Northern Virginia in September 1862 in regard to both subsistence and straggling presents an interesting exercise in historiography. The traditional view has been that this was a period of deficient diet (lack of food combined with the wrong foods) that resulted in a drastic reduction of the strength of the army. There is too much supporting evidence to doubt that this conclusion is true in very general terms. Indeed, conclusive and unbiased testimony may be cited from the enemy. As late as September 17, a reconnaissance by the 2d New York Cavalry reported: "The whole country, from Warrenton to Leesburg, is filled with sick soldiers, abandoned on the wayside by the enemy."[50]

Nonetheless, there is also a significant body of apparently conflicting evidence that somehow must be taken into account. Three modifications of the traditional view seem to reconcile most of the contradictions.

In the first place, it is incorrect to treat the entire Maryland campaign—from Ox Hill on September 1 to Shepherdstown on September 20—as an unvarying whole. Allowance must be made for changes in the availability of supplies and in marching conditions that occurred during the three weeks. It is also true that different parts of the army experienced different conditions. The two lowest points—both for lack of food and for straggling the ranks—came from September 1 through 3 (immediately after Second Manassas) and from September 14 through 17 (South Mountain to Sharpsburg).

In the second place, prior to crossing the Potomac the strength of the Army of Northern Virginia was not unlike a large revolving door. Soldiers both came and went in large numbers. The muster rolls that have survived from those units that bothered to keep them at this time (the practice was not yet uniform), show a continuing flow of returnees to the army—conscripts and recruits, convalescents from the battles around Richmond, men who had broken down in the earlier phases of the campaign, and men rejoining after official and unofficial furloughs. The fragmentary evidence suggests that as long as the army remained in Virginia, the numbers of those returning roughly balanced the number of those leaving.[51] The returns for the brigades of Hood and Law are particularly helpful in demonstrating this.

The flow of returnees was reduced to a trickle after the army crossed the Potomac. Fearing that soldiers following along behind would be captured by the enemy, Lee established a stragglers' camp at Winchester and ordered that all those attempting to rejoin the army be collected there. Even then, a few of the most determined made it back to their comrades.

The classic account is that of Berry Benson of the 1st South Carolina, who gradually weakened from dysentery and collapsed near Leesburg. After convalescing with a sympathetic family, Benson evaded the stragglers' net and rejoined Gregg's brigade in time for the capture of Harpers Ferry and the Battle of Antietam.[52] Joab Goodson of the 44th Alabama illustrates the story of a soldier who fell ill and sat out the campaign at Winchester.[53] Yet a different example is provided by Draughton Haynes of the 49th Georgia (A. P. Hill's division), who marched all the way from Richmond with neighbors in the 6th Georgia (D. H. Hill's division) to rejoin his comrades in time to enter Maryland.[54]

In the third place, even on September 2 (in the middle of the first of these critical periods) there is scattered evidence that the army's condition was not so uniformly dire as Confederate apologists (both veteran and descendent) have claimed. Alexander Hunter of the 17th Virginia of Kemper's brigade acknowledged that among the souvenirs of Second Manassas were captured saltpork, boiled beef, canned vegetables, and "a gallon of real coffee per man" and that enemy haversacks substituted for Confederate rations for several days.[55] George Wise of the same regiment remembered that breakfast on August 31 "consisted of beef, sliced off by us as we hurriedly passed the smoking carcass, slaughtered by the enemy a short time previous." Each soldier in the 17th Virginia also got rations of two biscuits and a quarter pound of bacon that evening. This fortunate unit had been recruited locally, and on the morning of the 2d a wagon arrived from Leesburg with "bread, hams, cakes, pickles and other delicious edibles."[56] In fact, Chaplain James Sheeran of the 14th Louisiana recorded in his diary of traveling down the Little River

Turnpike and meeting "many wagons loaded with provisions which the good people of the surrounding country were sending to our wounded soldiers."[57]

Jubal Early speculated that the men of Jackson's command were better off than those under Longstreet's because of their capture of the Federal supply depot at Manassas Junction a week before. Those delicacies had been limited to what each soldier could carry off on his person and were now finally exhausted, but Early was able to issue "boiled fresh beef" and corn to his brigade on the 2d.[58] Jed. Hotchkiss recorded in his diary that "the wagons came up on the 2nd, and the men cooked rations."[59] Other references to cooking rations may be found in scattered sources.[60]

Still, there can be no doubt that food for the army was generally scarce, many soldiers went to sleep hungry during these nights, and many of the estrays that reduced Lee's numbers to 75,000 present for duty were due to illness related to diet. For example, even George Wise observed his regiment had gone nearly two days without tasting food before the Leesburg provisions arrived; and Chaplain Sheeran noted in his same diary entry that "nothing but stragglers was to be seen in every direction," and "many of the fellows was broken down." Abundant further testimony exists.[61]

Gary Gallagher and Robert Krick have contributed two recent discussions of the causes and impact of straggling on the Maryland campaign, both highly informed and suggestive for further study.[62]

M. Lee's Entry into Maryland as a Turning Movement

Lee's crossing of the Potomac has customarily been viewed as an invasion, in spite of his statements to the contrary. (See *Taken at the Flood*, chap. 1, notes 21, 22, 24.) In Lee's mind, however, the campaign was a turning movement. In his report, he wrote plainly:[63]

> It was decided to cross the Potomac east of the Blue Ridge, in order, by threatening Washington and Baltimore, to cause the enemy to withdraw from the south bank, where his presence endangered our communications and the safety of those engaged in the removal of our wounded and the captured property from the late battle-fields. Having accomplished this result, it was proposed

> to move the army into Western Maryland, establish our communications with Richmond through the Valley of the Shenandoah, and, by threatening Pennsylvania, induce the enemy to follow, and thus draw him from his base of supplies.

After the war Lee told William Allan: "By crossing the river and thus threatening Washington and Baltimore, he drew the enemy from their works."[64]

Two contemporary writers—although neither had particular access to Lee's thinking at this point—grasped the essential nature of his strategy. William W. Blackford observed in his memoirs, "I suppose General Lee never entertained the idea of doing more than make a campaign in the enemy's territory of the 'offensively defensive' kind."[65] And Bradley Johnson concluded, "It was an offensive-defensive operation, having as its objective neither the invasion of Pennsylvania nor the redemption of Maryland, but only the relief of the Confederacy, as far as the means at his command would permit."[66]

Not surprisingly, the most incisive analysis of Lee's strategy came from William Allan, who got to know Lee well after the war and on several occasions heard him explain his intentions in the Maryland campaign:[67]

> None of these courses was possible [idleness or retreat] to a General who, though too weak to attack such a place as Washington, was at the head of a successful army which his enemies had been unable to match in the open field. Lee's victories in the field had greatly depressed his antagonists and had restored a great part of Virginia to his possession, and it was plainly his policy to compel the Federal army to further battle.
>
> As he was greatly outnumbered he must divide his adversaries; he must keep up, and increase if possible, their apprehensions for the safety of Washington, and thus detain a part of the Union army in the defensive lines of that City, while he drew the other part away and fought it at a distance from supports and strongholds.
>
> The great object of all Confederate campaigns was, of course, not to capture cities but to cripple the opposing army.
>
> The best and most direct way of effecting the object now sought was to cross the Potomac and advance into Maryland. Lee

> could thus turn the more formidable of the defences of Washington and threaten that City from its most vulnerable side. He would at the same time excite fears about the safety of Baltimore and Maryland, ill-affected as they were to the Union cause, and alarm Pennsylvania. No other course promised to hamper the Federal army so seriously.
>
> Large garrisons would be kept to secure the safety of Washington, Baltimore and other important places, while public sentiment would demand that the remainder be promptly led against the invaders. Lee could then, probably, choose his battle-field and fight when and where he thought best.

Allan's analysis is far superior to his account in his book, where he relies on quotations from Lee's reports and dispatches, or his version in "First Maryland Campaign, Review of General Longstreet," which gives an abbreviated summary but does not mention or imply a turning movement and is primarily concerned with refuting Longstreet's claim to undue influence over Lee.[68]

Among modern historical accounts, Stephen Sears has appreciated that Lee intended to draw the Federals away from Washington: "Lee was confident he would have the time to rest and recruit his forces and plot the kind of battle of maneuver, somewhere in the Cumberland Valley of Maryland or Pennsylvania, that had been so successful at Second Bull Run."[69] Sears accepts the move as invasion, however, that aimed at deep penetration of Pennsylvania.

And Robert K. Krick has written suggestively that "the verities of military geography in Virginia, which are ignored to an alarming degree in historical studies of the war, made Northern Virginia a poor stage upon which to strut. Maryland's narrow breadth offered little better prospect, to be sure, but Lee did not necessarily limit his trans-Potomac horizon to that state. Furthermore, the inalterable Federal ground rules about protecting Washington served to straiten enemy military options and broaden Lee's."[70]

The two historians who have rejected Lee's move as an invasion have done so on the grounds that it was a raid. Gary Gallagher has recently written that Pope's defeat "presented an opportunity to flank the Federal capital by marching into Maryland. This would not be an invasion—Lee had no intention of holding any Union territory indefinitely—but a great raid during which the Confederates would maintain a flanking posture northwest of Washington for most if not all of the fall season." And then a page later he adds: "When the approach of winter exhausted supplies in Maryland, Lee would withdraw to Virginia."[71]

In his admirable study of Civil War strategy, Archer Jones observed that Lee "took his weary army on another turning movement, this time into western Maryland." The phrase seems to be used in a limited sense, however, as Jones clearly describes the move as a raid: "Realizing McClellan's unexpected behavior had defeated his raid, Lee moved to recross the Potomac [on September 14] while delaying McClellan at the passes in the low mountains which separated the two armies." And finally Jones concludes that Lee had to retreat after the battle of Antietam: "He did so because, as a raider, he could not remain concentrated and unable readily to forage."[72]

It is interesting that two of McClellan's warmest supporters over the years, Isaac Heysinger and Thomas Frothingham, have also been strong proponents of Lee aiming for a deep penetration into Pennsylvania. The connection, of course, is simple. The grander the aims foiled, the greater McClellan's achievement.[73]

N. Lee's Expectations Regarding the Resources of Western Maryland

According to the 1860 census, the Maryland counties of Frederick and Washington possessed: 19,314 horses; 18,021 milk cows; 21,661 beef cattle; and 69,973 swine. They produced 1,858,957 bushels of wheat; 1,752,225 bushels of Indian corn; and orchard products valued at $31,720. If inserted into the ranking of Virginia counties, the two Maryland counties would have compared very favorably: in horses and wheat they would have ranked first and second; in milk cows, swine, and Indian corn Frederick would have ranked first and Washington in the top 5 percent.[74]

Of course, Lee could not know the details of the yet-unpublished eighth census, but clearly he did expect Maryland to provide him with plentiful provisions. On the 5th he would state plainly that he intended to supply himself with food and forage locally.[75] And after the war he would refer to the "abundant" and "ample" supplies he expected to obtain in Maryland.[76] The census simply proves that Lee correctly assessed the potential.

In contrast stands Longstreet's curious assertion that Lee "hesitated a little" to cross the Potomac "on account of our short supplies" and that he was forced to assure his commander the army could live off "roasting ears." The contradiction can be explained in two ways. First, Lee may have expressed misgivings before learning about Maryland from some of his officers who were natives; or, second, Longstreet may have misunderstood Lee's concerns about ordnance to apply to food. On the other hand, as William Allan pointed out in a sharp rebuttal to Longstreet, such a remark was redundant, since the army had been living on green corn "for some days" previously. Longstreet does not repeat the claim in his memoirs and may have decided he was in error.[77]

O. Jackson's Views on Crossing the Potomac

The evidence on Jackson's views is at best indirect. It was Capt. John Pelham of the Horse Artillery who wrote to his parents: "I understand that General Jackson wants to invade Pennsylvania in order to strike the coal mines and railroads so as to cripple the enemy's industry and transportation."[78] Pelham's information may have come by way of Jeb Stuart. Jed. Hotchkiss of Jackson's staff provides tenuous corroboration by writing many years after the war—when discussing the decision to cross the Potomac—that the "invasion of Pennsylvania . . . was one of the cherished designs of Stonewall Jackson."[79]

James Kegel, *North with Lee and Jackson: The Lost Story of Gettysburg*, has propounded the theory that Stonewall Jackson was the main force behind Confederate adventures beyond the Potomac. According to Kegel, Jackson's strategy to invade Pennsylvania and visit devastation upon the free state, especially its coal fields, was accepted by Davis and Lee in the spring of 1862. Thereafter Confederate operations, including the Maryland campaign of 1862 and the Pennsylvania campaign of 1863, were manifestations of the attempt to carry out Jackson's views.[80] At least in the case of the Maryland campaign, however, this would seem not to be the case. Kegel presents no evidence to show that Jackson exercised any seminal influence on Lee's decision to cross the Potomac. Moreover, Lee's more modest goals, including the desire to attract the support of Marylanders and his determination to protect civilians and their property, show that Lee was thinking along substantially different lines.

Biographer Bevin Alexander has proposed an interpretation similar to Kegel's and only slightly less modest in its claims for Jackson.

According to Alexander: (1) Jackson held a fully developed strategy for destruction on Northern soil; (2) Jackson held this view as late as September 1862; (3) Jackson presented his ideas to Lee, who rejected them; and (4) Jackson was correct and Lee wrong.[81] The problem with this theory is that the evidence Jackson held such views as late as September 1862 is tenuous at best; and there is no evidence that Jackson, if he held them, presented them to Lee to accept or reject. Alexander builds much of his case on the incorrect assumption that Jackson wanted Lee to cross the Potomac east of the mountains—when the opposite was true—thus weakening an already thin case.

Based upon currently available sources, the most that can be concluded is that Jackson's enthusiasm for a northward movement might have helped allay any concerns Lee may have held.

P. Confederate View of the Superiority of the Army of Northern Virginia

After the war Lee would tell Edward Gordon "he did not doubt . . . he could have crushed" the Federal army, "which was to a great extent disorganized and demoralized." And he told William Allan that had he not been caught with his army divided, he would have attacked the Federals, "hoping the best results from the state of my troops and those of the enemy."[82] The evidence does not indicate that Lee believed the Federal soldiers inherently inferior to their Confederate counterpart, as he is careful each time to qualify his remark with reference to the conditions prevailing in the Federal army at the time.

In his report Lee stated somewhat modestly that the Army of Northern Virginia was "believed to be strong enough to detain the enemy upon the northern frontier until the approach of winter should render his advance into Virginia difficult, if not impracticable."[83] James Longstreet asserted more forcefully—without explaining the basis for his insight—that Lee "knew from events of the past that his army was equal to the service which he thought to call it, and ripe for the adventure."[84]

On another occasion Longstreet exaggeratedly claimed, "We then possessed an army which, if it had been kept together, the Federals would never dared attack."[85] Hyperbole, to be sure, but the comment is interesting as a possible glimpse into the prevailing Confederate spirit at the time.

Q. Lee's Belief That He Had Caused the Federal Concentration at Washington

In his report of the Maryland campaign, Lee would make it plain that he fully appreciated what he had already accomplished by September 3:[86]

> The armies of Generals McClellan and Pope had now been brought back to the point from which they set out on the campaigns of the spring and summer. The objects of those campaigns had been frustrated and the designs of the enemy on the coast of North Carolina and in Western Virginia thwarted by the withdrawal of the main body of his forces from those regions. Northeastern Virginia was freed from the presence of Federal soldiers up to the entrenchments of Washington.

In June 1863, having launched his offensive into Pennsylvania, Lee made equally plain that he hoped to achieve the same results:[87]

> Last summer you will remember that troops were recalled from Hilton Head, North Carolina, and Western Virginia for the protection of Washington, and there can be little doubt that if our present movements northward are accompanied by a demonstration on the south side of the Potomac, the coast would again be relieved and the troops now on the Peninsula and south of the Potomac be withdrawn.

CHAPTER SIX

Research Appendixes on the Early Campaign, September 4–9

A. The Importance of Conscientious Straggling in the Maryland Campaign

It is asserted in *Taken at the Flood* (chap. 2) that there was but negligible impact on the strength of the Army of Northern Virginia from objections in the ranks to an "invasion." This conclusion is reached in spite of the fact that the two recent histories of the Maryland campaign have given some weight to the notion that Lee's decision to enter Maryland did hurt the morale of his army and did cost him a significant number of soldiers. The evidence uncovered thus far is slight and unconvincing. Stephen Sears and James Murfin both rely on a passage from Garland Ferguson's history of the 25th North Carolina Infantry, first cited by Douglas Freeman.[1] Ferguson wrote:

> When it was first made known to the men by General Lee's order that the army was to cross the Potomac there was a considerable murmur of disappointment in ranks. The men said they had volunteered to resist invasion and not to invade, some did not believe it right to invade Northern territory, others thought that the same cause that brought the Southern army to the front would increase the Northern army, still others thought the war should be carried into the North; thus the men thought, talked and disagreed.

Note that there is not one word about refusing to participate or dropping from the ranks. In fact, Ferguson's next sentence strongly implies the opposite: "This was the first dissension among the men of the regiment, but all were united in their confidence and love for Lee." It should be noted that Freeman limited himself to the following cautious speculation: "Those of extreme conscience may have found opportunity of leaving the ranks for the duration of the Maryland expedition."[2]

The only other evidence cited by both Sears and Murfin is a letter of September 30, 1862, from Rev. Joseph Clay Stiles, who was traveling as a civilian with the army:[3] "There were two opinions in the army as to the propriety of the move. A minority believed that as a matter of *prudence* at least we should not leave our own soil; that it looked a little like *invasion.* The consequence was a large number hung back and would not cross the river—while others were willing to retire from the fight sooner than they would have done on our own soil."

Not only is it questionable how the minister could have been in a position to make such a sweeping assertion, but his reference to faint-hearted fighting casts doubt on the whole statement. It scarcely seems applicable to any of Lee's units at either South Mountain or Sharpsburg.

Murfin cites a story related by Capt. Charles Walcott in the history of the 21st Massachusetts. After South Mountain, Walcott spoke to the dying lieutenant colonel of the 3d South Carolina Battalion, George W. James, who claimed that Col. William DeSaussure of the 15th South Carolina had refused to cross the Potomac, because "the regiment had enlisted to defend the South and not to invade the North." Allegedly, James had to shame DeSaussure into entering Maryland.[4] However, the fact is DeSaussure was present to command the 15th at Sharpsburg and would even cross the Potomac a second time to be killed in action at Gettysburg.

Finally, two similar stories might be noted. Lt. Col. Franklin Gaillard of the 2d South Carolina wrote home that an invasion of the North was "simply ridiculous," but the historian of the regiment found no evidence that "any of its members refused to cross the Potomac."[5] Also, when Isaac Hirsch of the 30th Virginia of Walker's division heard on September 5 that the army was entering Maryland, he recorded in his diary: "I dont like the idea as I dont like to invade anybodys Country." He did not consider dropping out of ranks on that account, however, nor does he relate that any of his colleagues did.[6]

B. D. H. Hill's Crossing of the Potomac on September 4: Its Location and Its Nature as a Raid

Just when Lee decided to send D. H. Hill's division across the Potomac and what he intended it to accomplish in Maryland remains, in part, speculation. It makes sense to assume that Lee sent orders to Hill at the same time he instructed Beverly Robertson to undertake the cavalry diversion in the vicinity of Lewinsville. Still, although Robertson reported receiving directions during the morning, it is barely possible that Lee waited until arriving in Leesburg at noon to issue the orders to D. H. Hill. With a quick response by Hill, there would have been time for his division to start crossing by three o'clock. Nevertheless, even in this less likely case, Lee must have reached his decision during the morning.[7]

Lee's official report, submitted almost a year later, made no mention of Hill's independent mission.[8] After the war Lee was quoted as saying that Hill "had been ordered by him to cross the Potomac and had done so in advance of the army."[9] In a similar conversation Lee indicated that he may have tentatively decided even earlier and ordered Hill to the vicinity of White's Ford "in anticipation of this."[10] In a letter he wrote to Hill at the time of the postwar conversations, Lee strongly implied the two-step decision he had made:[11] "Your division having joined the army after the 2nd battle of Manassas, was placed in front in its subsequent movement, & was the first to cross the Potomac. When the whole army was ready to cross, Genl Jackson was sent to the front and directed to take command of the advanced troops."

There is another and altogether different possibility that fits the known facts contemporaneous to the incident itself. Lee may have decided to undertake a raid by Hill *before* deciding fully to enter Maryland with the main body. Certainly Lee's later report and postwar testimony implies otherwise, but it would not be the only time his memory telescoped two events into one. In the absence of solid evidence to the contrary, *Taken at the Flood* accepts the more likely view that Hill's crossing was the intentional prelude to the Maryland campaign.

It is, perhaps, not inappropriate here to notice Lee's inclination to issue oral orders in lieu of written. This practice causes a two-fold problem for historians. First, undoubtedly many such orders have vanished without a mention of their existence. Secondly, even those whose existence is recorded (in this case by Hill and Robertson) are incapable of analysis as to their precise wording and intentions. It is a cautionary reminder of the thin trail events leave behind them.

All of Hill's brigades crossed considerably above White's Ford, where the main body would cross in the next two days. After the war Hill would claim he "had no knowledge whatever of the object of the expedition," by which he must have meant its larger purpose.[12] Brief references to the various crossings are scattered through many sources.[13] The knowledge of the rest of the army about Hill's activities was somewhat confused.[14]

It is likely Hill already had several companies of cavalry attached to his command, since on the 5th the squadron serving with him was ordered to rejoin its regiment with Stuart.[15]

It should also be mentioned that the historian of the 7th North Carolina would claim his regiment crossed at Point of Rocks on the 4th. This regiment was part of Branch's brigade of A.P. Hill and should have crossed on the 5th at White's Ford. While a number of aging memories got the date wrong, none other missed both the date and place.[16]

Finally, it is interesting to note that disrupting the B&O Railroad and C&O Canal had been a longtime goal for Lee. On May 6, 1861, while still in command of Virginia forces, he wrote from Richmond to Jackson (who commanded at Harpers Ferry) to suggest "confidential arrangements with persons in Maryland" to sabotage the railroad and the canal.[17] Also, reflective of current attitudes, on September 15, Virginia governor John Letcher would declare, "The Baltimore and Ohio rail road has been a positive nuisance to this state." He demanded that its ownership submit to the Confederacy, or the line "must be abated."[18]

C. Confederate Artillery Present in the Maryland Campaign

Lee had forty-seven batteries at Second Manassas, and thirty-three joined him in the reinforcing column from Richmond. Of the eighty batteries he took to Leesburg, seven were left behind, thus giving him seventy-three for the Maryland campaign. If the average battery had four guns, the total number available would have been 292. The organizational table in the *Official Records* is generally accurate, including the information on the units left behind at Leesburg.[19]

Jennings Wise gives Lee forty-three batteries at Second Manassas, but he states the total to be seventy-eight at Leesburg on September 4. Actually, Wise's tables add up to eighty batteries. When Nelson's Hanover Artillery is added and Carrington's Charlottesville Artillery is deducted, the total remains the same and is in agreement with the conclusions reached above. Wise counts six batteries as left at Leesburg, but when Nelson is included the sum is seven. He believed that Lee had about three hundred guns in the Maryland campaign.[20]

Porter Alexander concluded that there were sixty-seven batteries in the Maryland campaign with 284 guns.[21] A recent study claims there were 241 guns active at Sharpsburg, but this figure excludes those left at Harpers Ferry and Shepherdstown.[22]

A close survey of the caliber of the guns with Lee's army on September 17 is given in tabular form in Curt Johnson's *Artillery Hell;* for September 24, see a report by Pendleton.[23]

Of the seven batteries left behind at Leesburg, one was from North Carolina (Latham's Branch Artillery) and the other six from Virginia (Leake's Turner Artillery, Stribling's Fauquier Artillery, Rogers's Loudoun Artillery, Fleet's Middlesex Artillery, Anderson's Thomas Artillery, and Nelson's Hanover Artillery). At least thirty-two of the men from Leake's and Anderson's batteries, in spite of Confederate law, served in the Washington (La.) Artillery during the Maryland campaign, and it seems likely the men from the other detached units were similarly distributed. Pendleton's report covering his work in Leesburg is brief; and his special report dated September 24 gives more insight into the state of the artillery on the 4th, including his arrest of the officers of Fleet's battery for insubordination.[24]

D. Slaves and Free Blacks in Maryland in 1860

In 1860, with a total population of 687,049, Maryland had only 87,189 (or 12.7 percent) slaves and nearly as many free blacks, 83,942 (12.2 percent). Although it is common to read that Southern sentiment was strongest on the Eastern Shore and in Baltimore, slaves were most heavily concentrated in five counties south of Annapolis on the western shore, where the percentage to total population ran to 45.4 percent. The percentage of slaves in the population of the Eastern Shore was only 17.2 percent; and in Baltimore city and Baltimore County—although there was undeniably Confederate sympathy evident—the percentage ran only to 2.0 percent. In Montgomery County, which bordered the Potomac across from Leesburg, the percent of slaves was a surprising 29.6 percent, but in neighboring Frederick County it dropped to 7.0 percent; and in Washington, the next county to the west, where Hagerstown was located, it was 4.6 percent; and in far west Allegheny (Cumberland) there were only 666 slaves (2.3 percent).[25]

E. Lee's Strategy in Crossing the Potomac East of the Mountains

Lee stated his strategy so plainly in his final report it is a wonder there has been any controversy:[26]

> It was decided to cross the Potomac east of the Blue Ridge, in order, by threatening Washington and Baltimore, to cause the enemy to withdraw from the south bank, where his presence endangered our communications and the safety of those engaged in the removal of our wounded and the captured property from the late battle-fields. Having accomplished this result, it was proposed to move the army into Western Maryland, establish our communications with Richmond through the Valley of the Shenandoah, and, by threatening Pennsylvania, induce the enemy to follow, and thus draw him from his base of supplies.

In case there be any doubt that rationalization might have slipped in during the nine months that intervened before the report was written, it may be noted that Lee said the same thing almost as clearly in his dispatch to Davis from Hagerstown on September 12—before the lost orders had changed the nature of the campaign:[27]

> Before crossing the Potomac I considered the advantages of entering Maryland east or west of the Blue Ridge. In either case it was my intention to march upon this town. By crossing east of the Blue Ridge, both Washington and Baltimore would be threatened, which I believed would insure the withdrawal of the mass of the enemy's troops north of the Potomac. . . . I had also supposed that as soon as it was known that the army had reached Fredericktown, the enemy's forces in the Valley of Virginia . . . would retreat altogether from the State.

Three years after the close of the war, Lee briefly alluded to this stage in his thinking; and, although he telescoped a few of the details, he essentially confirmed the interpretation above:[28] "That in reference to this he talked to Gen. Jackson, who advised him to go up into the Valley and cross the Potomac at or above Harper's Ferry, clearing out Winchester, etc. He (Lee) opposed this, because it took him too far from McClellan, and might not induce the latter to cross over, which was his main object."

In his postwar remarks, Lee does not make clear if Jackson gave his advice during the evening meeting of the 4th, or earlier, or both, but the last is most probable. Second, Lee apparently forgot he already knew Winchester had been abandoned; and third, he superimposes his later knowledge that he would face McClellan onto a period when—at the time—he was referring to Pope as his opponent.

F. Confederate Recruitment in Maryland

Less than two hundred Marylanders volunteered to serve in the Confederate infantry during the September campaign.[29] On September 13 they would be mustered in as "Capt. Heard's company" and ordered to temporary duty with the 8th Virginia Infantry of Garnett's (Pickett's) brigade. On the 15th—with serious fighting pending—Lee had second thoughts about thrusting the newcomers into battle, and he transferred them into the ambulance corps.[30] The recruits would become the nucleus of Company A, 2d Maryland Infantry, formed at Winchester in the fall.[31]

According to a recent Maryland historian, a group of mounted volunteers from Poolesville became Company B of Lige White's cavalry battalion. The same author claims that four batteries of artillery were raised by Robert M. Chambers II, which not only fought at Antietam but suffered so heavily that they were absorbed into other units. Unfortunately, no sources are cited for the stories. In the latter instance it seems somewhat unlikely that the batteries were armed and trained in a week's time.[32]

The rumor in the ranks was that Bradley Johnson had recruited 1,500 at Frederick, a figure that was thought to augur well, since it came from such a stanch Union area of the state.[33]

G. Dating Davis's Proposed Proclamation

The editors of the *Official Records* published what purported to be a letter from Davis to Lee, which they headed "September 7 [?]."[34] This document was supplied by Davis in 1882, along with others, upon request for material pertinent to the series. Davis indicated there had been no date on the original and that he was supplying a probable date.[35]

The letter is simply an outline of a proposed proclamation Lee was requested to issue. Standing alone, therefore, it could not have been the dispatch to which Lee was replying on the 9th, since it makes no mention of a conference or of Davis traveling to Leesburg. At most it could have been an enclosure in another letter. Even this is not likely, however, for several reasons: (1) on the 9th, in reply, Lee would likely have mentioned issuing his own proclamation the previous day as a reason to dissuade the president from continuing his trip had the subject of proclamations been raised; and (2) on September 13 Lee would respond to a Davis letter of the 12th, which Lee indicates sent instructions in regard to a proclamation. It is reasonable to assume, therefore, that after the war Davis incorrectly suggested the 7th for a date for the letter that he sent on the 12th, and the letter is treated in the text based on that presumption.

H. Excerpt from the Report of John G. Walker

After the war Brig. Gen. John G. Walker would claim that he learned the details of the expedition against the garrisons at Harpers Ferry and Martinsburg from Lee on either September 8 or 9 and while still in Frederick. He asserted that he proceeded to the first part of his mission (destruction of the C&O aqueduct) and received S.O. 191, codifying what he already knew, while on the road.

A passage from his report, dated October 7, 1862, less than a month after the event, demonstrated that Walker had no specific foreknowledge of the Harpers Ferry expedition when he left Frederick. On the contrary, Walker was under the impression that the Army of Northern Virginia was marching to Hagerstown on the 10th. Since this was Lee's intention only on the morning of the 9th, the reference helps to place the time of the Lee-Walker meeting:[36]

> The movement of our main army from Frederick toward Hagerstown, which I had been officially informed would take place on the 10th, would leave my small division in the immediate presence of a very strong force of the enemy, and, while it would be engaged in destroying the aqueduct, in a most exposed and dangerous position. I therefore determined to rejoin General Lee by way of Jefferson and Middletown, as previously instructed by him. Before marching, however, I received instructions to cross the Potomac at

Cheek's Ford and proceed toward Harper's Ferry, and co-operate with Major-Generals Jackson and McLaws in the capture of the Federal forces at that point.

I. Lee's Knowledge of the Harpers Ferry Situation

The conclusion that Lee did not use his cavalry to obtain detailed and timely information about the Federal garrisons in the lower Valley needs to be amplified in several respects.

None of the cavalry reports state that any force was left behind to operate against Harpers Ferry. Munford would write, however, that the 17th Virginia Battalion was detached on an unspecified detached mission.[37] Also, the editors of the *Official Records* would amplify that the unit's service was in Berkeley County—where Martinsburg is located. A recent regimental history asserts that the 17th was engaged in recruiting and organizing.[38]

Moreover, there is no doubt that a Confederate cavalry force did operate in the lower Valley in early September, as the Federals at both Harpers Ferry and Martinsburg report skirmishing from time to time. Scattered references, including the capture of Lt. Milton J. Rouss, indicate that some of the horsemen were from the 12th Virginia Cavalry.[39] Since Munford reported that the 12th had only seventy-five men present at the Battle of Poolesville, because it "had been reduced by detail and other causes," it seems likely a portion of the regiment was in the Valley.[40]

According to the history of the Laurel brigade, the 17th Virginia Cavalry Battalion, with a company of the 12th attached, crossed the Blue Ridge at Snicker's Gap on August 30. They spent several days scouting Winchester and then operated against Harpers Ferry and Martinsburg.[41]

Nevertheless, such Confederate cavalry as was serving in the Valley seems to have been few in number, operating northward from Winchester, and neither gathering information, nor providing intelligence for Lee.[42]

J. The Number of Copies of Special Orders No. 191

There were at least seven copies made of S.O. 191, and there may have been as many as eleven.

Known copies:

(1) Longstreet reported receiving a copy. He chewed it up and swallowed it.[43]

(2) Walker reported receiving his copy by courier at around three on the morning of the 10th while at the C&O aqueduct. He pinned it inside his coat.[44]

(3) Jackson made a duplicate of his own, in his own hand, for D. H. Hill. The fate of Jackson's copy is unknown.

(4) McLaws received a copy on the night of September 9 after his meeting with Lee. The fate of McLaws's copy is unknown.[45]

(5) D. H. Hill's copy from Jackson is the only copy Hill acknowledged receiving, and it has survived.[46]

(6) D.H. Hill's copy from Lee's headquarters that Hill says was never delivered. This is the copy found with cigars and given to McClellan.[47]

(7) Davis's copy was enclosed by Lee in a dispatch of September 12. It was probably forwarded to the adjutant general for preservation in records.[48]

Possible copies:

(8) Stuart: It is clear from Stuart's report that he was familiar with the details of the order. It makes sense to believe that, as the subject of one of its articles, he would have received a copy.[49]

(9) Pendleton: From a veiled reference he seems to have been aware of Lee's plan. In a letter to his wife dated September 10, Pendleton wrote: "Today we go farther inward; I must not indicate where lest my letter fail and give some clue where I would not have information gotten. Suffice it that General Lee seems well to understand what he is about."[50] Of course, he might have gotten the information verbally from Lee, since he did not command an independent column. This copy would be less plausible than one for Stuart.

(10) Lee's headquarters: It seems almost certain that a copy would have been retained in the records of the headquarters of the Army of Northern Virginia. The fate of this copy is unknown.

(11) Cooper: The copy preserved by Adj. Gen. Samuel Cooper in the Confederate archives in Richmond may or may not be a separate document. It is most likely that Davis sent the copy he received from Lee to Cooper. It is possible, however, that Lee's staff routinely sent a copy of all orders and circulars directly to Richmond, including S.O. 191, in which case this is an additional copy.[51]

R. H. Anderson flatly stated after the war that he did not receive a copy but got verbal instruction from Lee.[52]

If Maj. Walter Taylor received anything, it was likely only the second article, which applied to him, as he left Frederick on his mission to visit Davis before the orders were prepared.

CHAPTER SEVEN

Research Appendixes on the Middle Campaign, September 10–13

A. Dr. Steiner's Comments on the Physical Condition of the Confederates

It is interesting that in his six days of observing the Confederates, the physician Lewis Steiner entered only one comment—and it somewhat indirect—on the physical evidence of the malnutrition that supposedly afflicted the Army of Northern Virginia during the Maryland campaign. On September he noted in his diary: "They ate everything offered them with a greediness that fully sustained the truth of their statement, that their entire subsistence lately had been *green corn, uncooked, and eaten directly from the stalk.*"[1]

On September 13, the day after the last Confederate had left Frederick, Steiner wrote a summary on the "Condition of the Rebels." In it, he confessed that the Confederate soldiers "looked sturdy when in ranks, yet a cachectic expression prevailed." He then went on to observe:[2] "Those who have fallen into our hands show worn-out constitutions, disordered digestions and a total lack of vital stamina. They do no bear pain with any fortitude, and their constitutions seem to have very little power of resistance to disease. The rate of mortality in the rebel sick and wounded is double or treble that found in the Hospitals containing our men."

It will be noted that the bulk of his observations do not relate to the Confederates he observed in Frederick, but to prisoners—many of which would have been stragglers—whom he had presumably examined at some earlier time.

B. Stonewall Jackson's Near Capture at Boonsboro

Traditionally, historians have relied upon Henry Kyd Douglas as the main source for Stonewall Jackson's brush with Federal cavalry that nearly resulted in his capture.[3] The incident seems to have been known in the ranks, however, as scattered references may be found in various diaries and memoirs.[4]

Douglas first told the story in an article published in 1886.[5] It quickly drew a rebuttal from M. M. Green in the *Baltimore Sun*—based on an account of the incident by Pvt. B. P. Green of the Black Horse Troop that claimed Douglas had unduly taken credit for what Jackson's cavalry escort alone had accomplished. When preparing his book-length memoirs, Douglas wrote for corroboration to Col. Bassett French, who had also ridden into Boonsboro and was witness to the event. French confirmed most of the details but awarded credit for Jackson's escape equally to Douglas and the Black Horse Troop.[6]

In the 1890s Jed. Hotchkiss and Surgeon Hunter McGuire, both of Jackson's staff, denied that Jackson himself had been involved in the affair.[7] The accounts of both men are essentially negative evidence, however—they do not recall Jackson ever leaving camp—and do not disprove the story of Douglas and French.

C. Size of the Trains of the Army of Northern Virginia in the Maryland Campaign

The exact number of wagons with Lee in Maryland in September of 1862 is not known but a basis for estimating exists.

In late September, after the Battle of Antietam, D. H. Hill's divisional, brigade, and regimental trains would number 212 wagons.[8] Extrapolating from these proportions would give a total of 1,671 wagons in all divisional, brigade, and regimental trains and another 243 wagons in the army reserve trains.

This combined total of 1,914 would not include, however, wagons in the booty train (that is, vehicles carrying goods captured or purchased in Maryland), the trains of the cavalry division or the Reserve Artillery, or reserve trains for the commands (corps) of Jackson and Longstreet, if such existed. Although the Federal cavalry escaping from Harpers Ferry would capture wagons said to be from Longstreet's ordnance train, it is not clear whether these were from a separate corps reserve or from the divisional trains.

Hence, the total number of wagons with Lee in Maryland may have reached 2,500. Although the Army of Northern Virginia undeniably suffered from inadequate transportation, this would still be an immense number of vehicles; and, if amassed in a single line with a modest allowance for intervals, it would have stretched over sixteen miles.[9]

D. The Question of Which Confederate Trains Remained at Boonsboro

After the war, D. H. Hill wrote that his duties upon reaching Boonsboro included "guarding the wagon trains and parks of artillery belonging to the whole army" and that he was directed "not only to protect the wagons and guns, but also to watch the roads leading from Harper's Ferry."[10] This assertion has been reasonably read to mean that Lee did not take either the Reserve Artillery or the trains of the army with him to Hagerstown but left them at Boonsboro.

Upon reflection this makes little sense, however. Why would Lee leave the most vulnerable part of his army behind, especially since he had no intention of returning to Boonsboro? And it seems he did not do so.

There is no doubt the bulk of the Artillery Reserve went on to Hagerstown. Not only does Pendleton's report so state, but the artillery chief himself wrote a letter home from Hagerstown on September 13.[11] Porter Alexander is also clear that the hundred-wagon ordnance train went to Hagerstown.[12] Finally, Ezra Carman claims that the wagons carrying supplies purchased in Maryland traveled to Hagerstown.[13] While no contemporary reference to the commissary and quartermaster trains has been found, it must be doubted that Lee would have left the valuable contents of these loaded wagons where they were not needed; or that he would not have taken empty wagons to fill with the flour, shoes, and other supplies he hoped to obtain in Hagerstown.

Yet, it is difficult to believe that Harvey Hill would be completely wrong in remembering this additional responsibility thrust upon him. It is possible that Jackson and McLaws had left behind some excess wagons in order to travel lighter, and that these were left in Boonsboro in anticipation of these commands returning there after the completion of their missions.

There is another possible explanation for the additional "parks of artillery" claimed by Hill. Pendleton took to Hagerstown the battalions of Brown, Nelson, and S. D. Lee (who had been assigned from Longstreet).[14] He specifically mentions leaving Cutts's battalion with D. H. Hill, which is confirmed by Cutts.[15] It is also possible that Pendleton left behind H. P. Jones's battalion in Boonsboro. (See chapter 2, Reserve Artillery, Jones's Battalion.) If so, this would have given Hill the four batteries of Jones (seventeen guns), the five of Cutts (nineteen guns), and the four (fifteen guns) regularly attached to his division—a total of fifty-one guns, which no doubt would have seemed like an impressive amount of artillery.

E. Copy of Special Orders No. 191 Sent to Davis

It is interesting to speculate—based on no evidence whatsoever—that the copy of S.O. 191 that Lee forwarded to Davis on September 12 theoretically could have been the copy that fell into Federal hands.[16] The following chain of events are at least possible: (1) the copy of S.O. 191 from Jackson reached D. H. Hill's headquarters first; (2) therefore, when the official document arrived, it was returned to Lee's headquarters as a duplicate. (3) When a copy was needed on the 12th to send to Davis, someone on Lee's staff simply availed himself of the duplicate conveniently at hand. (4) The dispatch was sent off at a reasonably early hour on the 12th. (5) The courier took the route through Frederick, arriving before the town fell to Federals, or, perhaps, even during the confusion of the skirmishing. How the dispatch and the orders became separated, or the cigars became involved, would require a new hypothesis of its own.

There is one series of possibilities, however, that makes the theory of a spy somewhat less than ridiculous. If the Federals were just minutes away from entering Frederick, a disloyal courier might have thrown the orders on the ground to be found by his compatriots—perhaps even baiting them with the cigars. Although, as stated, there is absolutely no evidence to directly support the notion that the September 12 copy to Davis was lost, neither can it be proven that it ever reached Davis.

The original of Lee's dispatch to Davis of the 12th is in the Lee-Davis Correspondence, Library of Virginia, Richmond, and a copy of S.O. 191 is not with it. Nor is there a copy of the Proclamation to Marylanders that Lee included. Davis may have simply sent both to Adj. Gen. Samuel

Cooper for preservation in the archives. In that case, they would be the copies presently in Orders and Circulars Issued by the Army of Northern Virginia, RG 109, National Archives (the copy referred to in chapter 3 as the Lee-DNA copy).

In 1922 Thomas Jackson Arnold, grandson of D. H. Hill and grandnephew of Stonewall Jackson, wrote a brief article for *Confederate Veteran* based on a speech he had heard Gen. Tom Rosser deliver a quarter-century earlier.[17] Rosser claimed to know who lost the orders and, while naming no one, indicated it was a cigar-smoking member of Jackson's staff. Recently, Wilbur D. Jones, basing his speculations on the Arnold article, has concluded that Henry Kyd Douglas was the responsible courier.[18]

According to Jones, (1) a copy of S.O. 191 was delivered to Jackson, (2) who then made a duplicate and had Douglas deliver it to D. H. Hill. (3) On his way back, for no known reason, Douglas stopped at Lee's headquarters. (4) D. H. Hill's copy from Lee, for no known reason, had not yet been delivered, and Adj. R. H. Chilton, who was out of couriers, for no known reason, asked Douglas to carry it to Hill. (5) Without revealing that Hill had a copy, for no known reason, Douglas took the document, (6) wrapped it around cigars, for no known reason, and placed it in his pocket. (7) Later the package was lost without his knowledge. The theory, while interesting, strains credulity.

F. The Activities of John Walker on September 13

The account presented in chapter 5 of *Taken at the Flood* of Brig. Gen. John Walker's activities on September 13 is based on five firsthand accounts.[19] Unfortunately, there are unresolvable discrepancies in these narratives.

(1) After the war Walker claimed his division commenced its march at daybreak (ca. 5:10 a.m.). But Isaac Hirsch recorded in his diary that he had fallen two miles behind his regiment the day before. He started at dawn (5:48 a.m.) and caught up with the 30th Virginia just as it was leaving camp.[20] This suggests Walker did not start as early as claimed.

(2) After the war, Walker claimed he had been in possession of Loudoun Heights by two in the afternoon. Accounts by two of his soldiers who climbed the heights state that they did not reach the summit until about five o'clock.[21]

(3) Of greater importance is Walker's postwar implication that he had no contact with Jackson on the 13th. He mentions meeting the signal party but does not say where they came from; nor does he indicate the additional presence of engineers in the party. He also claims nothing was seen of Jackson from the mountain. Unfortunately for Walker, the reliable Jed. Hotchkiss of Jackson's staff records in his diary that he and two other engineers were sent with the signal party, met Walker at the foot of the mountain, and ascended with Cooke's regiment.[22] Several firsthand accounts also indicate that Jackson's troops were visible from the summit.[23]

Walker's version of his activities on September 13 must be seen as another example—in addition to the alleged interview with Lee on the 9th—of the unreliability of his postwar recollections.

G. Lee's Sources of Information on the Night of September 13

Precisely what Lee knew on the night of September 13, and when he learned it, cannot now be known conclusively. Still, there is good basis for the speculation in chapter 5 of *Taken at the Flood.*

After the war, Lee made the following statements: (1) "he received dispatches almost simultaneously from Genl. Stuart and Genl. Hill stating that McClellan had changed his tactics and was endeavoring to drive back Genl. Hill who was near Boonsboro."[24] And (2) "he rec'd a dispatch from Stuart, saying that McClellan had taken the advance, and was pushing with his whole force and that he (Stuart), was falling back. Later, an alarming dispatch was also received from Hill to the same effect."[25]

In partial confirmation, Longstreet wrote in his memoirs, "A little after dark of the 13th, General Lee received, through a scout, information of the advance of the Union forces to the foot of South Mountain in solid ranks. Later information confirmed this report, giving the estimated strength at ninety thousand."[26]

It will be noted that Lee and Longstreet agree the information arrived in several stages. Neither general, however, mentioned that there was an essential contradiction in the reports from Stuart and Hill. The passing of time may have telescoped the events, but it is clear from the dispatches sent to McLaws and Stuart on the 13th that Lee was concerned about both Crampton's and Turner's Gap. It is equally clear that on the night of the 13th, Stuart was concerned almost exclusively with Crampton's Gap.

H. Lee's Plans on the Night of September 13

Three days after the fact Lee would explain to Davis that he had returned from Hagerstown "lest the enemy should fall upon McLaws' rear, drive him from the Maryland Heights, and thus relieve the garrison at Harper's Ferry."[27] Lee did not express fear of the destruction of any part of his army, even McLaws's division.

Eleven months later, in his official report, Lee correctly recalled his motivations, but he telescoped and rearranged sequences. Lee asserted that after McClellan found the lost orders:[28]

> He immediately began to push forward rapidly, and on the afternoon of the 13th was reported approaching the pass in South Mountain, on the Boonsborough and Frederick road. The cavalry under General Stuart fell back before him, materially impeding his progress by its gallant resistance, and gaining time for preparations to oppose his advance. By penetrating the mountain at this point, he would reach the rear of McLaws and be enabled to relieve the garrison at Harper's Ferry. To prevent this, General D. H. Hill was directed to guard the Boonsborough Gap and Longstreet ordered to march from Hagerstown to his support.

Although Lee continued to maintain that his intention was to protect McLaws and prevent the relief of Harpers Ferry, he fails to mention the threat to Crampton's Gap, indicates that Hill had sole responsibility for defending Turner's, and implies that Longstreet was intended to march directly to Turner's Gap.

According to Ezra Carman:[29]

> All this unlooked for and unpleasant information Lee received early in the evening and he acted promptly. He concluded that McClellan was acting with energy for the relief of Harper's Ferry and determined to press matters there to a conclusion and to protect and support the troops he had detached to reduce it, and to thwart McClellan in his effort to divide his army and beat it in detail, as he rightly divined that McClellan was endeavoring to do.

Although Carman correctly captures the essence of Lee's decision, he incorrectly implies—as will be argued in chapter 8—that Lee knew too early of the pro-Southern civilian's story as the source of Stuart's information.

I. Lee and the Loss of Special Orders No. 191

For many years it was assumed that Lee did not know until after the close of the Maryland campaign that a copy of S.O. 191 had found its way into McClellan's hands. Indeed, in the absence of hard evidence to the contrary, it made sense to assume that such information would not have crossed the lines quickly. In 1892 Col. William Allan narrated an anecdote which explained that Lee did learn of the lost orders:[30]

> A citizen friendly to the Confederate cause had accidentally been present when the order had been brought to McClellan, and had heard the expressions of gratification that followed, and had learned of the orders then issued. He lost no time in leaving Frederick, and, making his way through the lines, brought this information after night to Stuart, who at once forwarded it to General Lee. Thus informed before daylight on the 14th of the impending danger, Lee, to cover McLaws, ordered D. H. Hill to hold the mountain pass, and directed Longstreet to march rapidly to the assistance of the latter.

Although Allan cited no authority, his story was accepted for over forty years. In 1934 Douglas Southall Freeman rejected the anecdote, giving the following reasons:[31]

> It was asserted by William Allan that Stuart notified Lee during the evening of September 13 that a citizen of Frederick had come to him and had reported that McClellan had found a copy of Special Order No. 191 in Frederick. Nearly every writer has repeated this assertion and has assumed that Lee knew that evening that McClellan was in possession of his plans. The contrary is almost certainly the case. If Stuart had received such intelligence, he would surely have mentioned it in his report. Longstreet said nothing of it. Neither did Taylor. Marshall flatly asserted that "Lee did not become aware of the cause that led to the sudden ad-

> vance of the Federal army after he left Frederick until the official report of General McClellan was published some months later."[32] Lee mentioned in his official report the discovery of the order, but did not write the report until the summer of 1863, when the facts had become generally known. Colonel Allan was not at Hagerstown on the night of the 13th, as far as the records show. Although he is justly rated as one of the most accurate and painstaking writers on the campaigns of 1862, in this instance he must have accepted hearsay.

Nine years later Freeman changed his mind. In the interim he had discovered memoranda of two conversations Lee held—one with Allan and one with E. C. Gordon—on the morning of February 15, 1868. To Gordon, Lee said:[33]

> . . . another dispatch arrived from Stuart, stating that he (Stuart) had learned from a gentleman of Maryland, who was in McClellan's head quarters when the dispatch from Genl. Lee to Genl. Hill was brought to McClellan, who after reading it, threw up his hands and exclaimed—Now I know what to do—That he (Genl. Lee) had been much surprised at the sudden change in McClellan's tactics, until he learned that he (McC) had thus found out his (Lee's) position.

Later the same morning, in somewhat less detail, Lee commented to Allan: "Stuart informed him of report of Md. gentleman, who said he was at McClellan's head H. Qr.s when Lost Dispatch was found, and that he (McC) openly expressed his delight."[34]

In 1943, on the basis of the new information, Freeman wrote that "The memoranda prove . . . that Lee received during the night of September 13–14, or on September 14 information that McClellan was said on credible authority to have a copy of S.O. 191. Lee's movements thereafter took into account the probability, if not the certainty, that McClellan knew the disposition and plans of the Confederates."[35]

In 1958 Hal Bridges discovered in the D. H. Hill Papers at Chapel Hill a letter dated February 21, 1868, from Lee to Hill. The letter, as had been the conversations of a week earlier, was triggered by Hill's article in *The Land We Love.* Once again Lee commented on his knowledge of the lost orders, and this time he stated more clearly when he received the news: "Early on the morning of the 14th I recd a dispatch from [Stuart] stating that he had fallen back to the South Mountains; that Genl. McClellan was pressing forward on the roads to Boonsborough & Rohersville gaps, & that he had learned from a citizen of Maryland, that he was in possession of the order directing the movement of our troops."[36]

Here matters stood until 1983, when Stephen W. Sears reopened the question by dismissing Lee's testimony and asserting that "there is substantial evidence that in this instance Lee's memory had failed him."[37] Sears argued that the civilian could have known nothing more than that McClellan had received important intelligence on the Confederates and that Lee did not learn the document was a copy of S.O. 191 until 1863. His single piece of new evidence is a statement made by Charles Marshall in a letter to D. H. Hill in 1867: "I remember perfectly that until we saw [McClellan's] report, Gen. Lee frequently expressed his inability to understand the sudden change in McClellan's tactics which took place after we left Frederick."[38] Otherwise Sears argues by inference. He concludes that had Lee been informed of McClellan's possession of S.O. 191 at the time:[39]

> . . . it is scarcely credible that he would not have revealed it to Longstreet in their conversation on the night of September 13, yet Longstreet makes no mention of it in his postwar writings on the campaign. In fact there is no reference of any kind to the Lost Orders in the wartime reports of Longstreet, D. H. Hill, or Stuart, those best positioned to have learned about it. The omission is most significant in Stuart's case. Had the Marylander told him on September 13 that McClellan possessed all the Confederate plans, it seems completely out of character that he would have excluded such a counterintelligence coup from his official report.

Elsewhere Sears elaborated:[40]

> As important as anything else, Lee's actions over the next several days were hardly those of a general who knew his opponent had all his plans. Rather than ordering Jackson to give up the siege of Harpers Ferry and find safer ground, he allowed him to continue it. Instead of instantly marching from Hagerstown to block the South Mountain passes, he waited until morning to move. Rather than prudently withdrawing across the Potomac to reunite his scattered forces, he ran an immense bluff by standing at Sharpsburg and then challenging McClellan to fight there.

The conclusion reached herein, as narrated in chapter 5 of *Taken at the Flood* and based on a reevaluation of old information and the uncovering of new, agrees with Sears only in small part. It is probably true that the civilian did not know exactly what document had been handed to McClellan. A passage from Carman's history buttresses this belief:[41]

> When McClellan came into possession of the lost order a citizen, friendly to the Southern cause, was present and observed the great satisfaction it gave him and the exuberant spirits of the staff. He listened to some talk of what was to be done by the Union army and noted the activity of aides and orderlies. He did not know the character of the paper, whether it was an order to McClellan or some report from one of his corps commanders, but he knew that it was of some importance and that a rapid forward movement was to be ordered. It was but a few minutes till he was speeding out of Frederick in the direction of Stuart's cavalry outposts, and before sunset had found Stuart, near Turner's Gap, and told him what he had seen and heard.
>
> Stuart hastened a swift courier with the news to Lee, at Hagerstown, fifteen miles away, and was able to confirm them by reporting increased activity on the part of Pleasonton's cavalry during the afternoon; that cavalry affairs had taken place near Burkittsville and Jefferson and that Pleasonton had driven him back and then was in the immediate front of the Gap.

It will be noted that Carman gives details not to be found elsewhere on what the civilian knew and that the civilian reached Stuart before sunset near Turner's Gap. Unfortunately, Carman cites no authority for his information. It seems reasonable, however, that such details could have come only from the civilian himself, or, more likely, from someone on Stuart's staff who was present when the civilian reported to the cavalry chief. The story has a basic credibility and should be accepted.

On the more important matter of what Lee knew or assumed, however, Sears's conclusion that Lee knew nothing about the loss of S.O. 191 until 1863 cannot be accepted. Lee's comments in his two conversations and letter of 1868 are too clear on this point. In addition, a fourth unequivocal comment by Lee has been uncovered. On June 12, 1867, in response to a query from D. H. Hill, who was then collecting information for his article on the lost orders, in a letter overlooked by Sears, Lee wrote: "I . . . heard at the time that the order was address to you, and it was so stated by Gen. J. E.B. Stuart in his report of the change of advance of Gen. McClellan which he commented upon."[42]

It is highly unlikely that Lee would have misremembered so important a point as to whether at the time he was mystified by McClellan's behavior or that he had some knowledge that McClellan possessed a copy of S.O. 191. It is reasonably clear, therefore, that if the civilian did not know what the document was, but Lee heard from Stuart that it was S.O. 191, then Stuart must have made the assumption. It was, after all, an easy jump in logic. No other piece of paper could have provided McClellan with such important information.

If Lee's memory did telescope any part of the story, it was probably the knowledge that it had been D. H. Hill's copy that the Federals had been found. That detail may not have been learned until the publication of McClellan's report in 1863.

Most of the questions raised by Sears in his argument by inference are answered by an understanding of the sequence of events on the night of September 13 and the morning of the 14th. Why didn't Lee mention the lost orders to Longstreet in their conference on the night of the 13th? Because Lee did not know until early on the morning of the 14th. Why didn't Lee march at once to South Mountain? In a matter of several hours he did. Why didn't Lee not call off the siege of Harpers Ferry? In his last dispatch to McLaws he did raise that very possibility.

The question of why Stuart would fail to mention an intelligence coup in his report requires examination. In fact, the larger question that needs to be asked is why Stuart makes no mention of the lost orders at all in his report, even though by the time he got around to reporting in February 1864 the story was common knowledge in the army. Moreover, Lee remembered after the war that "Genl. Stuart and other officers in the army were very indignant about the matter."[43] So unusual is this absence of any reference to the lost orders by Stuart, or indeed by Longstreet, Jackson, or any other officer, that it suggests a form of cover-up.

That Lee himself did not reveal knowledge of the lost orders before the appearance of McClellan's report, therefore, as Marshall remembered, may not be proof of his ignorance but the result of his attempt to conceal an embarrassment to his army. In his own report, dated August 19, 1863, he included a single, nonaccusatory sentence: "A copy of the order directing the movement of the army from Fredericktown had fallen into the hands of General McClellan, and disclosed to him the disposition of our forces."[44]

Even thereafter Lee kept silent on the lost orders. By that point Hill and his staff had left the army, and apparently Lee saw no reason to pursue the matter. After the war, Lee would explain, he "had no grounds upon which to act."[45] Perhaps he did not wish to take action based on enemy evidence. As he would later note, it not until after the war that he knew "certainly" that it was the copy addressed to Hill which had been lost.[46]

Thus, in light of the evidence now known, it seems likely that Lee did know—or at least assumed—from a point early on the morning of September 14 that a copy of S.O. 191 had fallen into McClellan's hands. He dealt with the loss characteristically by doing and saying almost nothing.

CHAPTER EIGHT

Research Appendixes on South Mountain and Harpers Ferry, September 14–15

A. Lee's Mode of Travel on September 14

Douglas Freeman puts Lee back in the saddle on September 14, but his only evidence is Walter Taylor's postwar remark that Lee chafed at riding in the ambulance because he "could not go into many places where a horse would have carried him, and so his movements were greatly hindered." Not only was Taylor absent from the army until the 15th, but his remark makes no reference to a specific date when Lee abandoned his ambulance.[1]

No direct reference to Lee's mode of travel has been found for September 14. Alexander's ambiguous comment "I was riding with Gen. Lee" sheds no light.[2] But Hood's memory that he "found General Lee standing by the fence, very near the pike," as Hood approached South Mountain, suggests that the Confederate commander had been traveling by ambulance.[3] Had Lee been on horseback, he would likely have remained mounted for a better view. He might even have attempted going part way up the mountain.

In any case, as will be developed in chapter 9, appendix C, evidence suggests Lee traveled by ambulance on the 15th, and he did not try the saddle until the 16th.

B. Sights and Sounds of the Battle of South Mountain

The evidence of the battle in progress on September 14 to the marching column from Hagerstown is given graphically in the memoirs of Sam Hood and mentioned by William Owen.[4] Later in the afternoon, when the disabled cannon of Chew's battery from Crampton's Gap passed through Boonsboro on its way to Shepherdstown, gunner George Neese noted in his diary that "a portion of General Longstreet's forces were engaged, fighting desperately right in the gap, which the enemy was assaulting vigorously with a heavy force. The artillery fire was very heavy and the deep-toned thunder of Longstreet's guns, mingled with the crash of fierce and incessant musketry, raged and roared and rolled along the mountain slopes and made the craggy battlements of South Mountain tremble from base to crest."[5] According to a number of sources, the firing could be heard as far away as Hagerstown.[6]

C. The Posting of Colquitt's Brigade at South Mountain

A minor mystery exists over the position of Alfred Colquitt's brigade on the night of September 13 and the morning of the 14th. After the war Harvey Hill claimed he had found the brigade posted at the eastern foot of South Mountain on the morning of the battle and brought it about halfway back up the slope.[7] The implication is strong that Colquitt did not understand how to defend a mountain pass and that Hill had corrected a significant error.

A persuasive case is made by George D. Grattan, Colquitt's adjutant at the time, that Hill is mistaken and that on the morning of the 14th the brigade already occupied the intermediate position it held all day.[8] Yet Grattan's account of the battle is not without its own flaws. His assertion that Garland's brigade was not on the mountain during the night overstates the case. Although Garland did not reach the Mountain House until after daylight of the 14th, his brigade slept on the western slope.[9]

D. H. Hill's Knowledge of Longstreet's March to His Relief

There is no direct evidence Lee informed D. H. Hill that Longstreet's command was returning from Hagerstown to the Boonsboro area on the morning of September 14. There is only Hill's postwar comment that during the morning it was his purpose to delay the enemy "until General Longstreet could come up," which implies that he expected help was on the way.[10] In his report Hill noted that "in answer to a dispatch from General Longstreet, I urged him to hurry forward troops to my assistance."[11]

Hill makes it clear, however, that this exchange occurred after noon, when Longstreet would have been nearing Boonsboro. It was probably this message Hill was referring to in his postwar letter to Longstreet, when he wrote, "It was then I called so loudly for your help."[12]

In spite of the lack of documentation, it is not likely that Lee would have written to McLaws on the night of the 13th and to both McLaws and Stuart early on the morning of the 14th (as discussed in chapter 5 of *Taken at the Flood*) that Longstreet was returning to Boonsboro without sending the same news to Hill. Whether that news was communicated in the dispatch Hill received at midnight (now lost), or in a different message cannot be known.

E. Strength of D. H. Hill's Division at South Mountain

D. H. Hill would claim he had no more than 5,000 men in his division on September 14.[13] After the war he made a determined effort to reduce the estimate of Confederate troops at South Mountain.[14] It may be assumed that Hill reached the 5,000 figure after making every possible deduction and that it represented his guess of the fighting strength of his infantry. It is probably the category frequently referred to by Confederates as "muskets" and did not include either officers or artillery.

Mr. Thomas White, chief clerk of the Army of Northern Virginia, estimated Hill's division at 7,000 on the 14th.[15] And the Federal observer, Dr. Lewis Steiner, calculated Hill's division at 8,000 when it passed through Frederick on the 11th.[16] According to the September 1 tri-monthly estimate, Hill totaled 9,794 present for duty, and the division had seen no fighting and had easy marching subsequently.[17]

Ezra Carman, a careful statistician for the battle itself, gives Hill 5,795 infantry and artillery on September 17, after the losses from South Mountain and the straggling from the march from Boonsboro.[18]

F. Strength of Federal and Confederate Forces at Harpers Ferry

The Federal casualty returns, totaling 12,737, are synonymous with the strength of the garrison, since all of its troops, except the cavalry, which escaped, were killed, wounded, or captured.[19] Dixon Miles's force was thus approximately the size of either the Federal First or Ninth Corps and larger than the Twelfth Corps.

Jackson's strength of 15,000 is estimated on the basis of the September 1 tri-monthly estimate. It is also assumed that the heaviest straggling lay yet ahead in the forced marches to Sharpsburg.[20]

Nothing certain is known about Jackson's information on the size of the garrison prior to its surrender. It was clear even to privates in Walker's command looking down from Loudoun Heights, however, that the enemy numbered at least 10,000, and Jackson should have known at least that much by the time he heard from Walker in the evening.[21]

G. John G. Walker's Harpers Ferry Claim

In his October report, Walker stated that he opened fire on Harpers Ferry on September 14 without authorization in order to protect his own guns.[22] Not until twenty-four years later, however, would he add that he purposefully exposed his infantry and that no authorization ever arrived.[23] In the latter source Walker concluded the incident with another highly quotable—and highly suspect—personal revelation made to him by a semi-immortal Confederate. He claimed that in riding with Jackson to Sharpsburg on the 16th, he confessed his ruse to Stonewall:[24]

> When I had finished my confession he was silent for some minutes, and then remarked: "It was just as well as it was; but I could not believe that the fire you reported indicated the advance of McClellan in force. It seemed more likely to be merely a cavalry affair." Then, after an interval of silence, as if to himself, he continued: "I thought I knew McClellan" (they were classmates at West Point), "but this movement of his puzzles me."

As in the case of the interview with Lee on the 9th, this episode is so counter to other evidence that it ought not be accepted.

H. Effect of the Confederate Bombardment of Harpers Ferry

The conclusion in the text that the Confederate bombardment of Harpers Ferry, while terrifying, was largely nondestructive is buttressed by the testimony of a contemporary. After the war artillerist Porter Alexander commented on the cannonade of September 14–15:[25]

> Its effect, however, was more moral than physical. The rifled ammunition of the Confederates was decidedly inferior to that of the enemy, many of their shells failing to burst, or bursting prematurely, or tumbling; and even the smooth-bore shells often burst near the guns. The part of the town near the rivers was within effective range of McLaws and Walker, but Bolivar Heights, where the most of the Federal force was located, was beyond it.

While not at Harpers Ferry during the bombardment, Alexander arrived on the 16th to manage the captured ordnance. As Lee's chief of ordnance, he likely discussed the effectiveness of the firing with the artillerists who had participated.

I. Evolution of Jackson's Tactical Plan at Harpers Ferry

Exactly when Stonewall decided on his plan to post artillery across the Shenandoah River and to work around the end of the Federal line on Bolivar Heights and how the orders were issued to implement the plan is not clear. Some sort of turning or flanking movement is implied in his 7:20 A.M. dispatch to McLaws of September 14.[26] Unnumbered Special Orders have survived that include articles directing the operations of Walker's and McLaws's divisions, as well as Jackson's, and therefore give the impression of having been issued in the morning. They exist only in the report of Signal Officer Bartlett, however, where they appear as the last message he transmitted for the day, which necessarily would have been mid- or late afternoon.[27] A. P. Hill and Jubal Early (for Lawton) imply that they received orders in the afternoon just before moving, and J. R. Jones does not specify a time.[28]

One of two explanations would fit the facts as known. First, the Special Orders were written in the morning and issued to Jackson's divisions, were triggered by follow-up orders in midafternoon, and were sent to Walker and McLaws in the late afternoon. Second, whether written in the morning or early afternoon, they were sent to all parties concerned at two o'clock and later. In the latter case, McLaws and Walker were included simply to provide a record of the orders for the day.

Precedent for issuing orders after the fact may be found in Lee's Special Orders No. 181 of August 13, 1862.[29]

J. War Council at the Mountain House

In their memoirs, Generals Hood, D. H. Hill, and Longstreet give three slightly different versions of the war council on the evening of September 14.[30] Hill places the council at nine and Hood at after ten. It is assumed in *Taken at the Flood*, however, that the meeting was over by eight and provided the basis for Lee's decision to retreat that was embodied in his 8:15 dispatch to McLaws.

This earlier meeting time is also supported by Hill's postwar recollection that after the conference he and Longstreet heard the cheering associated with the final stage of Colquitt's fight in the center.[31] The lieutenant colonel of the 23d Georgia would later recall that Colquitt's fighting ceased altogether between 8:00 and 9:00 P.M.[32]

K. Lee's Decision to Retreat to Virginia

Most historians have followed the lead of Douglas Freeman in assuming that Lee passed through two simple stages in his plans on the night of September 14th. First, he decided to retreat to Virginia; then learning Harpers Ferry was about to fall, he decided to make a desperate stand along the Antietam to await the reunification of his army.[33] This interpretation ignores the fact that Lee's eleven-fifteen dispatch reiterates the order for McLaws to abandon Maryland Heights.

After the war, Lee himself so telescoped the events of the night as to make unrecognizable the evolution of his thinking—which is clear from his contemporary documents—when he stated in conversation: "This night Lee found out that Cobb had been pressed back from Crampton's Gap, and this made it necessary to retire from Boonsboro Gap, which was done next morning and position at Sharpsburg taken."[34]

The most plausible interpretation of the known evidence is that Lee's decision passed through five stages. First, during or immediately after the war council at eight, he decided he must abandon his campaign in Maryland, which meant he would both break off the siege of Harpers Ferry and return to Virginian with the portion of the army with him at Boonsboro. Second, when he learned around ten of the Battle of

Crampton's Gap and the plight of McLaws, Lee modified his plan, but only to the extent that he would interrupt his own return to Virginia with a temporary stand at Keedysville to secure McLaws's flank. Third, upon reaching Keedysville about sunrise the next morning, he decided not to pause there but to continue west another three miles to Sharpsburg. Fourth, on the way to Sharpsburg, he received Jackson's dispatch of the previous evening predicting the early surrender of Harpers Ferry. It was at this point that Lee began to glimpse the possibility that he might not have to abandon Maryland. Fifth, it was not until noon, however, when he received official word of the Federal garrison's capitulation, that he completely reversed his decision to retreat.

Thus, for sixteen hours Lee intended to return to Virginia with the entire army. What he planned to do once there is uncertain. It is at least possible that he had in mind an immediate reentry into Maryland at another point. Such a tactical retreat to regain the initiative is exactly what he would attempt four days later.

Many years after the war, Walter Taylor suggested that McClellan's acquiring S.O. 191 compelled Lee to revise Confederate strategy in this respect: from the night of September 14 until learning of the surrender of Harpers Ferry, Lee's first priority was "extricating" McLaws from danger; secondarily, Lee became flexible as to whether to accept battle north or south of the Potomac. Taylor was absent from the army at this time, however, and claimed no direct knowledge of the question.[35]

It seems highly likely that had D. H. Hill, Hood, or Longstreet known that Lee at one time intended to retreat to Virginia, they would have mentioned it in their memoirs. This is especially true of Longstreet, who could then have claimed this is precisely what Lee ought to have done.

L. Jackson's Message to Lee Announcing the Fall of Harpers Ferry

It is concluded in *Taken at the Flood* that Jackson's message announcing the fall of Harpers Ferry reached Lee on Cemetery Hill about noon.[36] William Owen recorded the courier "arrives in hot haste."[37] The time is provided by Armistead Long.[38] And the location on Cemetery Hill is given by George Breckenridge Davis.[39]

Davis was not only a member of the editorial board of the *Official Records* but also president of the Antietam Battlefield Board, so he (like

Carman) had access to special testimony by veterans. Davis's article reveals, nevertheless, defects in scholarship which dictate that it be used with care. For example, he claims that the loss of Crampton's Gap compelled Lee to abandon Keedysville, when, in fact, Lee decided to stand at Keedysville because of Crampton's Gap. It is curious—and perhaps significant—that Carman described Lee's receipt of Jackson's message without ascribing a location.[40]

The fact that the courier took four hours to cover thirteen miles and arrived in "hot haste," may be explained partly by the morning heat and partly by detours taken along the way. Henry Kyd Douglas sent a note announcing the victory by the same courier to his father at Ferry Hill.[41] While the Douglas plantation lay directly between Shepherdstown and Sharpsburg, it may not have been the only side errand foisted on the hapless messenger.

M. What Dixon Miles Knew on September 15

It seems likely that Miles knew there had been fighting in McLaws's rear the day before. Col. Daniel Cameron of the 65th Ohio testified before the Harpers Ferry Court of Inquiry that the Battle of Crampton's Gap could be heard "distinctly" in Harpers Ferry on the 14th.[42] Moreover, the firing could also be heard by Jackson's men at their greater distance beyond Bolivar Heights.[43]

There is also the strong possibility that Miles knew directly that relief was nearby. Paul Teetor has made a persuasive case that Capt. Henry Cole carried a message from Miles to McClellan and that the Marylander returned with a message from McClellan by the evening of the 14th in time to lead his cavalry battalion in the escape column. If Miles did not hear directly from McClellan that help was at hand, therefore, it can only be because Cole, for some reason, failed to deliver a message he knew to be of critical importance.[44]

Miles's performance was so bad that rumors of treason circulated at the time. Teetor's book attempts to prove that Miles was, in fact, a traitor. As is the case with most conspiracy theories, however, this one entangles itself in an intricate web of even greater implausibilities and falls of its own weight. That Miles was a moral, if not physical, coward is a distinct possibility, although it is the kind of judgment that can seldom be proven in retrospect.

N. The Question of Fog at Harpers Ferry on September 15

Without citing sources, secondary studies have persistently depicted Harpers Ferry as fog enshrouded at dawn on the 15th.[45] This presents an interpretative dilemma these studies do not resolve. Either all the Confederates fired blindly and presumably ineffectively, or they delayed their fire until the mist had cleared. While the former is possible, the latter is unlikely, because the timetable of the morning's events (see chapter 9) requires the artillery to have opened at about sunrise. Moreover, of all the official reports, only one mentions either fog or a delay in firing.

John Walker reported that owing to a "heavy mist" his cannon did not open until eight o'clock, but they continued firing until a white flag was spotted at 9:30.[46] In this version, Walker implies he waited until the fog lifted, providing visibility for targets and seeing the white flag. There is a problem in timing, however, as this would have him continue his firing two hours after Jackson's men viewed white flags and an hour and a half after Jackson sent his victory message to Lee.

In his already much-discussed article in *Century Magazine* in June 1886, Walker related a substantially different story. He indicates that he opened at daylight along with all of the other Confederate batteries, but, because of a mist that affected only his mountain, "my artillerists trained their guns by the previous day's experience and delivered their fire through the fog." Walker continues by adjusting his timing and insists that he ceased fire by eight, not because he saw any signs of the surrender but by "surmising it." Finally, he goes out of his way to point out that it was Lawton's batteries that continued to fire and undoubtedly were guilty of mortally wounding Miles after white flags had been hoisted.[47] This is seemingly another example in this same article of Walker's attempt to arrange his position in history to suit himself; and it is difficult to know what, if anything, to accept.

It may be significant that Jed. Hotchkiss, who had been sent by Jackson to Loudoun to help supervise the artillery and signals, and who was usually meticulous in his weather observations, indicated in his diary that the guns on Loudoun opened at about the same time as the other batteries, but he also added: "Our batteries kept up the fire for some little time, as the fog and smoke prevented their seeing the flag, and besides, they were some ways off."[48] Thus, the fog must not have been too dense, or the smoke and distance would have hardly mattered.

Finally, Edward Moore, who was with the Rockbridge Artillery on the Potomac with J. R. Jones's division, remembered that "the morning was still and clear, giving us a full view of the lines of the lofty mountains."[49] Hence the conclusion in the *Taken at the Flood:* there was a fog, but it affected only—and that just moderately—the firing from Loudoun Heights.

O. The Timing of the Surrender of Harpers Ferry

Confederate sources agree that the white flags were seen between 7:00 and 8:00, and nearer the earlier hour: at 7:00 John R. Jones; at 7:15 O. E. Edwards; and at 7:30 Samuel McGowan.[50] Most impressively, Ham Chamberlayne, who helped supervise the batteries east of the Shenandoah, wrote home four days later that his guns opened "at daylight for 1hr 35m when a white flag was waved."[51] Depending on his definition of daylight, of course, Chamberlayne probably meant about 7:30.

Federal sources put these events about an hour later, indicating that the white flags were displayed at 9:00 or later. (All sources below, except where noted, are from *OR*, vol. 19, pt. 1.) According to Adj. Henry Binney, Miles began to consult his officers only at 8:00, and the white flags were not displayed until sometime thereafter.[52] Gen. Julius White reported that the consultations started at 9:00; while Maj. Henry McIlvaine, chief of artillery, reported that the white flags were displayed about 9:00.[53]

It may be that the Federals, consciously or not, tried to make their brief struggle appear moderately longer than it was. In this case, the Confederate version is clinched by Jackson's contemporaneous dispatch to Lee, which was timed at 8:00.[54]

P. Jackson's Paroling of the Harpers Ferry Garrison

To understand that Jackson's handling of the surrender of Harpers Ferry was entirely appropriate, it is necessary to review briefly the development of policy regarding prisoners of war. Fort Sumter fell before hostilities were recognized. Although the fort was captured, its garrison technically was "evacuated." The flag was not surrendered, and the officers and men were not paroled.[55]

After McClellan captured nearly a thousand Confederates in western Virginia in June and July 1861, the prisoners were paroled to await exchange.[56] This may have been in the hope that leniency would promote reconciliation. After First Manassas, however, the Confederates established the practice of holding prisoners to wait for exchange.

An early large-scale capture of a garrison occurred in Burnside's North Carolina campaign in February 1862. The nearly 2,500 prisoners from Roanoke Island and New Berne were paroled, immediately exchanged for prisoners on hand, and released.[57] A contrary policy was followed almost simultaneously for the approximately 11,000 prisoners captured by Grant at Fort Donelson on February 17. Probably because there was nowhere near an equivalent number available for exchange, these Confederates were shipped north to prison camps.[58]

On July 22, 1862, a cartel was signed between John Dix and D. H. Hill, as agents for their respective governments, which provided a formula for exchange of officers and men by rank and which stated that all prisoners should be paroled and released within ten days of capture, regardless of whether an equivalent number were then available. Commissioners were to keep a balance sheet of pluses and minuses.[59]

It would have been under this agreement and quite within its spirit that Jackson operated on September 15. Harpers Ferry gave the Confederates a surplus that they maintained until after Vicksburg and Gettysburg in July 1863. Grant decided to suspend exchanges in 1864 to hasten the end of the war. It probably did, but it also led to gruesome prison camp conditions in both the North and South.

Q. Jackson's Message to Lee of Noon, September 15

In chapter 7 of *Taken at the Flood* it is related that Lee sent a message to Jackson on the night of September 14 advising him that the siege of Harpers Ferry was being abandoned. The dispatch reached Jackson on about noon of the 15th, after the Federal garrison had surrendered. Jackson simply endorsed the letter that he would join Lee and returned it to his chief. This story, with more or fewer details, is given by Ezra Carman, John C. Ropes, and Henry Kyd Douglas.[60]

Lee's message and Jackson's endorsement have never been found, and their existence seems to rest on the word of Henry Douglas, who is the sole source for all of the versions found. Still, it is common sense to believe that Lee would advise Jackson that the main body would recross into Virginia and that McLaws had been ordered to abandon Maryland Heights. Since the siege would be thereby lifted, there would have been no point in Jackson remaining at Harpers Ferry.

The time of the dispatch's arrival can also be constructed logically. If Jackson had received the orders before eight o'clock, he would not have asked in his own dispatch of that hour where he should march. Had he received them before eleven he would likely have mentioned them to Stuart. On the other hand, had they arrived much later—after Lee's subsequent approval of Jackson's proposed course of action—they would have required no reply. Carman's belief that Lee received the endorsed reply by "mid-day" seems a bit early.

Jackson's endorsement is another matter. There is no reason to believe Jackson knew Lee was at Sharpsburg. Douglas may have superimposed later knowledge on his memory of the event. Jackson may have simply written "I will join you in Maryland."

R. Charles Squires and the Confederate Retreat from Boonsboro

Capt. Charles Winder Squires, who commanded the 1st Company of the Washington (La.) Artillery, made the following claim in his memoirs:[61]

> On the retreat from South Mountain, my battery brought up the rear of the army, and, although not engaged prior to the battle of Antietam, I was continually thrown into position to retard the enemy's advance. It was a tiresome, hard retreat on my men and horses. I reached the Antietam and crossed to the west side about daylight of September 16, 1862, and was placed in position north east of the town of Sharpsburg.

Of course, Squires could not have "brought up the rear" on the 16th, but neither could he have done so and crossed the Antietam at daylight on the 15th. The only explanation that allows some factual basis for the account is that Lee (or possibly Longstreet) posted Squires in battery at various places on the road from Boonsboro to cover the retreat of the main body. Squires would have been unaware of the rear guard under Hood and the cavalry skirmishers under Rosser. Squires manuscript memoir, in the W. H. T. Squires Papers in the Southern Historical Collection at the University of North Carolina, Chapel Hill, has been published but with some errors in transcription.

S. Inconsistencies in Lee's Dispatch to G. W. Smith of September 15

The date and location of Lee's letter to Gustavus W. Smith on September 15 are obviously inconsistent.[62]

There are four possibilities: (1) Lee dictated the letter at Hagerstown and sent it on the 13th, but it was misdated; (2) Lee dictated the letter on the 13th, but it was not sent until two days later—with the date but not the location corrected; (3) Lee dictated it and sent it on the 15th, and a careless staff member wrote an incorrect location; or, (4) the possibility followed in *Taken at the Flood,* Lee started the letter in Hagerstown on the 13th and finished it in Sharpsburg on the 15th.

There is no evident reason to accept one of the possibilities over the others. If Lee did work on the letter on the 15th, however, it certainly reveals a measure of *sang froid* on his part, since its contents deal with such routine matters. Whatever the explanation, this minor glitch reveals an uncharacteristic confusion at Lee's headquarters.

CHAPTER NINE

Research Appendixes on the Battle of Antietam, September 16–17

A. Categories of Strength in Civil War Armies

To Civil War historians there is a no more vexing question than the size of Union and Confederate armies. Numbers abound, but they vary so widely that accuracy seems unobtainable. Credentialed and oft-published students have been known—with good reason—to throw up their hands in surrender and avoid the whole subject. Yet, at the same time, no topic is more important to understanding strategy, tactics, and operations or more necessary for an evaluation of performance than knowing the strength of contending forces.

Sloppy record keeping, missing documents, and a host of random factors will prevent us from ever knowing down to the last individual the number of men in any unit from a regiment up to an army. Educated and reasonable approximations—near enough to allow analysis and fair evaluations—ought to be possible, however. One of the chief obstacles to reaching such estimates has been ignorance or disregard of the categories in Civil War military record keeping. When a reader turns to the Field Returns and Abstracts in the *Official Records,* he will find headings such as "present," "aggregate present," "present for duty," and "effectives." What do these terms mean? Are any or all the same thing? When the reader examines the reports of commanders (today called after action reports), he will find such additional terms as "officers and men," "men," "muskets," "carried into action," "on the line of battle," and other creative variations. How can these be evaluated?

All of these categories are valuable for some or another purpose, and any can be used for the purpose of comparison of two opponents. But it is imperative that the categories not be mixed in the comparison. It is unfair, for example, to compare Federal present for duty totals (always a larger number) to Confederate effectives (always a smaller number.) Either the Federals must be lowered to effectives or the Confederates raised to present for duty before the comparison is meaningful.

The following working definitions, in descending order of size, are offered as a first step toward lessening the obstacles in understanding the strength of Civil War armies:

MUSTER ROLL STRENGTH: All of the officers and men appointed to or sworn into a particular unit. During the unit's term of service, this number would increase due to recruitment and receipt of permanent transfers. This figure was purely theoretical (i.e., paper strength), as it is doubtful that any unit on either side ever had all its officers and men together at one place at the same time.

STRICKEN FROM THE ROLLS: Names were dropped from the muster rolls only when there was no possibility of return to service because of death (due to any cause), discharge (due to any cause), permanent transfer (to another unit or branch of service), and resignation (an option available only to officers).

AGGREGATE PRESENT AND ABSENT STRENGTH: The number remaining when the names stricken were deducted from the number mustered in.

ABSENT OR AGGREGATE ABSENT: All of those officers and men not physically present with the army through furlough, official leave, sick or wounded at home or in hospitals in the rear, prisoners of war, and missing for unknown reasons, including both missing in action and absent without leave.

PRESENT OR AGGREGATE PRESENT STRENGTH: All of those officers and men physically present with the army, whether fit for duty or not. Those present but not fit for duty would include those in nearby hospitals with less serious illnesses or wounds, those under arrest, etc.

PRESENT FOR DUTY STRENGTH: All of those officers and men physically with the army and fit for duty of any kind.

EXTRA-DUTY: Officers and men assigned to responsibilities that would keep them from fighting during a battle. Extra-duty would include serving as orderlies, camp guards, hospital stewards, cooks, teamsters, signalmen, etc. The term was used most often by the Federals but practiced by both sides.

EFFECTIVES OR FIGHTING EFFECTIVES: The officers and men left after deducting those assigned to extra-duty. The Confederates used this term more frequently than the Federals, but the concept applies to both.

The preceding terms are found in Field Returns and Abstracts for larger units, including armies. The following terms, all of which are less rigorously defined, are found in commanders' reports and most often apply to regiments and batteries.

OFFICERS AND MEN: Includes commissioned officers, noncommissioned officers, and enlisted men.

MEN: The most confusing term, as it is frequently not clear if noncommissioned officers (sergeants and corporals) are included with enlisted men.

BATTLEFIELD DETACHMENTS: Officers and men detached for some purpose after leaving camp (and hence after the morning report) and thereby kept from fighting in the battle in order to guard knapsacks and blankets dumped on the march, guard prisoners, etc. It seems that at times the Confederates even deducted skirmishers.

MUSKETS: Enlisted men only, as commissioned and noncommissioned officers did not carry shoulder arms.

CARRIED INTO ACTION: The number left after deducting battlefield detachments. An ambiguous term when it is not clear if officers are included with men.

ON THE LINE OF BATTLE: Usually the same as carried into action, except that skirmishers were deducted.

Table 23 illustrates how a mythical regiment, Federal or Confederate, might have atrophied over a year's time.

TABLE 23
Numbers and Losses of a Typical Civil War Regiment

Number	*Description*
1,098	Total officers and men mustered into the regiment
105	Dropped from the rolls (death, discharged, etc.)

Number	*Description*
993	Total officers and men present and absent
542	Absent (furlough, hospital, POW, missing, etc.)
451	Total officers and men present
45	Unfit for duty (sick, jail, etc.)
406	Total officers and men present for duty
89	Extra-duty (guards, cooks, stewards, orderlies, etc.)
317	Total effectives (officers and men)
63	Battlefield detachments (guards, carrying supplies, etc.)
254	Total officers and men on line of battle (including skirmishers)
28	Officers
226	Total muskets carried into action (including skirmishers)

The challenge for the historian is twofold. First, as already stated, is to make certain that when comparisons are made between Federal and Confederate forces, the same categories are used. But, second, it is also necessary to know which category is most suitable for the purpose intended. In the early chapters of *Confederate Tide Rising*, where the topic was mobilization of manpower, it was appropriate to use the category of "present and absent." In this work, when discussing strategy, planning for campaigns, and noncombat situations, it has been thought correct to use present for duty strengths. This is also the category most easily obtained and most comparable for the two sides.

The latest "present for duty" numbers for Lee's army, however, are from the September 1 tri-monthly estimate, and these figures have become so obsolete by the 16th—due to straggling, casualties and other causes—that they can no longer provide a fair basis for comparison with the Federals.

In any case, "effectives" is the classification most appropriate for comparisons in battle. Regrettably, these are the very figures usually the most difficult to come by, except for the spotty and frequently ambiguous references in "after-action" reports. Fortunately, for students of Antietam, Ezra Carman devoted some two decades to collecting "effective" strengths at the regimental level from veterans of the battle. Carman's figures are used for strengths and casualties in chapters 7, 8, and 9 of *Taken at the Flood.*

B. Lee's Sleeping Quarters on the Night of September 15–16

There is no local tradition of Lee spending any night under a roof while at Sharpsburg. Even Carman assumed that Lee spent all four nights in his tent three-quarters of a mile west of Sharpsburg, just north of the road to Shepherdstown.[1] Nevertheless, William Owen, adjutant of the Washington Artillery, writes in his diary-based account, "The Colonel [Walton] and I quartered ourselves in a dwelling-house on the edge of town. Gen. Toombs was under the same roof, and Gens. Lee and Longstreet were in a house on the opposite side of the street."[2]

It is possible that Lee used the house as headquarters but slept in his tent. It is more likely, however, that his stay was so brief as to have been forgotten and that it is proper to take Owen's word "quartered" literally.

Since Longstreet is known to have stayed in the Jacob H. Grove house, and Lee is known to have used the same dwelling on several occasions for councils of war, it makes sense to believe it was this house he slept in on the night of September 15–16. While the Grove house was in the center, and not on the edge, of town, a close reading of Owen reveals ambiguity in that regard.

C. Lee's Return to Traveller, September 16

No contemporary source provides a precise date for when Lee abandoned his ambulance to return to Traveller's back. Lee still had both hands bandaged and his right arm in a sling, but he was so anxious to regain his mobility that he used an aide to hold the reins.

The following are the grounds for the conclusion that he started on the 16th: (1) it is generally accepted that he did ride a "little" on the 17th during the battle;[3] (2) he entered Sharpsburg by ambulance on the 15th;[4] and (3) he was seen during the day of the 16th in the streets of the town, walking but followed by Traveller.[5]

D. Lee and the Army Trains on September 16

Seldom have Confederate orders for strictly logistical movements survived, which suggests that such orders may have frequently been oral and not written down. Ironically, Lee's action on the morning of September 16 is known only because it was observed and reported by the signal station established on Elk Ridge early that morning.[6] The following report was flagged to McClellan's headquarters and, although untimed, was the first message sent on the morning of the 16th, possibly between eight and nine, after the fog had cleared: "An immense train of the enemy's wagons is moving on the road from Sharpsburg to Shepherdstown. They cross the Potomac and halt about a mile south of Shepherdstown."[7]

All of the army's reserve trains were already in Virginia on the morning of the 16th. Alexander's ordnance train had proceeded under Lee's orders on the night of the 14th from Boonsboro to Williamsport and was now at Shepherdstown.[8] Longstreet's reserve wagons had gone from Hagerstown to Williamsport to Shepherdstown. D. H. Hill's reserve trains (at least his commissary wagons) had been pushed forward for safety to Hagerstown during the battle on the 14th. Along with the vehicles carrying supplies collected in Maryland, Hill's wagons had then proceeded to Martinsburg by way of Williamsport.[9] The only trains remaining with Lee that could have been sent away on the morning of the 16th, therefore, were the regimental, brigade, and divisional wagons.

It is possible that observation of the movement of these Confederate trains contributed to the doubt at McClellan's headquarters as to whether Lee intended a serious stand at Sharpsburg. The problems caused by the absence of the subsistence wagons is discussed in *Taken at the Flood*, chapter 8 (including notes 34 and 37).

E. Walker's March from Harpers Ferry and Arrival in Sharpsburg

This is another incident of uncertainty about John G. Walker's movements, due largely to his postwar writings. Since Walker did not set out from Halltown until one o'clock (see *Taken at the Flood*, chap. 7), he could not have reached the bivouac on the Shepherdstown Road until about the time Jackson sounded reveille. In his report, Walker wrote that he reached Shepherdstown by daylight and crossed the Potomac "early in the day."[10] In his first postwar article, however, he claimed to overtake Jackson's rear at two in the morning and cross the river at eight—and here he is obviously confused—"on the day of the battle."[11] In his second article he asserted that he reported to Lee "a little past the hour of noon on the 16th."[12] The only contemporary source discovered records Walker's division as crossing the Potomac at 1:00 P.M.[13] Hence, there are inconsistencies in Walker's accounts that are difficult to resolve.

In both his postwar articles on the Maryland campaign, Walker claims to have ridden with Jackson from the Potomac and in his company reported to Lee. It is conjectured that Jackson reached Lee at Cemetery Hill at about eight while at least part of Walker's division was still crossing the Potomac as late as 1:00 P.M.

It is certainly possible that Walker abandoned his men to their rest and, without waiting to supervise their fording the river, rode ahead to join Jackson. It is also possible that Walker invented the whole episode. He claims that on this ride he confessed his ruse to force the Federals to open fire at Harpers Ferry and was forgiven by Stonewall with the eminently quotable statement: "I thought I knew McClellan, but this movement of his puzzles me."[14] Walker then continued with the often-cited report of his arrival with Jackson and their meeting with Lee:[15]

> The thought of General Lee's perilous situation, with the Potomac River in his rear, confronting with his small force, McClellan's vast army, had haunted me through the long hours of the night's march, and I expected to find General Lee anxious and care worn. Anxious enough, no doubt, he was; but there was nothing in his look or manner to indicate it. On the contrary, he was calm, dignified, and even cheerful. If he had had a well-equipped army of a hundred thousand veterans at his back, he could not have appeared more composed and confident. On shaking hands with us, he simply expressed his satisfaction with the result of our operations at Harper's Ferry, and with our timely arrival at Sharpsburg; adding that with our reenforcement he felt confident of being able to hold his ground until the arrival of the divisions of R.H. Anderson, McLaws, and A.P. Hill.

Not only does the passage seem to employ a postwar hindsight of overall operations that were unlikely available to Walker at the time, but it also credits the crippled Lee with a round of hand shaking. Once again, there may well be some grain of truth in Walker's account, but it is impossible to separate it from the chaff. It has not, therefore, been used to illuminate the Lee-Jackson meeting.

F. Jackson's Arrival in Sharpsburg, September 16

Ezra Carman wrote: "Some of Jackson's staff officers and others say that Jackson reported to Lee at daylight on Cemetery Hill."[16] No doubt Henry Kyd Douglas, a postwar resident of Hagerstown and member of the commission to place battlefield markers, is one of the staff members referred to. Then, without attempting to reconcile the differences, Carman mentions John Walker's two articles that contradictorily record Jackson as reporting at 8:00 A.M. and at midday.

Eight o'clock has been chosen in the text for the following reasons: (1) daylight is too early, while midday is unreasonably late considering Jackson's predawn start. (2) Lee probably did not return to Cemetery Hill after the artillery bombardment started at nine. (3) The famous note thanking "Miss Fairfield" for breakfast (related below) indicates a relatively early arrival for Jackson. (4) After the war, Lee would remember that Jackson "preceded his troops" to Sharpsburg.[17] (5) The latter part of the meeting of Lee, Jackson, and Longstreet (no mention of Walker) was witnessed by Douglas, who had left Harpers Ferry "very early" in the morning.[18]

An indication that Jackson reported to Lee early on the 16th is in one of the most famous anecdotes of the Maryland campaign. As Jackson rode back through the main street of Sharpsburg, the Grove family—who probably had learned of his arrival from conversations among the headquarters staffs of Lee, Longstreet, and Stuart, who were occupying their home—invited Stonewall to stop for breakfast. Anxious to return to his men, Jackson politely declined. Miss Julia, one of the light-haired daughters of the house, prepared a breakfast and sent it by one of Longstreet's servants to Jackson in the field. When the servant was unable to put a name to the gracious donor, Jackson penciled a note of thanks to "Miss Fairfield" for her kindness. The document was lithographed during the war and sold to raise funds for Confederate hospitals. After the war the original was exhibited at bazaars and fairs for the benefit of veterans' homes.[19]

The alleged arrival of Jackson's men is fancifully described in an account by Thomas Caffey.[20] Although quoted trustingly by Francis Palfrey, the account has Stonewall arriving after dark on the night of the 16th and should not be credited.[21]

G. The Artillery Bombardment of September 16

The artillery exchange on September 16, although largely ignored by historians of the battle, made quite an impression on both armies at the time. Only two Confederate batteries can be identified from the reports as having participated in the duel, Squires of the Washington (La.) Artillery and Reilly's (Rowan, N.C.), attached to Hood's division.[22] Each had two 3-inch rifles. A lieutenant of the Rowan Artillery remembered that his battery fired four rifles in the duel (probably two 10-pounder Parrotts were rifled) and expended 484 rounds, exhausting its supply.[23]

Battlefield Plaque No. 368, located near the National Cemetery, identifies thirty-three guns in the Confederate line: "Washington Artillery (15 guns), Hood's division artillery (14 guns) and Capt. J. S. Brown's Va. Battery (4 guns)." This list, however, gives the Washington Artillery one less gun than reported by Walton and does not include either the four guns of Moody's (Madison, La., Artillery) battery of S. D. Lee's battalion, which remained in position north of the Boonsboro Pike,[24] or Boyce's battery (Macbeth, S.C., Artillery) of Evans's brigade, which should have been in the line and is presumed to have had four guns. The new total would thus be forty-one. Of these, only seven were 3-inch rifles: Squires (2), Moody (2), Wise (1), and Reilly (2). Eubank is not included, as he was too far to the right covering the Lower Bridge to participate in the duel.

Lt. Samuel Benjamin, Battery E, 2d U.S. Artillery, estimated that the Confederates had "ten or twelve" pieces engaged.[25] There were four 10-pounder Parrots in the batteries of Squires and Reilly which presumably also participated and thus reached Benjamin's total. However, a soldier of the 17th Virginia reported in his diary that only eight Confederate guns engaged.[26] Jennings Wise gives an account that confuses the firing on the 15th with the that of the 16th.[27] For armament of the Confederate batteries, see Pendleton's report.[28]

The bombardment was most dramatically described by diarist George Wise, who noted that at "near noon" a "most terrific artillery duel" occurred, and in Sharpsburg "many houses suffered terribly."[29] In the official reports the cannonade was called "heavy" by David R. Jones and Joseph Walker; "quite heavy" by Durham of the 23d South Carolina;

"severe" by McMaster of the 17th South Carolina; and by Eppa Hunton as "very heavy."[30]

Casualties reported were as follows: 17th South Carolina, 1 killed and six wounded; 22d South Carolina, 1 wounded;[31] and Reilly's North Carolina battery, four wounded, with two horses killed and one wounded.[32] North of the Boonsboro Pike, Ripley's brigade also endured a "heavy" fire but reported no losses.[33]

H. Confederate Cavalry on the Evening of September 16

In addition to the five regiments of Fitz Lee's brigade, two other cavalry units were present on the Confederate left by the evening of September 16. The 7th Virginia Cavalry, which had been assigned to Jackson's column for the Valley expedition, recrossed the Potomac in the afternoon. The 7th's commander—either misunderstanding that his brigade (Munford's) was on the far right at Snavely's Ford, or believing he was still assigned to Jackson—rode behind Sharpsburg and headed north. Traveling parallel to but west of the Hagerstown Pike in the darkness, the regiment went past both the Confederate and Federal lines and bivouacked at Ground Squirrel Church, almost a mile north of Doubleday's division.[34]

The presence of the Jeff. Davis Legion is known based on an anecdote that one of its horses was spooked during the night for no apparent cause.[35] The battalion had been guarding Solomon's Gap at the far end of Pleasant Valley and had gotten separated from the remainder of Hampton's brigade during the chaos of the defeat at Crampton's Gap and darkness of the night of the 14th. Hampton, with the rest of his brigade, covered McLaws's passage of the Potomac, crossed on the pontoon bridge on the afternoon of the 16th, and, for unknown reasons, did not reach the battlefield until the 17th, when he reported to Stuart on the far left.[36]

I. R.H. Anderson's Division in the Maryland Campaign

R.H. Anderson's is the mystery division of the Maryland campaign, since the *Official Records* contain no report from Anderson or any from his six brigade commanders or from twenty-five of his twenty-six regimental commanders.

McLaws wrote in his report that Longstreet ordered him "to send Gen. Anderson's division direct down the road to the hill beyond Sharpsburg, where he would receive orders."[37] Assuming McLaws had taken the same route as Jackson and Walker, he crossed at Boteler's Ford, followed the canal path to the country road that led to the Shepherdstown Road, and proceeded on the latter to Sharpsburg. In that case, Longstreet's orders would have sent Anderson directly east through town, where the Shepherdstown Road becomes the Boonsboro Pike, and on to Cemetery Hill. Antietam Battlefield Plaque No. 344 indicates something possibly different: "Anderson's Division crossed the Potomac at Blackford's [Boteler's] Ford about sunrise on the 17th and, marching through the fields west and north of Sharpsburg reached this road [Hagerstown Pike] about 9:00 A.M."

Since McLaws wrote his report only a month after the event, it is likely that he remembered being told, and then necessarily repeating, the directions to send Anderson "direct down the road" and through town, rather than "through the fields west and north of Sharpsburg." Nonetheless, it is almost certain that Anderson's division neither marched through town nor spent any time on Cemetery Hill.

A plausible explanation would be that Longstreet did originally intend for Anderson to occupy the position on Cemetery Hill, which was strong in artillery but weak in infantry support. By the time Anderson had forded the Potomac in McLaws's wake and reached the vicinity of the battlefield, however, the Federals were threatening to break through the Confederate left. Without McLaws ever knowing it, Longstreet then changed his orders and sent Anderson northwest to bolster the line in the Sunken Road. This explanation is at least consistent with the ambiguous statement in the recently published report by Col. William Gibson for Wright's brigade: "We reached the banks of the Potomac opposite [*sic*] Shepherdstown, where we received orders to hurry forward all our available force, and by 7 o'clock a.m. we were near the battlefield in front and ordered immediately in."[38]

J. Lee's Movements on September 17

Sixty years ago Douglas Freeman lamented that "the sequence of Lee's movements on Sept. 17 is very difficult to establish."[39] While the present study is able to shed new light on his whereabouts at various times, gaps remain. Lee spent most of the morning prior to eight on Cemetery Hill, but when he went there is conjecture.

Staff member Armistead Long recalled: "Lee's position during the engagement was on a hill to the east of Sharpsburg, which gave him an oversight of the whole field."[40] This was probably true—except for several trips to threatened points in the line (detailed in chapter 9 of *Taken at the Flood*)—until the Federal advance from the Middle and Lower Bridges forced him to retire to a point near his headquarters west of Sharpsburg. It is conjectured that he went to his observation post on Cemetery Hill at earliest light.

It is also speculation that Lee moved to different points on Cemetery Hill at various times to gain better views of particular points. It seems a safe hypothesis, since there is no one spot that affords equally good vantages of the Middle Bridge, the Lower Bridge area, the Sunken Road, and the Dunkard Church. In fact, only from north of the Boonsboro Pike in what is now the civilian cemetery (Mountain View) is it possible to see the Hagerstown Pike and the scene of the morning's fighting.

According to Henry Kyd Douglas, a large rock was uncovered immediately after the war in clearing the land south of the Boonsboro Pike for the National Cemetery. A legend grew up that Lee had spent most of the day of the battle standing on this boulder. With bitter feelings still prevalent, it was decided that this was an inappropriate intrusion in the burial ground of loyal soldiers, and "Lee's Rock" was destroyed. Confederate veterans, who knew Lee had never seen the stone, were amused by the episode.[41]

K. Numbers and Losses of the Army of Northern Virginia at the Battle of Antietam, September 17

Ezra Carman, from his position as historian on the Antietam Battlefield Board, focused foremost on pinpointing where the various units fought. He tried to send a map to at least one survivor of every regiment and battery, asking each to locate the positions occupied by his command. He used this information as the basis for the text for the cast-iron plaques and to place the units on the Cope maps, which were published first in 1904 and revised in 1908.

Secondarily, and with only slightly less zeal, Carman collected data on the strength and casualties of the two armies. His conclusions may be found in chapters 23 and 24 of his manuscript "History of the Maryland Campaign." Based on correspondence, personal interviews, newspaper accounts, memoirs, and regimental histories, his figures are probably as close to the real numbers as later generations can hope to approach. The table below is based on Carman's statistics, rearranged to reflect the revised organization of the Army of Northern Virginia as presented in chapter 2 herein. A similar exhibit for the Army of the Potomac will be included in a future study.

TABLE 24
Confederate Numbers and Losses at Antietam

	Strength				*Casualties*			
Unit	*Officers & men*	*Artillery*	*Total*	*Guns*	*Killed*	*Wounded*	*Casualties/ Missing*	*Total*
LONGSTREET'S COMMAND								
D. R. Jones	3,311	81	3,392	4	103	605	50	758
Hood	2,000	304	2,304	18	123	815	87	1,025
Evans	284	115	399	6	13	60	11	84
Washington Artillery	–	278	278	16	4	28	2	34
TOTAL	5,595	778	6,373	44	243	1,508	150	1,901
JACKSON'S COMMAND								
Jackson	1,784	310	2,094	21	145	486	17	648
Ewell	3,904	223	4,127	15	196	1,102	40	1,338
A. P. Hill	2,231	337	2,568	18	70	341	6	417
TOTAL	7,919	870	8,789	54	411	1,929	63	2,403
UNATTACHED								
R. H. Anderson	3,672	328	4,000	16	172	954	152	1,278
D. H. Hill	5,449	346	5,795	24	352	1,439	519	2,310
McLaws	2,823	138	2,961	9	160	933	26	1,119
Walker	3,764	230	3,994	12	184	839	97	1,120
TOTAL	15,708	1,042	16,750	61	868	4,165	794	5,827
Reserve Artillery	–	939	939	58	14	122	0	136
Cavalry	4,500	–	4,500	4	10	28	11	49
TOTAL	33,722	3,629	37,351	221	1,546	7,752	1,018	10,316

Summary

Infantry	29,222	Killed	1,546	(4.1%)
Artillery	3,629	Wounded	7,752	(20.8%)
Cavalry	4,500	Missing	1,018	(2.7%)
TOTAL	37,351	TOTAL	10,316	(27.6%)

Comments: The most important thing to understand about Carman's figures is that they do not represent present for duty, effectives, or even "on the field," but rather only those actually engaged in the fighting. Hence, he includes only nine of McLaws's nineteen guns and four of the Horse Artillery's sixteen, and he excludes the brigades of Pender and Field of A. P. Hill's division. Whether he did so consciously or not, Carman probably adopted this approach because it favors the Federals. Since nearly all of the Confederate army was engaged, such exclusions reduce its total by merely several thousand. Yet, by counting only those who fought, Carman is able to give an aggregate of infantry, artillery, and cavalry for the Federal army of 55,596, a total of nearly 30,000 fewer than that traditionally accepted.

Most of Carman's figures are only slightly larger than the Confederates' own estimates, and many of the negligible increases are attributable to adding officers where the Confederates neglected to do so. There are several significant exceptions, however. The totals for the divisions of Walker and D. H. Hill are much larger than will be found elsewhere.

It will be noted that not only did the unattached divisions have more men engaged and lose more casualties than Longstreet's and Jackson's commands combined, but their percentage of casualties (37.1) was higher than either (34 and 30.3, respectively).

A minor flaw in the table results from the fact that Carman did not attempt to include casualties for September 17 only. He did not screen out the losses of the 16th (probably several hundred) or the 18th (not more than a handful).

The most serious weakness in the figures, as Carman clearly recognized, is in the category of captured/missing. It was in this area that already haphazard Confederate record keeping was most deficient. It is possible that the total (1,018) needs to be multiplied by a factor of three or four.

In *Taken at the Flood* (chap. 9) Carman's figures have been used for the summaries of the men engaged and casualties suffered in the various phases (Jackson versus Hooker, the Sunken Road, etc.) In doing so, wherever possible, allowances have been made for the detachment of forces: for example, Cobb was deducted from McLaws and added to the defenders of the Sunken Road; G. T. Anderson was subtracted from D. R. Jones and Armistead from R. H. Anderson and both added to the forces fighting around the Dunkard Church. Such refinements have limits, however. Where a unit, such as Colquitt's brigade, fought in more than one phase (primarily in the D. R. Miller's Cornfield, but a portion later in the Sunken Road), it has not been possible to separate the casualties, and the losses have been attributed to the phase where the unit engaged in its primary fighting.

L. The Wounding of D. H. Hill's Horse on September 17

This famous incident has been placed at various places and at times from eight in the morning to late afternoon. In the midst of a welter of contradictory evidence, the account in chapter 9 of *Taken at the Flood* is believed to be the most likely for the following reasons. Although Longstreet places the episode at "a little after one" and his adjutant Moxley Sorrel in the "early afternoon," other compelling evidence presented by both—and by other witnesses—makes this improbable. In the first place, the location is relatively certain. Both Longstreet and Federal surgeon Alfred Woodhull, who witnessed the shot from Weed's Battery I, 5th U. S. Artillery (which fired it), agree that it occurred on Cemetery Hill, twenty or so feet either north or south of the Boonsboro Pike. Sorrel insisted it took place before he and other staff members worked the abandoned guns of Miller's battery to repulse Richardson, which would place it before noon. Longstreet also remembered that the point was behind a portion of D. H. Hill's line, which means it was before George B. Anderson's brigade moved from its position on the heights to fill the eastern end of the Sunken Road—in other words, before ten o'clock. Finally, Woodhull puts the time between 8:00 and 9:00, and before there had been any movement by Burnside.

At any time from 8:00 to 1:00, however, Hill was unlikely to have been away from the left. From 8:00 to 9:30 he was fully engaged in supervising the advance, and subsequent retreat, of the brigades of Ripley, Colquitt, and Garland and around 9:00 would be near the Dunkard Church to help direct McLaws's advance. Thereafter, Hill would be engaged in a life-and-death struggle to hold the Sunken Road. Moreover, between 8:00 and about 9:30, Lee himself was not on Cemetery Hill.

Thus, assuming the incident occurred in the morning, it most likely took place between 7:00 and 8:00. Hill's men were not yet engaged, and he had ridden over to the far right flank of his own line to see Lee. If around 7:30, he may have been carrying Jackson's message for support for Hood. Or, Hill may have simply been requesting permission to send his division to Jackson as suggested in *Taken at the Flood.* Although Jackson was the ranking field director, both he and Hill may have been reluctant to strip troops placed by Lee to protect the hinge in the line without the express approval of their chief.

In this case, the Federal troop movement the generals on Cemetery Hill went forward to observe would have been Mansfield's 12th Corps forming behind the Cornfield and East Woods—the news of which Hill may have himself supplied. This would fit Longstreet's memory that they were looking at enemy movements in front of the Confederate "rear left." This would also explain Hill's refusal to dismount because of his desire to return to his troops; which also fits with Long's recollection that Hill "was in great haste to deliver an important communication"—a better explanation than Longstreet's that Hill "was a little out of strength and thinking a single horseman not likely to draw the enemy's fire."[42]

The secondary accounts by Douglas Freeman and Hal Bridges mistakenly imply that the incident occurred behind the Sunken Road.[43]

D. H. Hill never wrote an account of the episode. However, he reviewed Longstreet's version before it appeared in *Century Magazine* (June 1886) and proclaimed it "entirely accurate."[44] Hill also mentioned that he had five horses shot from under him on the 17th and that he had written a letter to Longstreet describing the incidents. Unfortunately, that letter has not been found.

The historian of Durell's Battery D, Pennsylvania Artillery, in 1903 made a tentative claim to credit for the shot to his unit. The description in his account, however, makes it likely that their episode occurred during the attack of McLaws, when Lee was absent from Cemetery Hill.[45]

M. The Summons of McLaws to Battle on September 17

Jackson's call for reinforcements from Lee is confirmed by both J. W. Ratchford and Sandy Pendleton.[46] Neither of Jackson's requests have been found, and both may have been oral.

Ratchford and Pendleton indicated no awareness of one another's mission, and their order of arrival cannot be fixed certainly. Ratchford's recollection of Lee's initial refusal is the basis for fleshing out the details as given in chapter 9 of *Taken at the Flood*.

The timing of events is derived from Lee's actions and the arrival of Lee's orders to McLaws (also nonexistent, and perhaps oral) around 8:00. That Jackson was expecting McLaws is clearly evident and suggests Lee sent him a reply, which is also not extant.

McLaws, who was awakened from a sound slumber to catch up with his already-moving division, named no hour for his start in his postwar article or in his report; but Kershaw remembered it was "about 9 o'clock"; Col. William MacRae reported it was "about 8 A.M."; Maj. P. M. Loud recorded "at 8 A.M."; Barksdale's account may not be relied upon, as he reports not arriving at Sharpsburg until 9 o'clock.[47]

In his manuscript history, Ezra Carman fails to mention a specific time for the orders to McLaws, but battlefield plaques covering the division all indicate that the four brigades started their march to the left at "nearly" nine o'clock.[48]

It seems reasonable, therefore, that Lee sent Taylor shortly after 8:00. Taylor spent some time in a fruitless search for McLaws before ordering the division's adjutant to issue the orders to the brigades, so they probably did form line and set out shortly before nine.

N. Walker's Claim to Espy Lee on September 17

In the tiresome catalog of John G. Walker's postwar attempts to associate himself with heroic figures and moments in Confederate history must be included his account of sighting Lee during the march to the left. According to Walker, "As I passed what is now known as Cemetery Hill, I saw General Lee standing erect and calm, with a field-glass to his eye, his fine form sharply outlined against the sky, and I thought I had never seen a nobler figure. He seemed quite unconscious that the enemy's shells were exploding around and beyond him."[49]

The authenticity of the passage should be measured against the following: (1) Walker's division marched west of Sharpsburg, and it is unlikely a solitary figure east of town would have been visible at any point on the route; (2) with two bandaged hands and one arm in a sling, it is unlikely Lee was holding a telescope to his eye; and (3) during the time in question (8:30–10:00), Lee was not on Cemetery Hill but was visiting the left at the Reel Ridge and the Sunken Road.

If one were dealing with a usually reliable witness, it would be tempting to speculate that Walker confused his locations and actually saw Lee—minus telescope—on the Reel Ridge. Walker's memoirs do not earn this benefit of the doubt.

O. Lee's Meeting with His Youngest Son on September 17

Four accounts claim to be firsthand witness to this famous encounter between Lee and his youngest son during the Battle of Antietam: both Lees, father and son; William T. Poague, commander of the Rockbridge (Va.) Artillery; and Henry Kyd Douglas of Jackson's staff.[50]

Lee (Sr.) made a passing reference to the incident in a letter to his wife almost a month later that gives no details beyond implying the battery was "going in" for the second time. In spite of the casual and belated word sent home, the episode clearly impressed Lee's memory, and he would later relate it to Jefferson Davis.[51]

All of the other accounts were written around the turn of the century. Rob's version gives neither precise time nor location, but, contrary to his father, has the battery retiring and its commander approaching the elder Lee for instructions.

Both Poague and Douglas assign a time and site for the incident, but regrettably they are contradictory. Douglas claims to have been with Jackson at Lee's headquarters on the Shepherdstown Road just before three o'clock. Burnside was on the move and A. P. Hill was not yet up. Lee ordered Jackson to transfer some guns from the left to slow the Federals' advance. Graham's section of the Rockbridge Artillery was one of the units brought forward, and thus the exchange between the father and son took place. According to Douglas, he himself then personally posted the section. Douglas related the episode with such confidence and detail that his version was accepted for years.[52]

Poague's manuscript memoirs were written in 1903 but not published until 1957. Therein the artillerist gives the version that—except for time—is accepted in *Taken at the Flood.* According to Poague, the three guns were resting in the rear of the Dunkard Church woods, when Lee rode up and inquired about the condition of the unit. The reason Poague's account must be accepted over Douglas's is that none of his guns were transferred to the right to fight against Burnside. On the contrary, his one mobile gun did participate in the attempted turning movement under Stuart. This was actually made quite clear in Poague's report at the time.[53]

Thus, the "going in" for a second time without a doubt refers to the abortive Jackson-Stuart offensive on the left. This would also mean, since none of Poague's guns were on the Shepherdstown Road, that the meeting must have occurred in the rear of the West Woods.

The only difficulty is that Poague places the incident at eleven in the morning. And, certainly, it is possible that in his wanderings during the forenoon Lee strayed as far as Jackson's position to check affairs. It is even possible—although just barely—that Poague's estimate of the time is two hours late and that Lee saw his son on the first trip to the left around the time of McLaws's deployment. The rest of Poague's report, as well as his memoirs, suggests this battery was not resting at this early hour, however. If it is assumed that Poague was two and a half hours early in his estimate of the time, everything else falls into place.

The fact that the meeting occurred after gunner Edward Moore of the battery was wounded and that he did not witness it strengthens the latter theory.[54]

P. Lee's War Council on the Evening of September 17

The account of the meeting between Lee and his officers on the evening of September 17 given in *Taken at the Flood*, chapter 9, is a synthesis of numerous sources. The manner in which the several inconsistencies and contradictions were resolved is as follows:

Sources

The first evidence of an assemblage of officers at Lee's headquarters after the battle appeared in 1885 in the diary-based memoirs of William Miller Owen, adjutant of the Washington (La.) Artillery.[55] The following year Longstreet wrote an article for *Century Magazine* in which he described being the last arrival to report to Lee.[56] Ten years later, Longstreet published an abbreviated version in his autobiography.[57]

In the December 20, 1896, issue of the *Richmond Dispatch*, Stephen D. Lee published an extended account of what amounted to a war council.[58] Before publishing his version, ex-artillerist Lee provided it in letters (with insignificant differences from his newspaper article) to Jed. Hotchkiss, George F. R. Henderson, and Ezra Carman to include in their historical works in progress.[59]

G. Moxley Sorrel's memoirs, written about 1901 and published in 1905, included a brief mention of Longstreet's participation. Sorrel's account is based on what other staff members told him, as he had been wounded late in the day and was not present.[60] The passing reference in James C. Nisbet's 1915 memoirs is probably entirely secondary and should not be trusted.[61]

Location

Owen, Longstreet, and S. D. Lee agree that the event took place in a field near Lee's headquarters on the Shepherdstown Road. This should settle the matter, although there is a local tradition that a Confederate war council was held that evening in the Jacob Grove house on the town square.

Time

S. D. Lee says "an hour or two after dark set in." Owen and Longstreet simply imply it was soon after dark. Eight o'clock is a reasonable supposition.

Participants

Owen says a "large number of general officers and staff officers were assembled about Lee." When Owen and Walton rode up together, Lee was talking to Jackson, and "the two Hills, Hood, Jones and Early" were already present. Lee asked about Longstreet, and Venable replied. Then Longstreet—among the last, if not *the* last—rode up.

In his memoirs, Longstreet explained his delay was due to helping wounded and a Sharpsburg family whose home was burning, "so that all the other officers had arrived, made their reports, and were lounging about on the sod, when I rode up." No elaboration is given to the "all," but the implication is clear that Longstreet was the very last.

According to S. D. Lee, all of the corps and division commanders reported, one by one, and he specifies the following, in the order of their speaking: Longstreet, D. H. Hill, Jackson, and Hood. It will be noted that by putting Longstreet first, he precludes Robert E. Lee's anxious inquiry and Old Peter's dramatic late entrance.

S. D. Lee also claims that the officers had been summoned to headquarters. While it is certainly possible that a few—such as the colonel of an artillery battalion—were called because they would not normally report, it is likely that the others were there from custom.

It is suggestive that apparently neither McLaws nor Walker seem to have been present. Both gave much thought to the campaign after the war and wrote detailed accounts of it, and yet neither mentioned the meeting. In the case of Walker, it may be assumed he did not even realize there was a meeting, since he did not claim to be there.

Was it a council of war?

Probably not. Owen witnessed only individual conversations between Lee and his subordinates. Longstreet does not indicate any discussions that involved give-and-take occurred either before or after he arrived. If read carefully, S. D. Lee is not in disagreement; he simply implies that he was near enough to hear the individual conversations.

Even though no general pronouncement by the Confederate commander is mentioned by Owen or Longstreet, it is not unreasonable to follow S. D. Lee on this point. It is believable that Lee took advantage of the assemblage of his subordinates to announce his orders and avoid sending out couriers later in the dark. Also, as mentioned in *Taken at the Flood*, it was a decision that had to be rendered immediately, since any retreat would have had to be started at once.

Freeman's objection

Historian Douglas Southall Freeman accepted the accounts of Longstreet, Owen, and Sorrel but refused to rely on S. D. Lee's version.[62] While he raised valid points about the artillerist's story, the historian probably went too far in rejecting it altogether. Freeman incorrectly assumed Sorrel was an eyewitness to the event; and misread the S. D. Lee account to mean that a loud and semi-public discussion took place. (It is possible that Freeman relied upon the summaries in Hotchkiss and /or Henderson and did not read the full story in the newspaper.)

Colonel Lee may well have overdramatized the event, but, except for having Longstreet arrive too early, his version is reasonably consistent with the others.

What Lee said

Even though S. D. Lee puts R. E. Lee's words in quotation marks, the artillerist cautioned that he gave only the "substance" and not the verbatim of what the general said. It is reasonable for historians to take the same approach. There is nothing exceptionable in the remarks. They simply verbalize the decision Lee made and the instructions he must have given in some form that night.

E. Porter Alexander, an advocate of the view that Lee had "read McClellan's inmost soul," wrote as if there had been no meeting at all: "Without a word of explanation or asking advice from Jackson or Longstreet or anyone else, he directed all to collect their stragglers, strengthen their lines, and be prepared to renew battle in the morning." Alexander was in Shepherdstown, however, and had no firsthand knowledge of what he wrote.[63]

The Longstreet encomium

Longstreet's recollection of the compliment from his commander is supported by the earlier published account by Owen. Sorrel, although admittedly not an unbiased source and not present at the meeting, may be given some weight, since he reports the incident as the talk of Longstreet's staff. The quotation used in *Taken at the Flood* is from Owen, which was at least based on a diary. According to Longstreet, Lee said, "Here is my old war-horse at last." Sorrel's version, as garnered from colleagues and perhaps embellished, was "Here comes my war horse just from the field he has done so much to save."

In regard to the physical contact, Owen wrote that Lee greeted Longstreet by "grasping him by the hand." Considering Lee's bandaged hands and sling, Longstreet's earliest version—Lee "threw his arms upon my shoulders"—is more likely correct.

Jackson's advice

The most controversial point in S. D. Lee's account is his claim that Jackson advised Lee to retreat on the night of the 17th. Although there is no firsthand contradictory evidence to controvert this claim, various members of Jackson's staff—none of whom were present at the meeting—would reject the idea.

Hunter McGuire argued that Jackson's calm assurance during the afternoon that the enemy had done their worst proved that Stonewall would not have suggested withdrawal that night, while Henry Kyd Douglas insisted that Jackson "seemed ready for a fight at the drop of a hat" the next morning.[64] Two secondary accounts of the meeting, one by Hotchkiss and one by an early Lee biographer, omit reference to Jackson advising in favor of retreat.[65]

The logic of the Jackson supporters is hardly convincing. Jackson might well have been satisfied that the danger had passed during the afternoon and still believed it unwise to remain another day. Moreover, Douglas's assertion is itself contradicted by Hood's recollection that on the following morning Jackson remarked that he had hoped the Federals had withdrawn during the night.[66]

Perhaps the most telling point for the doubters, although scarcely conclusive, is their belief that it would have been against Jackson's nature to advise retreat. It is also true that after the war Robert E. Lee seemed to imply that Jackson agreed with him at every step during the war. In the postwar letter to Mrs. Jackson, however, Lee's reference to Jackson's concurrence in offering battle in Maryland could apply to the 16th and 17th and not include remaining on the 18th.[67]

This evidentiary dilemma has been resolved in *Taken at the Flood* (chap. 9) by not specifically identifying Jackson as one of those who advised retreat on the night of the 17th but depicting him in chapter 10 as one who was willing, if not eager, to withdraw on the next day.

Q. Lee's News of Distant Events

It must again be cautioned that it has not been possible to discover what, if anything, Lee knew about the Confederate offensives in the West after Kirby Smith's victory at Richmond, Kentucky. It is reasonable to assume, however, that the more he knew, the more determined he became to keep his own offensive alive.

Channing Price, an aid to Stuart, made an intriguing comment in a letter he wrote from Sharpsburg on the day following the battle: "We are entirely cut off from the world; I have not seen a paper or heard any news from Richmond for 2 weeks. . . . We heard yesterday that G. W. Smith and Johnston with their forces occupied Arlington Heights & if so, the blow we struck McClellan yesterday may become a decided victory."[68]

Coming from a member of Stuart's staff, this suggests that news of wider events was indeed scarce among the high command. Even more intriguing is the rumor of a Confederate ghost army at the gates of Washington. If Lee heard the rumor—and gave it any credence at all—it too might have played a role in his decision to remain another day.

CHAPTER TEN

Research Appendixes on the Antietam Aftermath, September 18 and After

A. Firing on September 18

Existing sources unanimously agree that September 18 was a quiet day. Two studies overstate the case by claiming "not a gun was fired."[1] One diarist, who would have been located in the West Woods, more accurately recorded that "there has been no fighting today."[2] Many sources do mention widespread sniping, which seems to have occurred largely on the Confederate center and right.[3]

It was David Hunter Strother, a member of McClellan's staff, who noted that the Federals fired "four or five" cannon shots.[4]

In his report, Lt. Col. James Perrin (1st S.C. Rifles) noted intense Federal sharpshooter fire from behind the cover of a fence that not only annoyed his regiment but killed one of his men, and added, "As I had received orders early in the morning to do nothing to bring on a general engagement, I refrained from any attempt to dislodge them."[5] It would be revealing to know if the order had come from brigade (Gregg), division (A. P. Hill), or army (Lee) headquarters.

Winfield Hancock, appointed to command the 1st division of the Second Corps, after the wounding of Israel Richardson, claimed that McClellan ordered him "not to precipitate hostilities" on the 18th.[6]

B. Confederate Stragglers Brought Up by the Morning of September 18

The estimate that nearly 6,000 stragglers were brought up during the night to strengthen the Confederate line is provided by Ezra Carman.[7] Lee reported simply: "Our ranks were increased by the arrival of a number of troops, who had not been engaged the day before."[8] Walter Taylor more helpfully indicates that the number was large and that most belonged to the divisions most recently arrived from Harpers Ferry: "Many of those left behind in the rapid march to Sharpsburg had rejoined their commands, and so considerably increased their numerical strength."[9] Taylor's comments would apply to the divisions of Jackson, Ewell, McLaws, Walker, and A. P. Hill. Two sources put the figure at "some" or "about" 5,000, respectively.[10]

Jubal Early reported ordering four batteries (Chesapeake [Md.] Artillery, 1st Md. Battery, Courtney [Va.] Artillery, and Staunton [Va.] Artillery) to Sharpsburg from Harpers Ferry.[11] There may have been other miscellaneous batteries that crossed into Maryland on the 18th.

A. P. Hill had left Col. Edward Thomas's brigade of four Georgia regiments behind to hold Harpers Ferry. Why Lee did not order these 1,000 men to Sharpsburg is not known. Thomas remained in Harpers Ferry on the 18th, and he moved up the river to rejoin his division at Shepherdstown on the 19th.[12]

C. Strength of the Army of Northern Virginia on September 18

According to an Abstract of Field Returns, dated September 22, the Army of Northern Virginia then had 34,747 infantry present for duty.[13] Lee's army must have been weaker on the day after the battle. On the 18th, six brigades are known to have had less than 250 men: Hays, Garnett, Evans, Armistead, Trimble, and Lawton.[14] Based on their known strength on the 17th, less the casualties suffered in the battle, another eleven brigades almost certainly had 400 or less men: Winder, J. R. Jones, Taliaferro, Starke, Cobb, Semmes, Mahone, Kemper, Drayton, Wofford, and Archer. On the same basis, yet another four other brigades may have had around 400 men: Kershaw, Barksdale, G. T. Anderson, and Toombs.

In the case of five brigades, where strengths are known for both the 17th and 18th, as well as battle casualties, it is possible to reckon the number of men who should have been, but were not, with their colors on the 18th. It will be noted in the table below that, with one exception, the straggling ran 10 percent higher than the battle casualties, and the average straggling exceeded 50 percent. Since these may well have been the worst cases in the army, however, it is not reasonable to apply such a high rate to the whole.

TABLE 25
Comparison of Strengths and Losses of Select Confederate Brigades

Brigade	*Size on 9/17*	*Size on 9/18*	*Battle losses*	*Stragglers*
Hays	550	90	336 (61.1)	124 (57.9)
Garnett	234	90	78 (33.3)	66 (42.3)
Evans	255	120	65 (25.5)	70 (36.8)
Trimble	700	200	237 (33.9)	263 (56.8)
Lawton	1,150	250	567 (49.3)	333 (57.1)
TOTALS	2889	750	1,283 (44.4)	856 (53.3)

D. Flags of Truce and September 18

Apparently, during the Civil War the attitude prevailed that requesting a truce was an admission of defeat. After the war, Lee agreed with the statement that "in all of his contests with General McClellan, the flag of truce had to come from the other side;" and at Sharpsburg there had been merely a "tacit understanding."[15]

Immediately after the battle, Jed. Hotchkiss wrote: "We . . . refused to let the enemy come to bury their dead, etc., though they asked the privilege three times, which showed plainly who had the advantage."[16]

Mention of localized Federal flags of truce, which seem to have been more numerous, may be found in scattered Confederate sources.[17] There are fewer indications that the Confederates sent out flags.[18] Longstreet admitted, however, that a "quasi truce" prevailed at times during the day.[19]

The most famous and brutal instance of an impasse over calling a truce would occur at Cold Harbor in early June 1864 when Grant's intransigence would lead to appalling suffering for Federal casualties trapped between the lines.

E. The Proposed Turning Movement on September 18

The story of S.D. Lee's mission—indeed the entire existence of the proposed turning movement on September 18—seems to be based on a single source, the memoirs of Col. Stephen Dill Lee himself.[20] Prior to the appearance of his newspaper article, Lee wrote an account of this incident in letters to several authors.[21] Also, one brief secondary version gives Jackson credit for originating the idea.[22]

It would be desirable to have a second, independent source to verify such an important event. This is especially true because S. D. Lee's account at places seems somewhat self-serving. Yet, there is nothing impossible, or even improbable, about the story; and nothing is known that contradicts its major points. On the contrary, it fits well with the implacable determination that Robert E. Lee evinced every day after September 14 to keep his campaign alive and that he would even again demonstrate later on the 18th. It must be remembered, however, as *Taken at the Flood* cautions, that the colonel never claimed to do more than approximate the words of the conversations and capture their substance.

S. D. Lee believed that Stuart referred to this proposed attempt on the 18th by writing in his report: "On the next day, it was determined, the enemy not again attacking, to turn the enemy's right."[23] It is obvious from the remainder of the paragraph, however, that Stuart is describing the actual attempt made on the 17th and has confused the days. The most that can be said is that Stuart's confusion may support the view that the turning movement was considered on both days.

It should also be noted that there is a slightly different reading possible of the evidence S. D. Lee presents. It is possible that General Lee ordered the turning movement and sent Colonel Lee to Jackson only to receive instructions on organizing the artillery. In this version, Jackson on his own authority used the gunner to try to dissuade the army commander from the plan.

It cannot be positively known that the subject of the Lee-Jackson meeting on September 18 was the proposed turning movement.[24] It is possible there was another Lee-Jackson meeting during the morning, and it may have taken place at Lee's headquarters. It does seem likely, however, that the disagreement between the two generals, which produced the S. D. Lee mission, derived from a meeting and not correspondence.

F. Lee's Intended Reentry into Maryland via Williamsport

Previously, it has been assumed that Lee intended nothing more than a feint at Williamsport in order to cover his crossing into Virginia. This is supported by Stuart's reference to his expedition as a "diversion."[25] Stuart did not submit his report until February 1864, however, and by that time he may have remembered only the result of the move and not its intention. It is also possible—although less likely—that Lee may have never told his cavalry chief about the larger aim of recrossing the entire army.

That reentry into Maryland at Williamsport was part of Lee's plan in withdrawing from Sharpsburg is attested by three statements Lee made in writing at the time:

1. "The morning of the 19th found us satisfactorily over on the south bank of the Potomac, near Shepherdstown, when the army was immediately put in motion for Williamsport."[26] This statement was made early on the 20th, before Lee knew the full damage at Shepherdstown and while he still intended to recross at Williamsport.

2. "As stated to you yesterday, the march of the army toward Williamsport was arrested."[27] Lee's comment came on the day after the Battle of Shepherdstown.

3. "When I withdrew from Sharpsburg into Virginia, it was my intention to recross the Potomac at Williamsport."[28] After this forthright statement of the 25th, Lee seems never to have referred to his Williamsport plan again.

G. The Wounded That Lee Left Behind at Sharpsburg

It is sometimes asserted that the Confederates took with them all of the wounded except those whose injuries would not allow them to be moved.[29] Heros von Borcke, who had no particular means to know the overall situation, claimed that only 300 of the worst cases were left behind.[30] It seems almost certain, however, that several thousand of the 6,000 prisoners captured by the Federals in the Maryland campaign must have come from the abandoned wounded at Sharpsburg.[31]

The statement by Sandy Pendleton of Jackson's staff in a letter home on September 21 ("a good number of our wounded were unable to be moved and had to be left at the various hospitals") supports the larger figure and is ambiguous as to whether severity of injury or lack of transportation or both caused abandonment.[32]

The impression at the biggest Confederate hospital, located on the Capt. David Smith farm, was that "there was no possible means of taking the wounded along." One Mississippian, who suffered merely a broken leg, escaped only by ordering his servant to get him back to Virginia. The servant stole a horse.[33] Several other anecdotes, although less direct, support the notion of a large number of abandoned Confederates.[34]

H. The Timing of the Confederate Withdrawal from Sharpsburg

The narrative of the withdrawal of the main body of the Army of Northern Virginia from Sharpsburg on the evening of September 18, as presented in *Taken at the Flood*, is a synthesis of evidence that is sometimes ambiguous and occasionally contradictory. As might be expected, there is only general agreement in the accounts on the question of timing of the withdrawal.[35]

Several assumptions were used to provide a framework for the story: (1) that it was not until several hours after dark that the roads were clear enough for the pullback to begin; (2) that, unlike the retreat from South Mountain, this movement was well planned and executed; and (3) that, because of the expeditious crossing of the river, the bottleneck at the ford lessened with the press of the disciplined ranks of the army.

The information that Evans's brigade was the first to withdraw, followed by D. R. Jones, is from a diary entry.[36] The retirement upon a prearranged silent signal is from a soldier in Pender's brigade, and it is only projected that it applied to the entire army.[37] The building of campfires after dark for deception is attested by a member of Stuart's staff, although considering the continuing light rain some question might be raised about the effectiveness of the ruse.[38]

I. Walker and Lee in the Middle of the Potomac on the Morning of September 19

Once again John Walker's memoirs manage to put him in the right place at the right time to contribute to Lee lore and to reflect importance on himself. He states that he remained behind to supervise withdrawal of his wounded and was "among the last to cross." Thus far there is nothing implausible in the story. But next he claims that he passed Lee (on horseback in midstream), who asked about what yet remained in Maryland.

Walker allegedly replied that there were his own wagons of wounded and a single battery, and all were near at hand. Finally, Walker ended: "'Thank God!' I heard him say as I rode on."[39]

If the incident occurred at all, either Walker was misinformed about what remained behind him and misled Lee, or he crossed after Fitz Lee and Munford and was under enemy fire. Moreover, it seems highly unlikely that Lee, who had both hands bandaged and very limited ability to control his mount, would have sat on horseback in the middle of a boulder-strewn ford.

J. The Confederate Forces Assembled at Williamsport

The conclusion in *Taken at the Flood*, chapter 10, that Stuart's force included 1,500 cavalry, 500 infantry, and up to fourteen guns is a synthesis of scattered information.[40] Heros Von Borcke is the only source for including Pelham's Horse Artillery, and it has been assumed that Pelham crossed with Stuart at Boteler's Ford rather than with Hampton at the fish trap dam.[41]

The 2d Virginia (Stonewall brigade), under Capt. W. W. Randolph, and the 10th Virginia (Taliaferro's brigade) had been detached by Jackson on the 13th as a provost guard for Martinsburg.[42] The 11th Georgia (G. T. Anderson), it will be recalled, had been detailed on the same day as a guard for the trains leaving Hagerstown for Williamsport. The right wing had proceeded to Shepherdstown and then to Sharpsburg on the afternoon of the battle. The left wing, under Capt. John W. Stokes, had been stationed at Martinsburg with the wagons of D. H. Hill, was the battalion that now joined Stuart.[43]

It is assumed that Watson and Hupp had two guns each. Pelham may have had as many as ten guns, if he had all of his own and Hart's battery with him. It is clear that Chew's battery of Munford's brigade did not accompany the expedition.[44]

K. Lee and the Battle of Shepherdstown, September 20, 1862

A postwar controversy grew up between the partisans of Jackson and Lee over credit for the victory at Shepherdstown Ford. Harvey Hill and Robert L. Dabney maintained that Jackson acted entirely on his own initiative and that Lee was confused throughout the morning and contributed little, if any, coordination. Lee saw Dabney's version before it appeared in Mrs. Jackson's biography and scotched it with his own account. Hal Bridges has given a masterful analysis of the major evidence in this dispute.[45]

The extent to which the conclusions in chapter 10 of *Taken at the Flood* disagree with Bridges derive mostly from the insight gained into Lee's intention to march to Williamsport and continue his campaign. Also, it is clear that A. P. Hill did not receive orders to march until 6:30, several hours after Lee had sent word to Jackson to return to the ford. The account that would seem best to harmonize with the known evidence would allow that Jackson acted instantly to reconnoiter personally; that Lee did order the general instructions to both Jackson and Longstreet; that Lee may well have evidenced confusion for a period; and that credit for the tactical execution of the battle belongs solely to Jackson.

Hal Bridges's speculation that Lee "may have succumbed to the temptation to show himself in a better light than his knowledge of the facts warranted" rests largely on the assumption that Jackson acted entirely without orders.[46] Jackson probably did undertake his personal reconnaissance on his own initiative; and, if he had ordered his men to break camp and follow him in the predawn darkness, there would be serious grounds for believing he might have acted before hearing from Lee—although even then he could still have consulted first with Lee who was camped nearby. The fact that A. P. Hill and D. H. Hill (and presumably Early and Grigsby as well) did not receive Jackson's orders to march until 6:30, a half-hour after dawn, proves Jackson did not move his troops precipitously. Indeed, the delay is best explained by the assumption Jackson awaited Lee's authorization.

There is only one statement in Lee's postwar letter to Mrs. Jackson that is clearly wrong: "After crossing the Potomac, Gen. Jackson was charged with the command of the rear, and he designated the brigades of infantry to support Pendleton's batteries."[47]

Jackson may have been charged with the rear guard through ten in the morning and until the retirement of Early, but not after that time. Moreover, it was Longstreet who selected the brigades of Lawton and Armistead. This is no doubt simply a memory lapse on Lee's part and is of little consequence.

One question only remains. Since Jackson's corps was farthest from the river, why did Lee select it to return to the ford? It is possible, of course, that even on September 20 Lee mistakenly thought Jackson was at the rear of the army. This is not a likely explanation, however, since Lee knew Jackson was camped nearby. Probably some or all of the following were considerations: (1) Pendleton's report suggested that Longstreet's corps was in some disarray; (2) Pendleton reported that Jackson already knew of the crisis, and perhaps he added that Stonewall seemed ready for action; (3) Lee may not have known the certain whereabouts of Longstreet; and finally, (4) Lee knew that A. P. Hill had the freshest troops in the army. This would be consistent with his designation of A. P. Hill as the last division to leave Sharpsburg.

L. Confederate Movements after Shepherdstown on September 20

The story in chapter 10 of *Taken at the Flood* of the Confederates remaining during the day at Shepherdstown (Boteler's) Ford during September 20, withdrawing at night, and marching to Martinsburg is a synthesis of scattered sources.[48] Jed. Hotchkiss is the source on Tabler's Mill.[49]

In a letter written on the same day, Hotchkiss speculated, "I think we will go there [Maryland] tomorrow."[50] Further references to the army moving slightly beyond Martinsburg in the direction of Williamsport may be found in two diary entries.[51]

Chew's Battery of Munford's brigade, on the contrary, left midmorning for Bunker Hill on the way to Winchester. It found "a great many troops camped around Bunker Hill," presumably a straggler's camp or, less likely, a portion of Longstreet's command that did not get the word to return to the ford.[52]

It is also clear that Lee—as he had done at Sharpsburg—abandoned the wounded at Shepherdstown.[53]

M. Lee's Depot at Winchester

There is much yet to be learned about Winchester as the depot and stragglers camp for the Army of Northern Virginia during the Maryland campaign. Any study should start with the letter Joaab Goodson of the 44th Alabama wrote to his niece on September 14 from Winchester, in which he observes that "three or four thousand men already here, and numbers coming in daily."[54] Other suggestive information is provided by Berry Benson (1st S.C.), Henry Berkeley (Hanover [Va.] Artillery), and Drury Gibson (15th La.).[55]

Many of the soldiers at Winchester were not stragglers in the true sense. They were convalescents returning to their units from Richmond who had followed Lee's orders not to enter Maryland. It is not clear why Lee did not bring this force to his support at an earlier date.

Mary Mitchell graphically recorded her childhood memories of the Confederate stragglers who engulfed Shepherdstown from September 13 on. But these men seemed to have been traveling on the fringes of the army on the march, and likely they were constantly in and out of the ranks.[56]

N. Lee's Information on September 21–25

Lee had a variety of sources of information about affairs beyond his army after his return to Virginia. It is almost certain that he scoured every Northern newspaper he could get his hands on to discover the reaction of Northerners to his retreat and for any hint of what McClellan intended to do. On September 24 he would mention that he had seen no word of Heintzleman's Corps in the reports of Maryland operations.[57]

Also, on the 21st Lee had two visitors directly from Richmond, A. K. Shriver, medical purveyor, and Brig. Gen. George H. Steuart, who reported for duty, and both likely brought him information.[58] By the 25th his son, Custis, arrived bearing special messages from the president.[59] Finally, Davis and Lee would exchange letters between September 28 and October 2 that included casual references to Confederate forces in Kentucky, implying that each knew what the other was writing about. In the latter, Lee commented, "I am delighted to learn that the prospect of affairs in Kentucky and Louisiana is so bright."[60]

O. Douglas Freeman's Criticism of Lee in the Maryland Campaign

Historian Freeman leveled four criticisms against Lee: (1) he should have reduced Harpers Ferry before crossing Potomac; (2) he underestimated the time required to capture Harpers Ferry by allowing only two days; (3) he should have employed cavalry to investigate the rumored enemy threat from the direction of Hagerstown; and (4) he should have rested his men before starting the campaign.[61]

Information developed in *Taken at the Flood* would answer these criticisms as follows: (1) Lee at first expected the garrisons at Martinsburg and Harpers Ferry to evacuate on their own accord upon his advance northward; (2) he did not misjudge the length of time required for a siege of Harpers Ferry because he did not envision the necessity of a siege, expecting the garrisons would flee at the approach of Confederate forces; (3) Lee went to Hagerstown primarily to obtain supplies and not to counter a Federal threat; (4) Lee did allow his men one day's rest at Chantilly, an easy march to Leesburg, one to two days' rest (depending on the unit) at Leesburg, and three to four days' rest at Frederick. It is difficult to imagine that his army would have been much better off had he concentrated the five to seven days at Chantilly, where he could not provision the army, or that he could have permitted a rest longer than a week anywhere in Virginia and still have exerted pressure to force the Federals into a new campaign while still demoralized and disorganized.

P. Confederate Losses in the Maryland Campaign

Table 26
Summary of Engagements and Casualties

Date	*Action*	*Killed*	*Wounded*	*Missing/ Captured*	*Total*
Sept. 5	Poolesville	3	4	–	7
Sept. 7	Poolesville	–	–	2	2
Sept. 8	Monocacy Church	1	10	4	15
Sept. 9	Barnesville	–	–	27	27
Sept. 9	Monocacy Viaduct	1	–	2	3
Sept. 11–15	Maryland Heights/ Harpers Ferry	41	247	–	288
Sept. 12	Monocacy Bridge	2	–	–	2
Sept. 13	Frederick	2	3	–	5
Sept. 13	Fairview	–	8	3	11
Sept. 13	near Burkittsville	4	9	–	13
Sept. 14	Crampton's Gap	70	289	603	962
Sept. 14	Turner's Gap	248	1,013	662	1,923
Sept. 15	Boonsboro	28	20	15	63
Sept. 16–18	Antietam	1,546	7,752	1,018	10,316
Sept. 19–20	Boteler's Ford	33	252	-	285
TOTAL		1,979	9,607	2,326	13,922

Source: From Carman, "Maryland Campaign," chap. 26. A similar exhibit of Federal losses will be included in a future study.

Comments: The only change made in the table as given by Carman is that the figures for the Harpers Ferry operations (September 11–15) have been brought up from the end and inserted where they belong chronologically. Carman wanted to demonstrate that—except for Harpers Ferry—the Confederates suffered a much higher percentage of losses in the campaign.

Carman believed that the total (2,326) in the category of captured/missing was too low. He estimated that aggregate Confederate casualties reached at least 16,600.

The table certainly does not reflect the massive losses due to straggling.

Q. Strategy Conferences Attended by Lee

Table 27
List of Meetings and Their Topics

Date	*Attendees*	*Location*	*Topic*
7/14/61	Davis, Cooper, Lee, Chesnut	Richmond	Beauregard's proposed offensive
4/14/62	Davis, Randolph, Lee, Johnston,Smith, Longstreet	Richmond	plans for the Peninsula
5/13/62	Davis, Lee, Johnston	Johnston's headquarters	plans for an offensive
6/3/62	Lee, division commanders, Davis	Chimneys	plans for an offensive
6/7/62	Davis, Lee	Lee's headquarters	plans for an offensive
6/16/62	Lee, Longstreet	Lee's headquarters	Longstreet urges offensive
6/23/62	Lee, Longstreet, Jackson, D.H. Hill, A.P. Hill	Dabbs house	plans for Seven Days
7/4/62	Lee, Jackson	near Harrison's Landing	decision whether to attack
8/11/62	Lee, Longstreet	Lee's headquarters	instructions for Gordonsville
8/15/62	Lee, Longstreet, Jackson	Gordonsville	operations against Pope
8/19/62	Lee, Longstreet	Clark's Mountain	revised plans for Pope
8/24/62	Lee, Longstreet, Jackson, Stuart	Jeffersonton	Jackson's turning movement
8/29/62	Lee, Longstreet, Jackson	Lee's headquarters	attack by Longstreet
8/30/62	Lee, Longstreet, Jackson	Lee's headquarters	plans for pursuit of Pope
8/31/62	Lee, Longstreet, Jackson	Bull Run Bridge	plans for pursuit of Pope
9/2/62	Lee, Longstreet, Jackson	near Chantilly	plans for new operations
9/4/62	Lee, Jackson, Johnson	Leesburg	possibilities of entering Maryland

Date	*Attendees*	*Location*	*Topic*
9/5/62	Lee, Longstreet, Jackson, Stuart	Leesburg	planning for operations in Maryland
9/6/62	Lee, Longstreet	enroute in Maryland	situation at Harpers Ferry
9/9/62	Lee, Jackson, Longstreet	Frederick	details of S.O. 191
9/13/62	Lee, Longstreet	Hagerstown	return to South Mountain
9/14/62	Lee, Longstreet, D.H. Hill, Hood	Boonsboro	retreat
9/16/62	Lee, Longstreet, Jackson	Sharpsburg	resuming offensive operations
9/17/62	Lee, Jackson, Stuart(?)	Sharpsburg	proposed turning movement on left
9/17/62	Lee, D.H. Hill, Hood, D.R. Jones, Longstreet, Jackson, Early, Walton, S.D. Lee, and staff officers	Sharpsburg	battle reports and future plans
9/18/62	Lee, Jackson, S.D. Lee	Sharpsburg	proposed turning movement
9/20/62	Lee, Longstreet, Jackson	Shepherdstown	whether to continue operations

Comments: The above is a revised and extended version of Table 4 from *Confederate Tide Rising*, (app. 4, sect. A, pp. 191–92). It was there noted that Lee's reputation for aloofness—probably justified in regard to his avoidance of partisanship and intrigue—did not restrict his willingness to debate strategic questions freely and frequently. Additional information had been included for the fifteen meetings listed in the earlier table, and twelve new meetings have been added from the Maryland campaign. The table thus now covers the beginning of the war through September 20, 1862.

It should be noted that not all of the meetings Lee is known to have attended with superiors or subordinates have been included. Those in which Lee either simply gave or received reports or gave or received instructions have been omitted

CHAPTER ELEVEN

List of Research Notes in Taken at the Flood

Introduction

In addition to the research appendixes in chapters 5 through 10 of the present work, many of the endnotes of *Taken at the Flood* discuss questions of historiography and research, explain speculative conclusions, and suggest areas for further study. Just as did the appendixes, the notes grew from research studies; but, unlike the appendixes, such notes proved amenable to condensation and abridgment.

The list below identifies, describes, and locates the research notes in *Taken at the Flood.* Thus, anyone wishing to pursue a particular issue can do so in both works. For example, someone interested in the reliability of the testimony of John G. Walker will find six related appendixes in *Sounding the Shallows:*

Excerpt from the Report of John G. Walker (chap. 6, app. H)
Activities of John G. Walker on September 13 (chap. 7, app. F)
John G. Walker's Harpers Ferry Claim (chap. 8, app. G)
Walker's March from Harpers Ferry and Arrival in Sharpsburg (chap. 9, app. E)
Walker's Claim to Espy Lee on September 17 (chap. 9, app. N)
Walker and Lee in the Middle of the Potomac on the Morning of September 19 (chap. 10, app. I)

There are also, however, eleven research notes in *Taken at the Flood* that ought to be consulted:

Itinerary of Walker's Division, September 6–7 (chap. 2 n.75 and chap. 3 n.7)
The Itinerary of Walker's Division, September 11 (chap. 4 n.49)
The Itinerary of Walker's Division, September 12 (chap. 4 n.88)

Walker's Guns on Loudoun Heights (chap. 6 n.44)
Supposed Jackson Messages to McLaws and Walker Late on September 14 (chap. 6 n.60)
Walker Reports to Lee, September 16 (chap. 8 n.31)
The Activities of Walker's Division, September 16 (chap. 8 n.83)
Fourth Phase (Walker/Greene) of the Battle of Antietam (chap. 9 nn.36, 38–39)

Other examples of topics that could be pursued through both the appendixes and notes are the lost orders, strengths and casualties, organization, structure, and condition of the Army of Northern Virginia, Lee's reasons for entering Maryland, logistics, and military intelligence.

For the purposes of the following list, descriptive titles have been created for select notes from *Taken at the Flood:*

Introduction
Founding of the Battlefield Parks (nn.2–3)
Visitor Attendance at Antietam (n.4)
Reprise
Time of the Jackson-Stuart Meeting on September 1 (n.1)
The Lee-Munford Meeting on September 1 (n.10)
Chapter 1
The Lee-Longstreet-Jackson Meeting on September 2 (nn.4, 105)
Federal Rear Guard Actions on September 2 (n.9)
Lee on a Strategic Movement Southward (n.20)
The Lushness of Loudoun County (n.25)
The Confederate Multiprong Invasion of August–September (nn.30–41)
The March of the Reenforcing Column from Richmond (nn.50–66)
Forces at Richmond and in North Carolina on September 2 (n.67)
Percentage of All Confederate Forces in Army of Northern Virginia on September 2 (nn.68–69)
Regimental Averages in the Army of Northern Virginia on September 2 (n.72)
Number of Regiments and Their Combat Experience in the Army of Northern Virginia on September 2 (n.75)
Combat Experience of Brigades and Divisions in the Army of Northern Virginia on September 2 (nn.77, 79)

Attrition in the Officer Corps of the Army of Northern Virginia on September 2 (nn.82–83)
Clothing of the Army of Northern Virginia on September 2 (n.89)
Morale of the Army of Northern Virginia on September 2 (nn.92–93)
Lee on Giving Battle in Maryland (n.97)
Maryland in the Eyes of the Confederates (nn.100, 101; also chap. 2 n.31)
Itinerary of the Army of Northern Virginia on September 3 (nn. 108, 117, 124)
Skirmish at Leesburg, September 2 (n.112)
Lee's Headquarters, September 2–3 (n.118)
A. L. Long Misdates the Dranesville Dispatch (n.125)
Lee on Importance of Acquiring Supplies in Maryland (n.130)
Lee, Northern Newspapers, and News of Western Affairs (nn.131, 132)
Lee's Knowledge of Who Commanded the Federals, September 2–3 (n.134)
The Rumor of an Order Keeping Shoeless Men in Virginia (n.135)

Chapter 2

Itinerary of the Confederate Infantry on September 4 (n.1)
Activities of the Confederate Cavalry on September 4 (nn.2, 3)
The Arrest of A. P. Hill (n.4)
The Arrest of John B. Hood (n.5; also chap. 6 n.12)
Leesburg Reception of the Army of Northern Virginia (n.9)
Army of Northern Virginia Resupplies in Leesburg (nn.21, 22)
Cameo Biography of Bradley T. Johnson (n.26)
Maryland's Fall 1861 Elections (n.30)
Lee's Meetings on the Morning of September 5 (n.36)
Itinerary of Jackson's Command, September 5 (nn.37–41, 63)
Itinerary of D. H. Hill's Division, September 5 (n.42)
Slavery in Maryland (n.48)
Discipline of the Army of Northern Virginia and Its Reception by Marylanders (n.50; also chap. 3 n.9; chap. 4 n.63)
Lee's Communications with Davis, September 3–28 (n.56)
Itinerary of Longstreet, McLaws, R. H. Anderson, September 6 (nn.69–74)
Lee's Crossing the Potomac, September 6 (n.78)
Lee-Longstreet Conversation on Harpers Ferry, September 6 (n.81)
Lee's Activities on September 6 (nn.82–83)

Lee's News of Western Affairs, September 6 (n.84)
Confederate Cavalry Activities, September 6 (nn.86, 87)

Chapter 3

Itinerary of Walker's Division, September 6–7 (n.7; also chap.2 n.75)
Itinerary of the Reserve Artillery, September 6–7 (n.8; also chap. 2 n.75)
Lee on Straggling (nn. 18–20)
Confederate Proclamations in Frederick (nn. 34, 35)
Lee's Knowledge of Who Commanded the Army of the Potomac (n.62; also chap. 4 n.67)
Lige White's Cavalry Battalion Sent Back to Virginia (n.69)
Longstreet and the September 9 War Council (nn.80, 81)
Surviving Copies of Special Orders 191 (nn.85–87)
The Spy Theory of the Lost Orders (n.90)
D. H. Hill's Frederick Headquarters (n.91)

Chapter 4

Cameo Biography of Lewis Henry Steiner (n.2)
Confederate Blacks in the Maryland Campaign (n.3)
Estimates of Confederate Strength by Observers (n.5)
The Historical Barbara Frietchie (n.6)
The Itinerary of Jackson's Command, September 10 (nn.16, 17)
The Itinerary of Longstreet's Command, September 10 (nn.20–23)
The Itinerary of McLaws's Command, September 10 (nn.24–26)
The Itinerary of the Trains and Artillery, September 10 (n.27)
The Itinerary of D. H. Hill's Division, September 10 (n.28)
The Itinerary of Walker's Division, September 10 (n.29)
The Activities of Confederate Cavalry, September 10 (n.31)
The Itinerary of Jackson's Command, September 11 (n.36)
Lee's Decision to Move to Hagerstown, September 11 (nn.40, 41)
The Itinerary of Longstreet's Command, September 11 (n.43)
The Itinerary of D. H. Hill's Division, September 11 (nn.44–46)
The Itinerary of McLaws's Command, September 11 (nn.47, 48)
The Itinerary of Walker's Division, September 11 (n.49)
The Activities of the Confederate Cavalry, September 11 (nn.50–55)
The Itinerary of Jackson's Command, September 12 (nn.76–81)
The Activities of McLaws's Command, September 12 (nn.82–87
The Itinerary of Walker's Division, September 12 (n.88)
The Activities of the Confederate Cavalry, September 12 (nn.89–91)
Skirmish at Frederick, September 12 (nn.92–93)
D. H. Hill's Division at Boonsboro, September 12 (nn.94–96)

Chapter 5

Confederate Congressional Debate on the Maryland Campaign, September 12–13 (n.5)

Jefferson Davis's Proposed Proclamation (nn. 7–10)

The Itinerary of Jackson's Command, September 13 (nn.32, 72)

Skirmishes at Middletown and Hagan's Gap, September 13 (n.42)

D. H. Hill's Defensive Measures at Turner's Gap on the Evening of September 13 (nn.49–57)

Stuart's Knowledge of the Loss of Special Orders 191 (nn.66–70)

Lee's Dispatch to Jackson on the Night of September 13 (n.75)

Chapter 6

Longstreet's March from Hagerstown to Boonsboro, September 14 (nn.1–9)

D. H. Hill on the Early Morning of September 14 (n.16)

Garland's Brigade at South Mountain, September 14 (n.17)

George B. Anderson's Brigade at South Mountain, September 14 (n.24)

The Brigades of D. R. Jones, Pickett, and Jenkins at South Mountain, September 14 (n.25)

Ripley's Aberration at South Mountain, September 14 (n.30)

Rodes's Brigade at South Mountain, September 14 (n.17)

Evans's Brigade at South Mountain, September 14 (n.43)

Hood's Division at South Mountain, September 14 (n.35)

D. R. Jones's Division at South Mountain, September 14 (n.36)

Colquitt's Brigade at South Mountain, September 14 (n.36)

The Activities of Jackson's Command, September 14 (nn.39–43, 51–54)

Walker's Guns on Loudoun Heights (n.44)

Lee-Jackson Communications on September 14 (nn.55, 56)

Supposed Jackson Message to McLaws and Walker Late on September 14 (n.60)

Jeb Stuart's Activities on September 14 (nn.61–68, 72–74)

The Battle of Crampton's Gap, September 14 (nn.75–79, 84)

Lee's Criticism of D. H. Hill's Activities on September 14 (n.85)

Confederate Withdrawal from South Mountain, September 14 (n.102)

Confederate Rest Pause at Boonsboro, September 14–15 (n.104)

The Activities of Fitzhugh Lee's Brigade on September 14 (n.117)

The Federal Cavalry Escape from Harpers Ferry and the Capture of Confederate Ordnance Wagons (n.121)

Walter Taylor's Narrow Escape, September 14–15 (n.122)
Medical Director Guild's Report of Confederate Casualties in the Maryland Campaign (n.124)

Chapter 7

Lee at Keedysville, September 15 (nn.3, 4)
Lee in the High Meadow, September 15 (n.5)
D. H. Hill Takes Position at Sharpsburg, September 15 (n.6)
The Naming of Cemetery Hill (n.7)
Longstreet's Arrival at Sharpsburg, September 15 (n.8)
The Posting of Confederate Artillery at Sharpsburg, September 15 (nn.9, 10, 53)
The Arrival of D. R. Jones's Division at Sharpsburg, September 15 (nn.11–13)
The Arrival of the Confederate Rear Guard at Sharpsburg, September 15 (n.14)
Lee Learns of the Fall of Harpers Ferry, September 15 (nn.20, 21)
Lee's Dispatches to Jackson on September 15 (nn.22, 40)
Cavalry Battle at Boonsboro, September 15 (nn.26, 27)
Effect of Confederate Artillery at Harpers Ferry (nn.32, 33)
Jackson's Tactical Operations on the Morning of September 15 (n.34)
Jeb Stuart's Activities on September 15 (nn.38, 50)
The McLaws-Jackson Meeting on September 15 (nn.41–43)
The Itinerary of McLaws's Command on September 15 (n.45)
The Spoils Captured by Jackson at Harpers Ferry (n.46)
The Destruction of the Harpers Ferry Bridges (n.48)
Jackson's Endorsement on Lee's Dispatch, September 15 (n.51)
The Night March of Jackson's Command from Harpers Ferry (nn.65, 66)

Chapter 8

Confederate and Union Strengths on September 16 (n.1)
Fog on the Antietam on the Morning of September 16 (nn.5, 17)
Federal Capture of the Middle Bridge, September 16 (nn.6, 19, 20)
Stuart's Reconnaissance, September 16 (n.7)
Jackson Reports to Lee, September 16 (n.15)
Federal Bombardment, September 16 (nn.18, 21–30)
On Lee's Returning to Traveller, September 16 (n.31)
Walker Reports to Lee, September 16 (n.31)
Lee's Dispatch to McLaws on the Morning of September 16 (n.33)
Lee Sends Trains Back to Virginia, September 16 (n.34)

Scarcity of Food for Confederates, September 16 (n.37)
Skirmish on Smoketown Road, September 16 (n.63)
Jackson's Move to the West Woods, September 16 (nn.64, 65)
The Activities of Lawton's Division on September 16 (n.67)
The Activities of Hood's Division on September 16 (n.75, 76)
The Itinerary of McLaws's Command, September 16 (nn.79–82, 86)
The Activities of Walker's Division on September 16 (n.83)

Chapter 9

McLaws's Arrival at Sharpsburg, September 17 (n.1)
Note on the Tactical Account of the Battle of Antietam (n.8)
First Phase (Jackson-Hooker) of the Battle of Antietam (n.11)
Second Phase (Hood-Mansfield) of the Battle of Antietam (n.12)
D. H. Hill's Support of Jackson's Morning Fight (n.20)
Meeting between R. E. Lee and S. D. Lee, September 17 (n.27)
Stuart and the Confederate Artillery on Nicodemus Heights (n.33)
Third Phase (McLaws-Sedgwick) of the Battle of Antietam (nn.35, 36)
Fourth Phase (Walker-Greene) of the Battle of Antietam (nn.36, 38, 39)
Fifth Phase (French/Richardson–D. H. Hill) of the Battle of Antietam (nn.42, 43)
Sixth Phase (Burnside–A. P. Hill) of the Battle of Antietam (n.46)
Questions about Burnside at the Lower Bridge (n.48)
Longstreet during the Battle of Antietam (n.59)
Lee's Message from an Engineer during the Battle of Antietam (nn.60, 61)
Lee's Journey to Confer with Jackson in the Early Afternoon (n.62)
The Confederate Stragglers' Brigade (n.67)
Lee's Proposed Turning Movement in the Midafternoon (nn.68, 71–79)
Thomas's Brigade and the Battle of Antietam, September 17–19 (n.91)
The Confederate Patchwork Line on the Evening of September 17 (n.95)
Robert Toombs and the Battle of Antietam (n.106)

Chapter 10

Confederate Supplies on September 18 (n.6)
Jackson's Moral Support of Lee in the Maryland Campaign (n.41)
Confederate Infantry Rear Guard Operations, September 18 (n.57)

Notes

1. Confederate Almanac for the Maryland Campaign of 1862

1. John Gruber, *J. Gruber's Hagers-town Almanack for the Year of Our Lord 1862* (Hagerstown: John Gruber, 1861).

2. U.S. Weather Bureau, Records of Surface Land Observations, 1819–1941, RG 27, National Archives, Washington, D.C. For a convenient guide, see Lewis J. Darter, Jr., *List of Climatological Records in the National Archive* (1942; reprint, Washington, D.C.: National Archives, 1981).

3. Jedadiah Hotchkiss, *Make Me a Map of the Valley: The Civil War Journal of Stonewall Jackson's Topographer*, ed. Archie McDonald (Dallas: Southern Methodist Univ. Press, 1973), 77.

4. John H. Worsham, *One of Jackson's Foot Cavalry, His Experience and What He Saw during the War, 1861–65*, ed. Bell Irvin Wiley (Jackson, Tenn.: McCowat-Mercer Press, 1964), 81.

5. John Hampden Chamberlayne, *Ham Chamberlayne, Virginian: Letters and Papers of an Artillery Officer in the War for Southern Independence, 1861–1865*, ed. C. G. Chamberlayne (Richmond: Dietz Print Co., 1932), 102.

6. James Fitz James Caldwell, *The History of a Brigade of South Carolinians, Known First as "Gregg's" and Subsequently as "McGowan's Brigade"* (Philadelphia: King & Baird, 1866), 68.

7. James Henry Lane, "Twenty-Eighth Infantry," *Histories of the Several Regiments and Battalions from North Carolina in the Great War 1861–65, Written by Members of the Respective Commands*, ed. Walter Clark, 5 vols. (Wendell, N.C.: Broadfoot's Bookmark, 1982), 2:473 (hereafter cited as *North Carolina Regiments*).

8. James A. Weston, "Thirty-Third Infantry," *North Carolina Regiments* 2:552.

9. William Dorsey Pender, *The General to His Lady: The Civil War Letters of William Dorsey Pender to Fanny Pender*, ed. William W. Hassler (Chapel Hill: Univ. of North Carolina Press, 1965), 170.

10. T. D. Lattimore, "Thirty-Fourth Infantry," *North Carolina Regiments* 2:585.

11. McIntire 's report in *Supplement to the Official Records of the Union and Confederate Armies*, ed. Janet B. Hewitt et al. [to be ca. 100 vols.] (Wilmington, N.C.: Broadfoot Publishing Co., 1984–), 3:778 (hereafter cited as *SOR*).

12. William Miller Owen, *In Camp and Battle with the Washington Artillery of New Orleans: A Narrative of Events during the Late Civil War, from Bull Run to Appomattox and Spanish Fort* (Boston: Ticknor and Co., 1885), 128.

13. Alexander Hunter, "A High Private's Account of the Battle of Sharpsburg," *Southern Historical Society Papers*, 52 vols. (Richmond: Southern Historical Society, 1876–1959), 10:505–6 (hereafter cited as *SHSP*).

14. Henry Walter Thomas, *History of the Doles-Cook Brigade, Army of Northern Virginia, C.S.A., Containing Muster Rolls of Each Company of the Fourth, Twelfth, Twenty-First and Forty-Fourth Georgia Regiments, with a Short Sketch of the Services of Each Member, and a Complete History of Each Regiment* (Atlanta: Franklin Print. and Pub. Co., 1903), 220.

15. William Willis Blackford, *War Years with Jeb Stuart* (New York: Charles Scribner's Sons, 1945), 135.

16. Calvin Leach, Diary, Sept. 1, 1862, Southern Historical Collection, University of North Carolina, Chapel Hill.

17. John S. Tucker, "The Diary of John S. Tucker: Confederate Soldier from Alabama," ed. Gary Wilson, *Alabama Historical Quarterly* 43 (1981): 19.

18. Mike M. Hubbert, "The Travels of the 13th Mississippi Regiment: Excerpts from the Diary of Mike M. Hubbert of Attala County," ed. John E. Fisher, *Journal of Mississippi History* 45 (1983): 306.

19. Isaac Hirsch, Diary, Sept. 1, 1862, Fredericksburg Area Museum, Fredericksburg, Va.

20. Owen, *In Camp and Battle*, 128.

21. Hotchkiss, *Make Me a Map*, 78.

22. Hubbert, "Diary," 306.

23. Hotchkiss, *Make Me a Map*, 78.

24. Tucker, "Diary," 19.

25. Hubbert, "Diary," 307.

26. Hotchkiss, *Make Me a Map*, 78.

27. Hubbert, "Diary," 307.

28. Hotchkiss, *Make Me a Map*, 79.

29. Ibid., 79.

30. Chamberlayne, *Letters*, 103.

31. James T. Shinn, Diary, Sept. 6, 1862, Osborne Papers, Southern Historical Collection, University of North Carolina, Chapel Hill.

32. Hubbert, "Diary," 307.

33. Hirsch, Diary, Sept. 6.

34. Hotchkiss, *Make Me a Map*, 79.

35. Hubbert, "Diary," 307.

36. Ibid.

37. Hotchkiss, *Make Me a Map*, 80.

38. Chamberlayne, *Letters*, 106.

39. Hubbert, "Diary," 307.

40. Owen, *In Camp and Battle*, 133.

41. Hotchkiss, *Make Me a Map*, 80.

42. Hubbert, "Diary," 307.

43. Hotchkiss, *Make Me a Map*, 80.

44. Shinn, Diary, Sept. 11.

45. Hubbert, "Diary," 307.

46. Hirsch, Diary, Sept. 11.

47. Heros von Borcke, *Memoirs of the Confederate War for Independence*, 2 vols. (New York: Peter Smith, 1938), 1:200.

48. Hotchkiss, *Make Me a Map*, 80.

49. Leach, Diary, Sept. 12.

50. Shinn, Diary, Sept. 12.

51. Tucker, "Diary," 19.

52. Hubbert, "Diary," 308.

53. Hotchkiss, *Make Me a Map*, 81.

54. Hubbert, "Diary," 308.

55. Leach, Diary, Sept. 13.

56. Gary W. Gallagher, ed., *Lee the Soldier* (Lincoln: Univ. of Nebraska Press, 1996), 8.

57. James Longstreet, *From Manassas to Appomattox: Memoirs of the Civil War in America*, ed. James I. Robertson, Jr. (Bloomington: Indiana Univ. Press, 1960), 220.

58. James Longstreet, "The Invasion of Maryland," in Robert Underwood Johnson and Clarence Clough Buel, eds., *Battles and Leaders of the Civil War . . . Being for the Most Part Contributions by Union and Confederate Officers Based upon "The Century War Series,"* 4 vols. (New York: Thomas Yoselof, 1956), 2:666 (hereafter cited as *Battles and Leaders*).

59. Hotchkiss, *Make Me a Map*, 81.

60. Hubbert, "Diary," 308.

61. Edward Alexander Moore, *The Story of a Cannoneer under Stonewall Jackson, in which Is Told the Part Taken by the Rockbridge Artillery in the Army of Northern Virginia* (New York: Neale Publishing Co., 1907), 139.

62. Hubbert, "Diary," 309.

63. Hotchkiss, *Make Me a Map*, 82.

64. Walker's report, in U.S. War Department, *The War of the Rebellion: A Compilation of the Official Records of the Union and Confederate Armies*, 128 vols. (Washington, D.C.: GPO, 1880–1901), ser. 1, vol. 19, 1:914 (hereafter cited as *OR*, with series 1 understood unless otherwise stated).

65. John George Walker, "Sharpsburg," *Battles and Leaders* 2:610.

66. Ezra A. Carman, "The Maryland Campaign of 1862," unpublished manuscript, chaps. 8 (pp. 14–15) and 13 (p. 9), Carman Papers, Library of Congress, Washington, D.C.

67. Edward Porter Alexander, *Military Memoirs of a Confederate: A Critical Narrative*, ed. T. Harry Williams (Bloomington: Indiana Univ. Press, 1962), 251.

68. Longstreet, *From Manassas to Appomattox*, 238.

69. Von Borcke, *Memoirs of the Confederate War* 1:229.

70. Hotchkiss, *Make Me a Map*, 82.

71. Hubbert, "Diary," 309.

72. William H. Hill, Diary, Sept. 16, quoted in Allan L. Tischler, *The History of the Harpers Ferry Cavalry Expedition, September 14 & 15, 1862* (Winchester, Va.: Five Cedars Press, 1993), 261.

73. Leach, Diary, Sept. 17.

74. John Brown Gordon, *Reminiscences of the Civil War* (New York: Charles Scribner's Sons, 1903), 84.

75. Hubbert, "Diary," 309.

76. Thomas R. Roulhac, "Forty-Ninth Regiment," *North Carolina Regiments* 3: 129.

77. Hotchkiss, *Make Me a Map*, 83. This suggests there may have been no rain at Harpers Ferry on either the 16th or 17th.

78. Owen, *In Camp and Battle*, 159–60.

79. Hotchkiss, *Make Me a Map*, 83.

80. Hubbert, "Diary," 309.

81. Walter Clark, "Sharpsburg," *North Carolina Regiments* 5:79.

82. Von Borcke, *Memoirs of the Confederate War* 1:240.

83. Blackford, *War Years with Jeb Stuart*, 153.

84. Hotchkiss, *Make Me a Map*, 84.

85. Hubbert, "Diary," 309.

86. Hotchkiss, *Make Me a Map*, 84.

87. Hubbert, "Diary," 310.

88. Ibid., 310.

89. Hotchkiss, *Make Me a Map*, 84.

90. Hubbert, "Diary," 310.

91. Hotchkiss, *Make Me a Map*, 84.

92. Hubbert, "Diary," 310.

93. Hotchkiss, *Make Me a Map*, 85.

94. Ibid.

95. Ibid.

96. Ibid.

97. Ibid.

98. Ibid.

99. Ibid., 86.

2. Organization of the Army of Northern Virginia in the Maryland Campaign, September 2–22, 1862

1. *OR*, ser. 4, vol. 2:198.

2. *OR*, vol. 19, 2:618–19, 621.

3. Ibid., 628–29.

4. Ibid., 633–34.

5. Ibid., 643–44.

6. Ibid., 683–84.

7. Ibid., 698–99.

8. For a contrary conclusion—that the view Lee harbored doubts about Jackson is "nonsense at the least"—see James I. Robertson, Jr., *Stonewall Jackson: The Man, the Soldier, the Legend* (New York: Macmillan Publishing, 1997), 631. For the traditional version see Frank Everson Vandiver, *Mighty Stonewall* (New York: McGraw Hill Book Co., 1957), 406. And for the view that Lee wrote solely to convince a skeptical Davis, see Byron Farwell, *Stonewall: A Biography of General Thomas J. Jackson* (New York: W. W. Norton, 1992), 456.

9. *OR*, vol. 19, 2:643.

10. Longstreet's report, ibid., 1:842; W. T. Hamilton, "Eleventh Mississippi Regiment," *Confederate Veteran* 14 (1906): 62–63; Joseph H. Crute, Jr., *Units of the Confederate States Army* (Midlothian, Va.: Derwent Books, 1987), 255.

11. D. R. Jones's report, *OR*, vol. 19, 1:885.

12. Toombs's report, ibid., 888.

13. Ibid., 893; Benning's report, ibid., vol. 51, 1:161; William C. Davis, ed., *The Confederate General*, 6 vols. (N.p.: National Historical Society, 1991), 6:51.

14. G. T. Anderson's report, ibid., vol. 19, 1:908–10.

15. Ibid., 910; Little's report, ibid., 911–12.

16. Ibid., 804; Carman, "Maryland Campaign," chaps. 23 (p. 33) and 24 (p. 9). *Confederate Veteran* 18 (1910): 138; 20 (1912): 241; 23 (1915): 71–72. Robert Kenneth Krick, *Lee's Colonels: A Biographical Register of the Field Officers of the Army of Northern Virginia*, 3d ed. (Dayton, Ohio: Morningside Bookshop, 1991), 207, 271; Mac Wyckoff, *A History of the 2nd South Carolina Infantry: 1861–1865* (Fredericksburg, Va.: Sergeant Kirkland Museum and Historical Society, 1994), 238.

17. *OR*, vol. 19, 1:804; Carman, "Maryland Campaign," chap. 11 (p. 38); *SOR* 19: 258–60; *Confederate Veteran* 4 (1896): 71; ibid. 20 (1912): 421; Krick, *Lee's Colonels*, 176; John J. Hennessy, *Return to Bull Run: The Campaign and Battle of Second Manassas* (New York: Simon & Schuster, 1993), 561; *Battles and Leaders* 3:146.

18. D. R. Jones's report, *OR*, vol. 19, 1:885.

19. *OR*, vol. 19, 2:595.

20. Ibid., 1:903–4.

21. Ibid., 805; additional information from ibid., 2:649.

22. Confirmed in S.O. No. 193, Headquarters Army of Northern Virginia, Sept. 14, ibid., 2:609.

23. G. T. Anderson's report, ibid., 1:909.

24. Hood's report, ibid., 924.

25. S.O. No. 236, Headquarters Army of Northern Virginia, Nov. 8, ibid., 2:705.

26. Jennings Cropper Wise, *The Long Arm of Lee: or, the History of the Artillery of the Army of Northern Virginia. With a Brief Account of the Confederate Bureau of Ordnance*, 2 vols., intro. by Gary W. Gallagher (Richmond: Owens Publishing Co., 1988), 1:259.

27. *OR*, vol. 19, 1:806.

28. Ibid., 2:697.

29. Ibid., 1:143.

30. Jackson's report, ibid., 952; Henry Kyd Douglas, *I Rode with Stonewall, Being Chiefly the Experiences of the Youngest Member of Jackson's Staff from the John Brown Raid to the Hanging of Mrs. Surratt* (Chapel Hill: Univ. of North Carolina Press, 1940), 152.

31. Franklin McIntosh Myers, *The Comanches: A History of White's Battalion, Virginia Cavalry, Laurel Brig., Hampton Div., A.N.V., C.S.A.*, intro. by Lee Wallace (Alexandria, Va.: Stonewall House, 1985), 107–9; John E. Divine, *35th Virginia Cavalry Battalion* (Lynchburg: H. E. Howard, Inc., 1985), 11.

32. Williams's report, *OR*, vol. 19, 1:1011, 1013; Dennis E. Frye, *2nd Virginia Infantry* (Lynchburg: H. E. Howard, Inc., 1984), 43–44.

33. Carman, "Maryland Campaign," chap. 11 (p. 52); Terrence V. Murphy, *10th Virginia Infantry* (Lynchburg: H. E. Howard, Inc., 1989), 53–54.

34. Krick, *Lee's Colonels*, 99.

35. *Confederate Veteran* 25 (1917): 86.

36. *OR*, vol. 19, 1:809; Carman, "Maryland Campaign," chap. 11 (p. 59); Wise, *Long Arm of Lee* 1:283.

37. Wise, *Long Arm of Lee* 1:258; *OR*, vol. 19, 1:964.

38. *OR*, vol. 19, 1:836, 964; ibid., 2:629, 632; Curt Johnson and Richard C. Anderson, Jr., *Artillery Hell: The Employment of Artillery at Antietam* (College Station: Texas A&M Univ. Press, 1995), 52, 60, 95, 102; U.S. Engineer Corps, *Atlas of the Battlefield of Antietam, Prepared under the Direction of the Antietam Battlefield Board* (1904; 2d rev. ed., Washington, D.C.: GPO, 1908), map no. 14.

39. *OR*, vol. 19, 1:836, 964; ibid., 2:629, 632; C. Johnson, *Artillery Hell*, 102; Robert H. Moore II, *The Danville, Eighth Star, and Dixie Artillery* (Lynchburg: H. E. Howard, Inc., 1989), 71.

40. *OR*, vol. 19, 1:808.

41. Ibid., 963.

42. Carman, "Maryland Campaign," chap. 11 (p. 52); Early's report, *OR*, vol. 19, 1:972.

43. William Thomas Poague, *Gunner with Stonewall, Reminiscences of William Thomas Poague . . . A Memoir Written for His Children*, ed. Monroe F. Cockrell (Jackson, Tenn.: McCowat-Mercer Press, 1957), 41–43; also, Moore, *The Story of a Cannoneer*, 129, 296.

44. Early's report, *OR*, vol. 19, 1:967, 969.

45. Carman, "Maryland Campaign," chap. 19 (pp. 37–39).

46. Rufus W. Wharton, "First Battalion (Sharpshooters)," *North Carolina Regiments* 4:225.

47. *OR*, vol. 19, 1:807n; Carman, "Maryland Campaign," chap. 11 (p. 46).

48. Robert H. Moore II, *The Charlottesville, Lee Lynchburg, and Johnson's Bedford Artillery* (Lynchburg: H. E. Howard, Inc., 1990), 14; *OR*, vol. 19, 1:807n; and Stuart's report, ibid., 821.

49. Crutchfield's report, *OR*, vol. 19, 1:963; and Early's report, ibid., 972.

50. Crutchfield's report, ibid., 963.

51. Ibid.; and Early's report, ibid., 972; also, Carman, "Maryland Campaign," chap. 11 (p. 46).

52. *OR*, vol. 19, 2:595; and ibid., 1:982.

53. Archer's report, *OR*, vol. 19, 1:1000–1001.

54. Ibid., 1000, 1003; *Confederate Veteran* 25 (1917): 171.

55. Louise Porter Daly, *Alexander Cheves Haskell: The Portrait of a Man* (Norwood, Mass.: Plimpton Press, 1934), 77–78.

56. In Pender's report, *OR*, vol. 19, 1:1004; also repeated in A. P. Hill's report, ibid., 980.

57. Ibid., 807, 982.

58. Pender's report, ibid., 1005; Pender, *The General to His Lady*, 168; and Francis Bernard Heitman, *Historical Register and Dictionary of the United States Army, from Its Organization, September 29, 1789, to March 2, 1903*, 2 vols. (Washington, D.C.: GPO, 1903), 1:243.

59. A. P. Hill's report, *OR*, vol. 19, 1:980.

60. Walker's report, ibid., 984.

61. Crutchfield's report, ibid., 963; and Walker's report, ibid., 984–85; Peter S. Carmichael, *The Purcell, Crenshaw, and Letcher Artillery* (Lynchburg: H. E. Howard, Inc., 1990), 97.

62. Walker's report, *OR*, vol. 19, 1:984.

63. Ibid.

64. R. H. Anderson to D. H. Hill, Nov. 14, 1867, D. H. Hill Personal Papers, North Carolina State Archives, Raleigh.

65. General Orders (G.O.) No. 103, Headquarters Army of Northern Virginia, Sept. 6, *OR*, vol. 19, 2:596; G.O. No. 102, Headquarters Army of Northern Virginia, Leesburg, Va., Sept. 4, ibid., 592.

66. Carman, "Maryland Campaign," chap. 18 (p. 20).

67. Ibid.

68. *OR*, vol. 19, 1:804; Carman, "Maryland Campaign," chap. 11 (p. 34); *OR*, vol. 18: 750–51; and Newton McAlpine, "Sketch of Company I, 61st Virginia Infantry, Mahone's Brigade, C.S.A.," *SHSP* 24 (1896): 98–108; Benjamin F. Trask, *61st Virginia Infantry* (Lynchburg: H. E. Howard, Inc., 1988), 6–8.

69. W. C. Davis, ed., *The Confederate General* 6:161.

70. Ibid., 139; 2:44–45.

71. *OR*, vol. 19, 1:804; Carman, "Maryland Campaign," chap. 11 (p. 36).

72. Krick, *Lee's Colonels*, 99.

73. *OR*, vol. 19, 1:804; Carman, "Maryland Campaign," chap. 11 (p. 35); W. C. Davis, ed., *Confederate General* 2:119; and *OR*, vol. 19, 1:855.

74. *OR*, vol. 19, 1:809; Carman, "Maryland Campaign," chap. 11 (p. 59); Wise, *Long Arm of Lee* 1:283.

75. Wise, *Long Arm of Lee* 1:257.

76. *OR*, vol. 19, 1:836; ibid., 2:650; C. Johnson, *Artillery Hell*, 103.

77. *OR*, vol. 19, 1:836; ibid., 2:650, 653; C. Johnson, *Artillery Hell*, 87–88; Moore, *The Danville, Eighth Star, and Dixie Artillery*, 75.

78. *OR*, vol. 19, 2:649, 653; and Wise, *Long Arm of Lee* 1:357, 422.

79. *OR*, vol. 19, 1:836.

80. Ibid., 804; and Carman, "Maryland Campaign," chap. 11 (p. 37).

81. J. W. Ratchford, Memoirs, pp. 45–46, D. H. Hill, Jr., Personal Papers, North Carolina State Archives, Raleigh.

82. D. H. Hill to Longstreet, Feb. 14, 1885, Longstreet Papers, Duke University, Durham, N.C.

83. *OR*, vol. 19, 1:809; Carman, "Maryland Campaign," chap. 11 (p. 56); and Lee A. Wallace, *A Guide to Virginia Military Organizations, 1861–1865*, rev. 2d ed. (Lynchburg: H. E. Howard, 1988), 3.

84. Nance's report, *OR*, vol. 19, 1:869.

85. Ibid., 809; Carman, "Maryland Campaign," ch. 11 (p. 59); and Wise, *Long Arm of Lee* 1:283.

86. *OR*, vol. 19, 1:873 (Semmes's report), 881 (Montague's report); Robert H. Moore II, *Miscellaneous Disbanded Virginia Light Artillery* (Lynchburg: H. E. Howard, Inc., 1997), 55.

87. McLaws's report, *OR*, vol. 19, 1:854.

88. Carman, "Maryland Campaign," chap. 23 (p. 24).

89. *OR*, vol. 19, 1:836; ibid., 2:650, 654; Wise, *Long Arm of Lee* 1:357–58.

90. *OR*, vol. 11, 2:488, 912.

91. S.O. No. 235, Headquarters Army of Northern Virginia, Nov. 7, 1862, ibid., vol. 19, 2:703; and S.O. No. 264, Adj. and Inspector General's Office, Richmond, Va., Nov. 11, 1862, ibid., 731.

92. Davis to Lee, Nov. 7, ibid., 703.

93. Ibid., vol. 5:1031; 9:451, 460; vol. 11, 2:488.

94. Walker's report, ibid., vol. 19, 1:913.

95. *SOR* 18:105; see also James Augustus Graham, "Twenty-Seventh Infantry," *North Carolina Regiments* 2:438; and idem, "Cooke's Brigade," ibid. 4:504.

96. Crute, *Units of the Confederate Army*, 414.

97. Walker's report, *OR*, vol. 19, 1:913.

98. Carman, "Maryland Campaign," chap. 19 (p. 39).

99. *OR*, vol. 9:447, 460; vol. 11, 2:488.

100. Walker's report, ibid., vol. 19, 1:913; Carman, "Maryland Campaign," chap. 19 (p. 39).

101. Clarke to Benjamin, Feb. 24, 1862, *OR*, vol. 11, 2:488, 3:539, 652; ibid., vol. 19, 1:921; ibid., vol. 51, 2:483; ibid., ser. 4, vol. 1:949–50; *North Carolina Regiments* 1:77.

102. *OR*, vol. 11, 2:912.

103. A. S. Cutts, "Cutts' Battalion at Sharpsburg," *SHSP* 10 (1882): 430–31.

104. Ransom to Chilton, Sept. 25, *OR*, vol. 19, 1:921.

105. Ibid., 2:649, 653.

106. *North Carolina Regiments* 4:653.

107. *OR*, vol. 19, 1:809; Wise, *Long Arm of Lee* 1:282; and Carman, "Maryland Campaign," chap. 11 (p. 57).

108. *OR*, vol. 11, 3:652; Wise, *Long Arm of Lee* 1:242. See also William Allan, "Confederate Artillery at Second Manassas and Sharpsburg," *SHSP* 11 (1883): 289–91.

109. *OR*, 19, vol. 2:595.

110. Cutts to Pendleton, Sept. 8, ibid., 2:599–600.

111. A. S. Cutts, "Cutts' Battalion at Sharpsburg," *SHSP* 10 (1882): 430–31; also John William Jones, "Did Cutts' Bttn Have Sixty Guns at Sharpsburg?" ibid., 190.

112. *OR*, vol. 19, 1:809.

113. Pendleton's report, ibid., 829–31.

114. Henry Robinson Berkeley, *Four Years in the Confederate Artillery: The Diary of Private Henry Robinson Berkeley*, ed. William H. Runge (Chapel Hill: Univ. of North Carolina Press, 1961), 23–24, 27.

115. *OR*, vol. 19, 1:806, 840, 844; ibid., 2:621; Carman, "Maryland Campaign," chap. 11 (p. 43); and Wise, *Long Arm of Lee* 1:358.

116. Wise, *Long Arm of Lee* 1:257; *OR*, vol. 12, 2:577–78; ibid., vol. 19, 1:829, 830; Stephen Dill Lee, "New Lights on Sharpsburg," *Richmond Dispatch*, Dec. 20, 1896, 12.

117. Pendleton's report, *OR*, vol. 19, 1:829; ibid., 2:595.

118. Ibid., 1:809; Wise, *Long Arm of Lee* 1:283; Carman, "Maryland Campaign," chap. 11 (p. 59).

119. Robert J. Driver, Jr., *1st Virginia Cavalry* (Lynchburg: H. E. Howard, Inc., 1991), 47.

120. Michael P. Musick, *6th Virginia Cavalry* (Lynchburg: H. E. Howard, Inc., 1990), 21–22.

121. Nelson Harris, *17th Virginia Cavalry* (Lynchburg: H. E. Howard, Inc., 1994), 1–14. Also see below chap. 6, sect. I, "Lee's Knowledge of the Harpers Ferry Situation."

122. See below chap. 9, sect. H, "Confederate Cavalry on the Evening of September 16."

123. Carman, "Maryland Campaign," chap. 11 (p. 60); H. R. Berrier, "Company B, Tenth Virginia Cavalry," *North Carolina Regiments* 5:627–28; Robert J. Driver, Jr., *10th Virginia Cavalry* (Lynchburg: H. E. Howard, Inc., 1992), 23–24.

124. Carman, "Maryland Campaign," chap. 11 (p. 61); *OR*, vol. 19, 1:810.

125. Krick, *Lee's Colonels*, 302; William Woods Hassler, *Colonel John Pelham, Lee's Boy Artillerist* (Richmond: Garrett & Massie, 1960), 52.

4. Gazetteer for the Maryland Campaign of 1862

1. Lee to Davis, Sept. 12, Hagerstown, *OR*, vol. 19, 2:605.

2. Ibid.

3. Certificate of Maj. John F. Edwards, Oct. 10, 1885, McLaws Papers, Southern Historical Collection, University of North Carolina, Chapel Hill.

4. Richard Duncan, "Marylanders and the Invasion of 1862," *Civil War History* 9 (1965): 370–83; Festus Paul Summers, *The Baltimore and Ohio Railroad in the Civil War* (New York: G. P. Putnam's Sons, 1939).

5. McLaws's report, *OR*, vol. 19, 1:856; Certificate of Maj. John F. Edwards, Oct. 10, 1885, McLaws Papers.

5. Research Appendixes on Lee's Decision to Enter Maryland

1. Lee to Davis, Sept. 3, *OR*, vol. 19, 1:590–91.

2. Lee's report, ibid., 144.

3. Lee to to Seddon, June 8, 1863, ibid., vol. 27, 3:868–69.

4. Lee to Davis, June 25, 1863, ibid., 931–33.

5. Charles Marshall, *An Aide-de-camp of Lee, Being the Papers of Colonel Charles Marshall, Sometimes Aide-de-camp, Military Secretary, and Assistant Adjutant General on the Staff of Robert E. Lee, 1862–1865*, ed. Sir Frederick Maurice (Boston: Little, Brown and Co., 1927), 145–47. For a discussion of Marshall as a source for understanding Lee's strategic thinking, see Joseph L. Harsh, *Confederate Tide Rising: Robert E. Lee and the Making of Southern Strategy, 1861–1862* (Kent, Ohio: Kent State Univ. Press, 1998), app. 3, sect. A, 185–86.

6. Editorial, *Richmond Examiner*, July 21, 1862.

7. Longstreet, "Maryland," 663; Gilbert Moxley Sorrel, *Recollections of a Confederate Staff Officer* (New York: Neale Pub. Co., 1905), 98; and William Allan, "Strategy of the Campaign of Sharpsburg or Antietam, September 1862," in *Papers of the Military Historical Society of Massachusetts*, 16 vols. (Boston: Various pubs., 1881–1916), 3:76. In Gary W. Gallagher, ed., *Antietam: Essays on the 1862 Maryland Campaign* (Kent, Ohio: Kent State Univ. Press, 1989), see Robert Kenneth Krick, "The Army of Northern Virginia in September 1862: Its Circumstances, Its Opportunities, And Why It Should Not Have Been at Sharpsburg," 36–37. And in Gallagher, ed., *Lee the Soldier*, see D. Scott Hartwig, "Robert E. Lee and the Maryland Campaign," 331–32.

8. Lee to Davis, Sept. 3, 1862, *OR*, vol. 19, 2:590.

9. Report on Second Manassas, ibid., vol. 12, 2:558.

10. Allan Memorandum of Feb. 15, 1868, in Gallagher, ed., *Lee the Soldier*, 7.

11. Allan Memorandum of Apr. 15, 1868, in ibid., 13.

12. Robert Edward Lee, "Letter from General R. E. Lee [to William McDonald]," *SHSP* 7 (1879) 445.

13. Gallagher, ed., *Lee the Soldier*, 13.

14. Chilton for Lee, Sept. 2, 1862, *OR*, vol. 19, 2:588.

15. Lee to Davis, Sept. 3, 1862, ibid., 590.

16. Lee to Davis, Sept. 3, 1862, Robert Edward Lee, *The Wartime Papers of R. E. Lee*, ed. Clifford Dowdey and Louis H. Manarin (Boston: Little, Brown and Co., 1961), 269–70.

17. Henry Heth, "Causes of Lee's Defeat at Gettysburg," *SHSP* 4 (1877): 153.

18. Robert Edward Lee [Jr.], *Recollections and Letters of General Robert E. Lee, by His Son* (Garden City, New York: Garden City Pub. Co., 1926), 416.

19. Marshall, *Aide-de-Camp of Lee*, 144.

20. For a discussion of Lee's use of the fear for the safety of Washington, see Harsh, *Confederate Tide Rising*, app. 3, sect. D, 188.

21. Allan, "The Campaign of Sharpsburg or Antietam," 76; and Bradley Tyler Johnson, "First Maryland Campaign," *SHSP* 12 (1884): 502.

22. Lee to Davis, Sept.3, 1862, *OR*, vol. 19, 2:590.

23. Lee's report, ibid., 1:144.

24. Gallagher, ed., *Lee the Soldier*, 13.

25. Lee, "McDonald Letter," 445. See also Armistead Lindsay Long, *Memoirs of Robert E. Lee, His Military and Personal History, Embracing a Large Amount of Information Hitherto Unpublished* (Philadelphia: J. M. Stoddart & Co., 1886), 204; and Longstreet, *From Manassas to Appomattox*, 200.

26. Heth, "Letter," 153.

27. Gallagher, ed., *Lee the Soldier*, 7.

28. Ibid., 13.

29. Comte de Paris, *History of the Civil War in America*, 4 vols. (Philadelphia: Porter & Coates, 1876–88), 2:308–9.

30. Johnson, "Maryland," 505.

31. James V. Murfin, *The Gleam of Bayonets: The Battle of Antietam and the Maryland Campaign of 1862* (New York: Thomas Yoseloff, 1965), 67.

32. John Owen Allen, "The Strengths of the Union and Confederate Forces at Second Manassas" (master's thesis, George Mason Univ., 1993), 186–209.

33. Walter Heron Taylor, *Four Years with General Lee*, ed. James I. Robertson, Jr. (Bloomington: Indiana Univ. Press, 1962), 61, 73.

34. Allan, "The Campaign of Sharpsburg or Antietam," 75.

35. Long, *Memoirs of R. E. Lee*, 205.

36. Johnson, "Maryland," 507.

37. Stephen W. Sears, *Landscape Turned Red: The Battle of Antietam* (New Haven: Ticknor & Fields, 1983), 69.

38. Sorrel, *Recollections of a Confederate Staff Officer*, 98.

39. Murfin, *Gleam of Bayonets*, 88.

40. R. H. Anderson to D. H. Hill, Nov. 14, 1867, D. H. Hill Personal Papers, North Carolina State Archives, Raleigh.

41. Alexander, *Military Memoirs*, 225.

42. Gallagher, ed., *Lee the Soldier*, 26.

43. Krick, "The Army of Northern Virginia in September 1862," 49–51.

44. Quoted in Hal Bridges, *Lee's Maverick General: Daniel Harvey Hill* (New York: McGraw Hill Book Co., 1961), 90.

45. W. E. Lee to mother, Sept. 5, Laura Elizabeth Battle, *Forget-Me-Nots of the Civil War: A Romance Containing Reminiscences and Original Letters of Two Confederate Soldiers* (St. Louis: Fleming Print. Co., 1909), 75.

46. See Leach, Diary, Sept. 1, for 1st N.C. of Ripley; for the 2d and 3d S.C. of Kershaw, Richard Wright Simpson, *"Far, Far from Home": The Wartime Letters of Dick and Tally Simpson, Third South Carolina Volunteers*, eds. Guy R. Everson and Edward H. Simpson, Jr. (New York: Oxford Univ. Press, 1994), 146–47; Wyckoff, *History of the 2d S.C.*, 39; and Draughton Stith Haynes (of the 49th Georgia but marching with Colquitt), *The Field Diary of a Confederate Soldier, Draughton Stith Haynes, while Serving with the Army of Northern Virginia, C.S.A.* (Darien, Ga.: Ashantilly Press, 1963), 14.

47. McLaws to wife, Sept. 4, McLaws Papers.

48. Berkeley, *Four Years in the Confederate Artillery*, 26.

49. Emmett M. Morrison, "Fifteenth Virginia," *SHSP* 33 (1905): 100–101.

50. Davies's report, *OR*, vol. 19, 1:1092.

51. War Department Collection of Confederate Records, RG 109, National Archives. See also Allen, "Second Manassas Strengths."

52. Berry Benson, *Berry Benson's Civil War Book: Memoirs of a Confederate Scout and Sharpshooter*, ed. Susan Williams Benson (Athens: Univ. of Georgia Press, 1962), 24–27.

53. Joab Goodson "The Letters of Captain Joab Goodson, 1862–64," ed. W. Stanley Hoole, *Alabama Review* 10 (1957): 130.

54. Haynes, *Diary*, 13–14. For another example, see Talley Simpson to sister, Sept. 24, Simpson, *Far, Far from Home*, 148.

55. Hunter, "Sharpsburg," 505.

56. George Wise, *History of the Seventeenth Virginia Infantry, C.S.A.* (Baltimore: Kelly, Piet & Co., 1870), 105–7.

57. James B. Sheeran, *Confederate Chaplain: A War Journal of Rev. James B. Sheeran, C.S.S.T, 14th Louisiana, C.S.A.*," ed. Rev. Joseph T. Durkin (Milwaukee: Bruce Pub. Co., 1960), 21.

58. Jubal Anderson Early, *War Memoirs, Autobiographical Sketch and Narrative of the War Between the States*, ed. Frank E. Vandiver (Bloomington: Indiana Univ. Press, 1960), 134.

59. Hotchkiss, *Make Me a Map*, 78.

60. See the diary of Calvin Leach of the 1st North Carolina, University of North Carolina; a letter of Kittrell Warren of the 11th Georgia in Aurelia Austin, *Georgia Boys with "Stonewall" Jackson—James Thomas Thompson and the Walton Infantry* (Athens: Univ. of Georgia Press, 1967), 45; and the official report of Capt. Murdock McLauchlin of the 38th North Carolina, *SOR* 2:776.

61. See McLaws to wife, Sept. 4, McLaws Papers; Johnson, "Maryland," 507; Pender to wife, Sept. 7, in Pender, *The General to His Lady*, 173; William Allan, *The Army of Northern Virginia in 1862* (Boston: Houghton Mifflin and Co., 1892), 324; Douglas, *I Rode with Stonewall*, 142–43; Worsham, *One of Jackson's Foot Cavalry*, 82; Marion Hill Fitzpatrick, *Letters to Amanda from Sergeant Major Marion Hill Fitzpatrick, Company K,*

45th Georgia Regiment to His Wife Amanda Olive Elizabeth White Fitzpatrick, 1862–1865 (Culloden, Ga.: Privately printed, 1976), 19–20; H. C. Kearny, with reference to "green beef," "Fifteenth Infantry," *North Carolina Regiments* 1:739–40. And see in ibid., vol. 2, V. E. Turner and Henry Clay Wall, "Twenty-Third Infantry" (p. 217), and Lane (p. 473). See also the collected witnesses cited in Murfin, *Gleam of Bayonets*, 92–97.

62. See Gary W. Gallagher, "The Autumn of 1862: A Season of Opportunity," Gallagher, ed., *Antietam Essays*, 10–11; and Krick, "The Army of Northern Virginia in September 1862," ibid., 40–47.

63. *OR*, vol. 19, 1:145.

64. Gallagher, ed., *Lee the Soldier*, 13. For variant statements see ibid., 6; and Lee, "McDonald Letter," 445.

65. Blackford, *War Years with Jeb Stuart*, 142.

66. Johnson, "Maryland," 504–5.

67. Allan, "The Campaign of Sharpsburg or Antietam," 76.

68. Allan, *Army of Northern Virginia*, 322–23; and idem, "First Maryland Campaign, Review of General Longstreet," *SHSP* 14 (1886): 102–4.

69. Sears, *Landscape Turned Red*, 82–83.

70. Krick, "The Army of Northern Virginia in September 1862," 37.

71. Gallagher, "The Autumn of 1862: A Season of Opportunity," 7–8.

72. Archer Jones, *Civil War Command and Strategy: The Process of Victory and Defeat* (New York: The Free Press, Macmillan, 1992), 83–84, 95; see also Jones's "Military Means, Political Ends: Strategy," in Gabor S. Boritt, ed., *Why the Confederacy Lost* (New York: Oxford Univ. Press, 1992), 59–60; Richard C. Beringer, Herman Hattaway, Archer Jones, and William N. Still, Jr., *Why the South Lost the Civil War* (Athens: Univ. of Georgia Press, 1986), 165–67; and Herman Hattaway and Archer Jones, *How the North Won: A Military History of the Civil War* (Urbana: Univ. of Illinois Press, 1983), 232–34.

73. See Isaac Winter Heysinger, *Antietam and the Maryland and Virginia Campaigns of 1862, from the Government Records, Union and Confederate, Mostly Unknown and Which Now First Disclosed the Truth* (New York: Neale Pub. Co., 1912), 55–58; and Thomas Goddard Frothingham, "The Crisis of the Civil War, Antietam," *Massachusetts Historical Society Proceedings* 56 (1922–23): 177–78.

74. 8th Census, *Agriculture*, 72–73, 154–63.

75. Lee to Davis, Sept. 5, *OR*, vol. 19, 2:594.

76. Gallagher, ed., *Lee the Soldier*, 7, 13.

77. Longstreet, "Maryland," 663; and Allan, "First Maryland Campaign," 102.

78. See Hassler, *Pelham*, 77.

79. See Jedidiah Hotchkiss, *Virginia*, in Clement A. Evans, ed., *Confederate Military History: A Library of Confederate States History*, 10 vols. (Atlanta: Confederate Publishing Co., 1899), 3:337. For a similarly suggestive statement, see John Esten Cooke, *Stonewall Jackson* (New York: G. W. Dillingham, 1899), 308–9.

80. James A. Kegel, *North with Lee and Jackson: The Lost Story of Gettysburg* (Mechanicsville, Pa.: Stackpole Books, 1996).

81. For a different, but no more fetching, Jackson-centered argument, see Bevin Alexander, *Lost Victories: The Military Genius of Stonewall Jackson* (New York: Henry Holt & Co., 1992), 207–10.

82. Gallagher, ed., *Lee the Soldier*, 26, 8.

83. Lee's report, *OR*, vol. 19, 1:144.

84. Longstreet, *From Manassas to Appomattox*, 200.
85. Longstreet, "Maryland," 663.
86. Lee's report, *OR*, vol. 19, 1:144.
87. Lee to Davis, June 23, 1863, ibid., vol. 27, 3:925.

6. Research Appendixes on the Early Campaign, September 4–9

1. Sears, *Landscape Turned Red*, 71; Murfin, *Gleam of Bayonets*, 96; and Douglas Southall Freeman, *Lee's Lieutenants: A Study in Command*, 3 vols. (New York: Charles Scribner's Sons, 1942–44), 2:151–52.
2. Garland S. Ferguson, "Twenty-Fifth Infantry," *North Carolina Regiments* 2:296.
3. Original in Stiles Papers, Henry E. Huntington Library, San Marino, California.
4. Charles Folsom Walcott, *History of the Twenty-First Regiment Massachusetts Volunteers in the War for the Preservation of the Union, 1861–1865* (Boston: Houghton, Mifflin, 1882), 191.
5. Wyckoff, *2nd S.C.*, 90; and idem, *A History of the 3rd South Carolina Infantry: 1861–1865* (Fredericksburg, Va.: Sergeant Kirkland's Museum and Historical Society, 1995), 66.
6. Hirsch, Diary, Sept. 5.
7. See Daniel Harvey Hill, "The Lost Dispatch," *Land We Love* 4 (1867–68): 274; and see in *OR*, vol. 19, 1, the reports of Robertson (p. 828) and D. H. Hill (p. 1019).
8. Lee's report, *OR*, vol. 19, 1:144–45.
9. Gallagher, ed., *Lee the Soldier*, 26.
10. Ibid., 7.
11. Lee to D. H. Hill, Feb. 21, 1868, Robert Edward Lee, "A Lee Letter on the 'Lost Dispatch,' and the Maryland Campaign of 1862," ed. Hal Bridges, *Virginia Magazine of History and Biography* 66 (1958): 164.
12. D. H. Hill, "Lost Dispatch," 274.
13. See D. H. Hill's report, *OR*, vol. 19, 1:1019; H. W. Thomas, *History of the Doles-Cook Brigade*, 469; DeRosset, "Additional Sketch Third Regiment," *North Carolina Regiments* 1:224; and Turner, ibid., 217 (where the account is one day off and places Noland's Ford too far east); Shinn, Diary, Sept. 6; Leach, Diary, Sept. 4–6; and Leonidas Torrence, "The Road to Gettysburg, The Diary and Letters of Leonidas Torrence of the Gaston Guards," ed. Haskell Monroe, *North Carolina Historical Review* 36 (1959): 499.
14. See Hotchkiss, *Make Me a Map*, 78; and Chamberlayne, *Letters*, 102.
15. S.O. No. 188, Headquarters, Dept. of Northern Virginia, Sept. 5, *OR*, vol. 19, 2:595.
16. James Sidney Harris, "Seventh Infantry," *North Carolina Regiments* 1:372.
17. Lee, *Wartime Papers*, 20.
18. Summers, *The Baltimore and Ohio in the Civil War*, 118.
19. *OR*, vol. 19, 1:803–10.
20. J. Wise, *Long Arm of Lee* 1:259, 277–83.
21. Alexander, *Military Memoirs*, 226.
22. C. Johnson, *Artillery Hell*, 128.
23. Ibid., 129; Pendleton's report, *OR*, vol. 19, 1:836–37.

24. *OR*, vol. 19, 1:829; ibid., 2:647–52.

25. 8th Census, *Population*, 210–14.

26. Lee's report, *OR*, vol. 19, 1:145.

27. Lee to Davis, Sept. 12, ibid., 2:604–5.

28. Gallagher, ed., *Lee the Soldier*, 7.

29. For the numbers of volunteers, see Duncan, "Marylanders," 188–89. See also Evans, ed., *Confederate Military History* 2:87–91; Hotchkiss, *Make Me a Map*, 79; and Lewis Henry Steiner, *Report of Henry Lewis Steiner, M.D., Inspector of the Sanitary Commission, Containing a Diary Kept during the Rebel Occupation of Frederick, Md., and an Account of the Operations of the U.S. Sanitary Commission during the Campaign in Maryland, September 1862* (New York: Anson D. F. Randolph, 1862), 12–13.

30. Special Orders, Nos. 192 (Sept. 13) and 194 (Sept. 15), Orders and Circulars of the Army of Northern Virginia, RG 109, National Archives.

31. Lee to Steuart and Lee to Randolph, Sept. 30, *OR*, vol. 19, 2:636–37.

32. Daniel D. Hartzler, *Marylanders in the Confederacy* (Westminster, Md.: Family Line Publications, 1986), 31.

33. Price to mother, Sept. 10, Robert J. Trout, *With Pen and Saber: The Letters and Diaries of J. E. B. Stuart's Staff Officers* (Mechanicsburg, Pa.: Stackpole Books, 1995), 97.

34. *OR*, vol. 19, 2:598–99.

35. Louis H. Manarin, "A Proclamation To the People of ——," *North Carolina Historical Review* 41 (1964): 246–47.

36. *OR*, vol. 19, 1:913.

37. Munford's report, ibid., 825.

38. See *OR General Index*, (p. 1149) correction for vol. 19, 1:810; Harris, *17th Virginia Cavalry*, 1–14.

39. In *OR*, vol. 19, 1, see Voss's report (p. 517), Binney's diary (pp. 532–33), and testimony before the Harpers Ferry court of inquiry (pp. 725, 737, 738). Also, see White to Wool, Sept. 7, ibid., 2:205.

40. Ibid., 1:825.

41. William Naylor McDonald, *A History of the Laurel Brigade, Originally the Ashby Cavalry of the Army of Northern Virginia and Chew's Battery*, ed. Bushrod C. Washington (Baltimore: Sun Job Print. Office, 1907), 94.

42. See also Miles to White and Miles to Ford, Sept. 9, *OR*, vol. 51, 1:804.

43. Longstreet, *From Manassas to Appomattox*, 213.

44. Walker's report, *OR*, vol. 19, 1:912–13; John George Walker, "Jackson's Capture of Harper's Ferry," in Johnson and Buel, eds., *Battles and Leaders* 2:607.

45. LaFayette McLaws, "The Maryland Campaign," in *Addresses Delivered before the Confederate Veterans Association of Savannah, Ga.*, 4 vols. (Savannah: Braid & Hutton, 1893–1902), 3:6.

46. Copy in the D. H. Hill Personal Papers.

47. Copy in George Brinton McClellan Papers, Library of Congress, Washington, D.C.

48. Lee to Davis, Sept. 12, *OR*, vol. 19, 2:605.

49. Stuart's report, ibid., 1:816.

50. Susan Pendleton Lee, *Memoirs of William Nelson Pendleton* (Harrisonburg, Va.: Sprinkle Publications, 1991), 211.

51. Orders and Circulars Issued by the Army of the Potomac and the Army and Department of Northern Virginia, RG 109, National Archives.

52. R. H. Anderson to D. H. Hill, Nov. 14, 1867, D. H. Hill Personal Papers; see also D. H. Hill, "Lost Dispatch," 275.

7. Research Appendixes on the Middle Campaign, September 10–13

1. Steiner, *Diary*, 10.

2. Ibid., 26–27.

3. Douglas, *I Rode with Stonewall*, 152–54; idem, "Stonewall Jackson in Maryland," in Johnson and Buel, *Battles and Leaders* 2:622–23. The Federal version is given in White to Wool, Sept. 10, 9:00 P.M., *OR*, vol. 19, 2:249.

4. Hotchkiss, *Make Me a Map*, 80; Poague, *Gunner with Stonewall*, 43; and Worsham, *One of Jackson's Foot Cavalry*, 83, where Jackson is said to have ridden all the way into the town and entered a house.

5. *Century Magazine* 10 (1886): 285–95, later reprinted in Johnson and Buel, *Battles and Leaders* 2:620–29.

6. See Douglas, *I Rode with Stonewall*, 367–68. The newspaper clipping and the French letter of June 28, 1886, are in the Douglas Papers, which are privately owned and not open to scholars.

7. See Dennis E. Frye, "Henry Kyd Douglas Challenged by His Peers," *Civil War* (Sept.–Oct. 1991): 41–42, based on correspondence in the Hotchkiss Papers, Library of Congress.

8. Lee to Jackson, Oct. 1, *OR*, vol. 19, 2:641.

9. For a generalized study of Lee's trains see, Tischler, *Harpers Ferry Cavalry Expedition*, 88–90.

10. Daniel Harvey Hill, "The Battle of South Mountain, or Boonsboro': Fighting for Time at Turner's and Fox's Gaps," in Johnson and Buel, *Battles and Leaders* 2:560.

11. Pendleton's report, *OR*, vol. 19, 1:829; Pendleton to wife, Sept. 13, S. P. Lee, *Memoirs*, 211–12.

12. Edward Porter Alexander, *Fighting for the Confederacy: The Personal Recollections of General Edward Porter Alexander*, ed. Gary W. Gallagher (Chapel Hill: Univ. of North Carolina Press, 1989), 142.

13. Carman, "Maryland Campaign," chap. 9 (p. 509).

14. Pendleton's report, *OR*, vol. 19, 1:829.

15. Ibid.; Cutts, "Letter," 430.

16. Lee to Davis, Sept. 12, *OR*, 19, 2:604–5.

17. Thomas Jackson Arnold, "The Lost Dispatch—A War Mystery," *Confederate Veteran* 30 (1922): 317.

18. Wilbur D. Jones, "Who Lost the Lost Order? Stonewall Jackson, His Courier, and Special Orders No. 191," in Mark A. Snell, ed., *Antietam: The Maryland Campaign of 1862*, special issue of *Civil War Regiments: A Journal of the American Civil War* 5 (1997): 1–26.

19. Walker's report, *OR*, vol. 19, 1:913; Walker, "Harper's Ferry," 608–9; Hirsch, Diary, Sept. 13, 14; Graham, *North Carolina Regiments* 2:433–34; and Hotchkiss, *Make Me a Map*, 80–81.

20. Hirsch, Diary, Sept. 13.

21. Graham, *North Carolina Regiments* 2:433–34; and Hirsch, Diary, Sept. 13, 14.

22. Hotchkiss, *Make Me a Map*, 80–81.

23. Graham, *North Carolina Regiments* 2:433–34; and Hirsch, Diary, Sept. 13, 14.

24. Gallagher, ed., *Lee the Soldier*, 26.

25. Ibid., 8, 27.

26. Longstreet, *From Manassas to Appomattox*, 219.

27. Lee to Davis, Sept. 16, *OR*, vol. 19, 1:140.

28. Lee's report, ibid., 146.

29. Carman, "Maryland Campaign," chap. 7 (p. 394).

30. Allan, *Army of Northern Virginia*, 345–46.

31. Douglas Southall Freeman, *R. E. Lee: A Biography*, 4 vols. (New York: Charles Scribner's Sons, 1934–35), 2:369n.72.

32. Marshall, *Aide-de-Camp to Lee*, 160.

33. Gallagher, ed., *Lee the Soldier*, 26.

34. Ibid., 8.

35. Freeman, *Lee's Lieutenants* 2:722.

36. Lee, "Hill Letter," 166. Bridges discovered a retained copy in the Lee Papers, Library of Congress.

37. Sears, *Landscape Turned Red*, 351.

38. Marshall to D. H. Hill, Nov. 11, 1867, D. H. Hill Papers, Library of Virginia, Richmond.

39. Sears, *Landscape Turned Red*, 351.

40. Stephen W. Sears, "The Last Word on the Lost Order," in *Experiences of War: An Anthology from MHQ, the Quarterly Journal of Military History* (New York: Dell, 1992), 208.

41. Carman, "Maryland Campaign," chap. 7 (pp. 393–94).

42. Lee to Hill, June 12, 1867, Lee Family Papers, Virginia Historical Society, Richmond.

43. Gallagher, ed., *Lee the Soldier*, 27.

44. Lee's report, *OR*, vol. 19, 1:146.

45. Gallagher, ed., *Lee the Soldier*, 27.

46. Lee, "Hill Letter," 166.

8. Research Appendixes on South Mountain and Harpers Ferry, September 14–15

1. See, Freeman, *R. E. Lee* 2:369; and Walter Taylor, *General Lee, His Campaigns in Virginia, 1861–1865, with Personal Reminiscences* (Norfolk: Nusbaum Book and News Co., 1906), 115.

2. Alexander, *Fighting for the Confederacy*, 142.

3. John Bell Hood, *Advance and Retreat, Personal Experiences in the United States and Confederate States Armies*, ed. Richard N. Current (Bloomington: Indiana Univ. Press, 1959), 39.

4. Ibid., 39; and Owen, *In Camp and Battle*, 136.

5. George Michael Neese, *Three Years in the Confederate Horse Artillery* (New York: Neale Pub. Co., 1911), 122–23.

6. Sorrel, *Recollections of a Confederate Staff Officer*, 100; William Nathaniel Wood, *Reminiscences of Big I*, ed. Bell Irvin Wiley (Jackson, Tenn.: McCowat-Mercer Press, 1956), 35; Neill W. Ray, "Sixth Infantry," *North Carolina Regiments* 1:306.

7. Hill, "South Mountain," 561–62.

8. George D. Grattan, "The Battle of Boonsboro Gap, or South Mountain," *SHSP* 39 (1914): 35–38; buttressed by the slight reference in Colquitt to D. H. Hill, July 4, 1885, D. H. Hill Personal Papers.

9. Iverson to D. H. Hill, Aug. 23, 1885, D. H. Hill Personal Papers.

10. Hill, "South Mountain," 565.

11. Hill's report, *OR*, vol. 19, 1:1020.

12. Hill to Longstreet, Feb. 14, 1885, Longstreet Papers, Duke University.

13. *OR* 19.1: 1022; and Hill, "Lost Dispatch," 277.

14. See D. H. Hill's letters to Longstreet of May 21, June 8, Aug. 4, and Aug. 31, 1885, Longstreet Papers, Duke University.

15. Taylor, *Four Years with General Lee*, 158.

16. Steiner, *Diary*, 21–22.

17. Allen, "Second Manassas Strengths," 186.

18. Carman, "Maryland Campaign," chap. 23 (pp. 31–34).

19. Federal casualty returns for Harpers Ferry, *OR*, vol. 19, 1:549.

20. Allen, "Second Manassas Strengths," 194–201.

21. Hirsch, Diary, Sept. 13.

22. Walker's report, *OR*, vol. 19, 1:913.

23. Walker, "Harper's Ferry," 609–10.

24. Ibid., 611.

25. Alexander, *Military Memoirs*, 235.

26. Jackson to McLaws, 7:20 A.M., Sept. 14, *OR*, vol. 19, 2:607.

27. Bartlett's report, ibid., 1:959.

28. Ibid., 966, 980, 1007.

29. See Harsh, *Confederate Tide Rising*, 197–99.

30. Hood, *Advance and Retreat*, 41; D. H. Hill, "South Mountain," 571; and Longstreet, *From Manassas to Appomattox*, 227; and idem, "Maryland," 666.

31. D. H. Hill to Longstreet, Feb. 11, 1885, Longstreet Papers.

32. Statement [1885] of Emory F. Best, ibid.

33. Freeman, *R.. E. Lee* 2:372–76; and idem, *Lee's Lieutenants* 2:203.

34. Gallagher, ed., *Lee the Soldier*, 8.

35. Taylor to Ropes, Jan. 28, 1898, John Codman Ropes Papers, Boston University.

36. The message itself, timed near 8:00 A.M., Sept. 15, may be found in *OR*, vol. 19, 1:951.

37. Owen, *In Camp and Battle*, 139.

38. Long, *Memoirs of R. E. Lee*, 216.

39. George Breckenridge Davis, "The Antietam Campaign," *PMHSM* 3:51.

40. Carman, "Maryland Campaign," chap. 9 (p. 559).

41. Douglas, *I Rode with Stonewall*, 163.

42. *OR*, vol. 19, 1:636.

43. E. A. Moore, *The Story of a Cannoneer*, 142–43.

44. Paul R. Teetor, *A Matter of Hours: Treason at Harper's Ferry* (Rutherford, N.J.: Fairleigh Dickinson Univ. Press, 1982), 156–58, 176–77. For a good brief study, see Dennis E. Frye, "The Siege of Harper's Ferry," *Blue and Gray Magazine* 5 (1987): 8–27, 47–54.

45. Murfin, *Gleam of Bayonets*, 201; Sears, *Landscape Turned Red*, 152; and Dennis E. Frye, "The Siege of Harper's Ferry," *Blue and Gray Magazine* 5 (1987): 51.

46. Walker's report, *OR*, vol. 19, 1:914.

47. Walker, "Harper's Ferry," 610.

48. Hotchkiss, *Make Me a Map*, 81.

49. E. A. Moore, *The Story of a Cannoneer*, 139.

50. In *OR*, vol. 19, 1, see the reports of: J. R. Jones (p. 1007), Edwards (p. 998), and McGowan (p. 987).

51. Letter to mother, Sept. 19, Chamberlayne, *Letters*, 109.

52. *OR*, vol. 19, 1:539.

53. Ibid., 528, 548.

54. Jackson to Lee, Sept. 15, near 8:00 A.M., ibid., 951.

55. Samuel Wylie Crawford, *The Genesis of the Civil War: The Story of Sumter, 1860–1861* (New York: Charles L. Webster & Co., 1887), 439–49.

56. *OR*, ser. 2, vol. 2:9–10.

57. Ibid., 264.

58. Ibid., 271–72, 278.

59. Robert Ould, "The Exchange of Prisoners," in *The Annals of the War, Written by Leading Participants, North and South, Originally Published in the Philadelphia Weekly Times* (Philadelphia: Times Pub. Co., 1879), 32–34.

60. Carman, "Maryland Campaign," chap. 9 (pp. 559–60); see also John Codman Ropes, *The Story of the Civil War: A Concise Account of the War in the United States of America Between 1861 and 1865*, 2 vols. (New York: G. P. Putnam's Sons, 1894–98), 2:348; Douglas, *I Rode with Stonewall*, 164–65; and idem, "Maryland," 627. Confirmation, but little in the way of new details, may be found in Douglas to Ropes, Jan. 23 and 25, 1898, Ropes Papers.

61. In Charles W. Squires, "Boy Officer of the Washington Artillery—Part I," *Civil War Times Illustrated* 14 (1975): 19.

62. Lee to G. W. Smith, Sept. 15, Hagerstown, Md., *OR*, vol. 19, 2:609.

9. Research Appendixes on the Battle of Antietam, September 16–17

1. Carman, "Maryland Campaign," chap. 8 (p. 1).

2. Owen, *In Camp and Battle*, 139.

3. Lee [Jr.], *Recollection*, 78–79.

4. Carman, "Maryland Campaign," chap. 9 (pp. 518–20).

5. Owen, *In Camp and Battle*, 141. See also Sorrel, *Recollections of a Confederate Staff Officer*, 96; Douglas, *I Rode with Stonewall*, 143; Taylor, *General Lee*, 115; and F. Lee, *Lee*, 210.

6. Carman, "Maryland Campaign," chap. 13 (p. 27).

7. *OR*, vol. 19, 1:137.

8. Alexander, *Fighting for the Confederacy*, 147–48; and *Military Memoirs*, 242.

9. Carman, "Maryland Campaign," chap. 9 (pp. 509–10); and report of Little, *OR*, vol. 19, 1:911.

10. Walker's report, *OR*, vol. 19, 1:914.

11. Walker, "Harper's Ferry," 611.

12. Walker, "Sharpsburg," 675.

13. Hirsch, Diary, Sept. 16.

14. Walker, "Harper's Ferry," 611.

15. Walker, "Sharpsburg," 675.

16. Carman, "Maryland Campaign," chap. 13 (p. 20).

17. Lee to Mrs. Jackson, Jan. 25, 1866, Lee Family Papers.

18. Douglas, *I Rode with Stonewall*, 166–67. Douglas relates two credible anecdotes of the meeting: first, speculation in the ranks about Jackson's arrival; and second, the myth of the "Lee Rock" in the cemetery—upon which Lee never stood.

19. Ibid., 167.

20. Thomas E. Caffey, *Battle-fields of the South: From Bull Run to Fredericksburg, with Sketches of the Confederate Commanders and Gossip of the Camps, by an English Combatant* (New York: John Bradburn, 1864), 482–83.

21. Francis Winthrop Palfrey, "The Battle of Antietam," *PMHSM* 3:2.

22. In *OR*, vol. 19, 1, see the reports of Walton (p. 849) and Frobel (p. 925). See also Squires, "Boy Officer," 19.

23. John A. Ramsay, "First N. Ca. Artillery: Additional Sketch, Light Batteries A, D, F [E] and I," *North Carolina Regiments* 1:574.

24. S. D. Lee's report, *OR*, vol. 19, 1:844.

25. Benjamin's report, ibid., 436.

26. G. Wise, *History of the 17th Va.*, 115.

27. J. Wise, *Long Arm of Lee* 2:297.

28. Pendleton's report, *OR*, vol. 19, 1:836–37.

29. G. Wise, *History of the 17th Va.*, 115.

30. In *OR*, vol. 19, 1, see the reports of D. R. Jones (p. 886), Walker (p. 903), Durham (p. 950), McMaster (p. 945), and Hunton (p. 898).

31. Ibid., 949.

32. Ramsay, *North Carolina Regiments* 1:574. See also, Osmun Latrobe, Diary, Sept. 16, Virginia Historical Society, Richmond; and W. H. Andrews, *Diary of W. H. Andrews, 1st Sergt., Co. M, 1st Georgia Regulars, from February 1861, to May 2, 1865* (East Atlanta: Privately printed, 1891), 7.

33. Ripley's report, *OR*, vol. 19, 1:1032; H. W. Thomas, *History of the Doles-Cook Brigade*, 469; and in *North Carolina Regiments* vol. 1, see Hamilton A. Brown, "First Infantry (State Troops)" (p. 141), John Cowan and James I Metts, "Third Infantry" (p. 184); and DeRosset (p. 225). See also Leach, Diary, Sept. 16; and Thruston's report, *SOR* 3:586.

34. Carman, "Maryland Campaign," chap. 13 (pp. 46–47).

35. Sorrel, *Recollections of a Confederate Staff Officer*, 103–4.

36. Hampton's report, *OR*, vol. 19, 1:824.

37. McLaws's report, *OR*, vol. 19, 1:857; and repeated verbatim in McLaws, "Maryland," 24.

38. Gibson's report, *SOR* 3:568.

39. Freeman, *R. E. Lee* 2:39n.9.

40. Long, *Memoirs of R. E. Lee*, 221.

41. Douglas, *I Rode with Stonewall*, 166–67.

42. The sources referred to in this discussion are: Longstreet, *From Manassas to Appomattox*, 254; Longstreet, "Maryland," 671, where Alfred Woodhull's "Letter," which makes reference to an unpublished letter from Longstreet, is printed in a footnote. Also, Long, *Memoirs of R. E. Lee*, 221; Sorrel, *Recollections of a Confederate Staff Officer*, 104–5; and Oliver T. Reilly, *The Battlefield of Antietam* (Sharpsburg: Privately printed, 1906), [20].

43. Freeman, *R. E. Lee* 2:392; and Bridges, *Lee's Maverick General*, 118–19.

44. Hill to Longstreet, Mar. 12, 1885, Longstreet Papers.

45. Charles A. Cuffel, *History of Durell's Battery in the Civil War (Independent Battery D, Pennsylvania Volunteer Artillery): A Narrative of the Campaigns and Battles of Berks and Bucks Counties' Artillerists in the War of the Rebellion* (Philadelphia: Craig, Finley & Co., 1903), 78–79.

46. Ratchford, Memoir, pp. 39–40, D. H. Hill, Jr., Personal Papers; and A. S. Pendleton to mother, Sept. 21, S. P. Lee, *Memoirs*, 216.

47. In *OR*, vol. 19, 1, see the reports of Kershaw (p. 865), MacRae (p. 871), Loud (p. 877), and Barksdale (p. 883).

48. Antietam Battlefield Plaques nos. 357, 358, 359, 363, typescript at Visitors Center, Sharpsburg, Maryland.

49. Walker, "Sharpsburg," 676–77.

50. Lee [Jr.], *Recollections*, 77–79; Poague, *Gunner with Stonewall*, 48; Henry Kyd Douglas, *I Rode with Stonewall*, 173; and idem, "Maryland," 629.

51. John W. Daniel, ed., *Life and Reminiscences of Jefferson Davis by Distinguished Men of His Time* (Baltimore: Eastern Pub. Co., 1890), 409–10, where the secondhand details are considerably confused.

52. Freeman, *R. E. Lee* 2:396–97.

53. Poague's report, *OR*, vol. 19, 1:1010.

54. E. A. Moore, *The Story of a Cannoneer*, 153.

55. Owen, *In Camp and Battle*, 152.

56. First published. in *Century Magazine* 33 (1886): 314; and reprinted in Longstreet, "Maryland," 671–72.

57. Longstreet, *From Manassas to Appomattox*, 262.

58. S. D. Lee, "New Lights on Sharpsburg," 12.

59. S. D. Lee to Hotchkiss, July 20, 1896, Hotchkiss Papers; Hotchkiss in *Confederate Military History* 3:556–57; George Francis Robert Henderson, *Stonewall Jackson and the American Civil War* (New York: Longmans, Green and Co., 1949), 540–41; and Carman, "Maryland Campaign," chap. 22 (pp. 3–5).

60. Sorrel, *Recollections of a Confederate Staff Officer*, 108.

61. James Cooper Nisbet, *Four Years on the Firing Line*, ed. Bell Irvin Wiley (Jackson, Tenn.: McCowat-Mercer Press, 1963), 108.

62. Freeman, *R. E. Lee* 2:403–4, esp. n.44.

63. Alexander, *Military Memoirs*, 269.

64. Hunter McGuire, "General T. J. (Stonewall) Jackson, Confederate States Army: His Career and Character," *SHSP* 25 (1897): 102; and Douglas, *I Rode with Stonewall*, 179.

65. Hotchkiss in *Confederate Military History* 3:556–57; and Henry Alexander White, *Robert E. Lee and the Southern Confederacy, 1807–1870* (New York: Haskell House Pub. Ltd., 1968), 224–25.

66. Hood, *Advance and Retreat,* 45; discussed in chapter 10 of *Taken at the Flood.*

67. Lee to Mrs. Jackson, Jan. 25, 1866, Lee Family Papers.

68. Price to mother, Sept. 18, Trout, *With Pen and Saber,* 101.

10. Research Appendixes on the Antietam Aftermath, September 18 and After

1. Evans, ed., *Confederate Military History* 3:357 225; White, *Lee,* 224–25.

2. Hirsch, Diary, Sept. 18.

3. See Early, *War Memoirs,* 152; Owen, *In Camp and Battle,* 159; George H. Mills, "Sixteenth N.Ca. Infantry, Additional Sketch, *North Carolina Regiments* 4:166; Neese, *Three Years in the Confederate Horse Artillery,* 126; G. Wise, *History of the 17th Va.,* 119; Andrews, "Diary," 7; Tucker, "Diary," 20; and Latrobe, Diary, Sept. 18. Also, in *OR,* vol. 19, 1, are the reports of Longstreet (p. 841), D. R. Jones (p. 887), Jos. Walker (p. 907), Hilton (p. 949), Lane (p. 986), Neal (p. 1003), and Pender (p. 1004). In *SOR* vol. 3 see the reports of McRae (p. 575) and McIntire (p. 577).

4. David Hunter Strother, *A Virginia Yankee in the Civil War: The Diaries of David Hunter Strother,* ed. Cecil D. Eby (Chapel Hill: Univ. of North Carolina Press, 1961), 112.

5. Perrin's report, *OR,* vol. 19, 1:994.

6. Hancock's report, ibid., 280.

7. Carman, "Maryland Campaign," chap. 22 (p. 7).

8. Lee's report, *OR,* vol. 19, 1:151.

9. Taylor, *General Lee,* 136.

10. Evans, ed., *Confederate Military History* 3:357; and White, *Lee,* 225.

11. Early's report, *OR,* vol. 19, 1:972.

12. Haynes, *Diary,* 20; Fitzpatrick, *Letters,* 21; and Record of Events, 35th Georgia, *SOR* 18:652.

13. *OR,* vol. 19, 2:621.

14. In ibid., 1, see the reports of Pendleton (p. 832), McLaws (pp. 861–62), and Early (p. 972); and Lee to Davis, Sept. 21 (p. 143). See also Early, *War Memoirs,* 152.

15. John William Jones, *Personal Reminiscences, Anecdotes, and Letters of Gen. Robert E. Lee* (New York: D. Appleton and Co., 1876), 239.

16. Hotchkiss to wife, Sept. 21, Hotchkiss Papers.

17. Early, *War Memoirs,* 152; Neese, *Three Years in the Confederate Horse Artillery,* 126; John C. Gorman, "Memoirs of a Rebel, Part I," *Military Images* 3 (1981): 6; and Sandie Pendleton to Mother, Sept. 21, S. P. Lee, *Memoirs,* 217.

18. See Leach, Diary, Sept. 18; and Hancock's report, *OR,* vol. 19, 1:280–81.

19. Longstreet, *From Manassas to Appomattox,* 263.

20. S. D. Lee, "New Lights on Sharpsburg," 12.

21. Evans, ed. *Confederate Military History* 3:357; and Henderson, *Stonewall Jackson,* 542–44.

22. White, *Lee,* 225.

23. Stuart's report, *OR*, vol. 19, 1:820.

24. Von Borcke, *Memoirs of the Confederate War* 1:237–38.

25. Stuart's report, *OR*, vol. 19, 1:820.

26. Lee to Davis, Sept. 20, ibid., 142.

27. Lee to Davis, Sept. 21, ibid.

28. Lee to Davis, Sept. 25, ibid., 2:626.

29. Carman, "Maryland Campaign," chap. 22 (p. 8).

30. Von Borcke, *Memoirs of the Confederate War* 1:240.

31. McClellan's report, *OR*, vol. 19, 1:67.

32. S. P. Lee, *Memoirs*, 217.

33. James Dinkins, "Griffith-Barksdale-Humphrey Brigade and Its Campaigns," *SHSP* 32 (1904): 264; and idem, *1861 to 1865, by an Old Johnie: Personal Recollections and Experiences in the Confederate Army* (Cincinnati: Robert Clarke Co., 1897), 62–63.

34. See also Hirsch, Diary, Sept. 21; Hubbert, "Diary," 309; and Austin, *Georgia Boys*, 51.

35. In *OR*, vol. 19, 1, see the reports of D. R. Jones (p. 887), Jos. Walker (p. 907), Stevens (p. 942), Hilton (p. 949), Jackson (p. 957), Early, (p. 972), A. P. Hill (p. 981), Lane (p. 986), McGowan (p. 988), and Perrin (p. 994). In *SOR* vol. 3 see the reports of McIntire (p. 577) and Thruston (p. 588). See also Longstreet, *From Manassas to Appomattox*, 263–64; Early *War Memoirs*, 152–53; G. Wise, *History of the 17th Va.*, 119; Andrews, *Diary*, 7; Tucker, "Diary," 21; Carman, "Maryland Campaign," chap. 22 (p. 8); Hotchkiss to wife, Sept. 21, Hotchkiss Papers; and Leach, Diary, Sept. 19.

36. Latrobe, Diary, Sept. 18.

37. Mills, *North Carolina Regiments* 4:166.

38. Blackford, *War Years with Jeb Stuart*, 153.

39. Walker, "Sharpsburg," 682.

40. Stuart's report, *OR*, vol. 19, 1:820–21; Carman, "Maryland Campaign," chap. 25 (p. 13); Brown to Pendleton, Sept. 17, *OR*, vol. 19, 2:610–11.

41. Von Borcke, *Memoirs of the Confederate War* 1:242, 250–51.

42. Carman, "Maryland Campaign," chap. 11 (p. 50); Murphy, *10th Virginia*, 53–54.

43. Little's report, *OR*, vol. 19, 1:911.

44. Neese, *Three Years in the Confederate Horse Artillery*, 126–27.

45. Bridges, *D. H. Hill*, 127–41.

46. Ibid., 141.

47. Lee to Mrs. Jackson, Jan. 25, 1866, Lee Family Papers.

48. In *OR*, vol. 19, 1, see the reports of Jackson (p. 957), Early (p. 972), Lane (p. 986), McGowan (p. 989), Hamilton (p. 992), Perrin (p. 995), McCorkle (p. 997), Brown (p. 999), Johnston (p. 1003), Pender (pp. 1004–5), and Thomas (p. 1006). See also Early, *War Memoirs*, 162; Owen, *In Camp and Battle*, 163; Ramsay, *North Carolina Regiments* 1:577; and G. Wise, *History of the 17th Va.*, 121.

49. Hotchkiss, *Make Me a Map*, 84; location of the mill from U.S. War Department in *The Official Atlas of the Civil War* (New York: Arno Press, 1978), plate 69, map 1.

50. Hotchkiss to wife, Sept. 21, Hotchkiss Papers.

51. See the September 21 entries in the Leach and Latrobe diaries.

52. Neese, *Three Years in the Confederate Horse Artillery*, 127.

53. Alexandria Lee Levin, ed., "A Wounded Confederate Soldier's Letter from Fort McHenry," *Maryland Historical Magazine* 73 (1978): 394–96.

54. Goodson, "Letters," 128.

55. Benson, *Berry Benson's Civil War Book*, 26–27; Berkeley, *Four Years in the Confederate Artillery*, 27–29; and Drury P. Gibson, "Letters from a North Louisiana Tiger," ed. Debra Nance Laurence, *North Louisiana Historical Association Journal* 10 (1979): 141–42. See also Joel C. Blake, "Letters of Joel C. Blake," ed. J. Russell Reaver, *Apalachee* 5 (1957–62): 5; Randolph Harrison McKim, *A Soldier's Recollections: Leaves from the Diary of a Young Confederate, With an Oration on the Motives and Aims of the Soldiers of the South* (New York: Longmans, Green, and Co., 1910), 120; and Steuart to Randolph, Oct. 13, *OR*, vol. 19, 2:664–65.

56. Mary Bedinger Mitchell, "A Woman's Recollections of Antietam," in Johnson and Buel, *Battles and Leaders* 2:687–88.

57. Lee to Randolph, Sept. 24, *OR*, vol. 19, 2:625.

58. In *OR*, vol. 19, 2, see Lee to Randolph, Sept. 21 (p. 614) and S.O. 196 Headquarters Army of Northern Virginia (pp. 614–15).

59. Custis Lee to Davis, Sept. 25, Jefferson Davis, *The Papers of Jefferson Davis*, eds. Lynda Lasswell Crist and Mary Seaton Dix, 8 vols. to date (Baton Rouge: Louisiana State Univ. Press, 1971–), 8:405–6.

60. In *OR*, vol. 19, 2, see Davis to Lee, Sept. 28 (pp. 633–34) and Lee to Davis, Oct. 2 (p. 644).

61. Freeman, *R.. E. Lee* 2:411–12.

Works and Sources Cited

Addresses Delivered before the Confederate Veterans Association of Savannah, Ga. 5 vols. Savannah: Braid & Hutton, 1893–1902.

Alexander, Bevin. *Lost Victories: The Military Genius of Stonewall Jackson.* New York: Henry Holt & Co., 1992

Alexander, Edward Porter. *Fighting for the Confederacy: The Personal Recollections of General Edward Porter Alexander.* Ed. Gary W. Gallagher. Chapel Hill: Univ. of North Carolina Press, 1989.

———. *Military Memoirs of a Confederate: A Critical Narrative.* Ed. T. Harry Williams. Bloomington: Indiana Univ. Press, 1962.

Allan, William. *The Army of Northern Virginia in 1862.* Dayton: Morningside Bookshop, 1984.

———. "Confederate Artillery at Second Manassas and Antietam." *Southern Historical Society Papers* 11 (1883): 289–91.

———. "First Maryland Campaign, Review of General Longstreet." *Southern Historical Society Papers* 14 (1886): 102–18.

———. "Strategy of the Campaign of Sharpsburg or Antietam, September, 1862." *Papers of the Military Historical Society of Massachusetts* 3 (1888): 73–103.

———. "Strategy of the Sharpsburg Campaign." *Maryland Historical Magazine* 1 (1906): 247–71.

Allen, John Owen. "The Strength of the Union and Confederate Forces at Second Manassas." Master's thesis. George Mason University, 1993.

Andrews, W. H. *Diary of W. H. Andrews, 1st Sergt. Co. M, 1st Georgia Regulars, from February, 1861, to May 2, 1865.* East Atlanta: Privately published, 1891.

The Annals of the War, Written by Leading Participants, North and South, Originally Published in the Philadelphia Weekly Times. Philadelphia: Times Publishing Co., 1879.

Antietam National Battlefield Plaques. Typescript at Visitors Center, Sharpsburg, Maryland.

Arnold, Thomas Jackson. "The Lost Dispatch—A War Mystery." *Confederate Veteran* 30 (1922): 317.

Austin, Mildred Aurelia. *Georgia Boys with "Stonewall" Jackson—James Thomas Thompson and the Walton Infantry.* Athens: Univ. of Georgia Press, 1967.

Battle, Laura Elizabeth. *Forget-Me-Nots of the Civil War: A Romance Containing Reminiscences and Original Letters of Two Confederate Soldiers.* St. Louis: Fleming Printing Co., 1909.

Benson, Berry. *Berry Benson's Civil War Book: Memoirs of a Confederate Scout and Sharpshooter.* Ed. Susan Williams Benson. Athens: Univ. of Georgia Press, 1962.

Beringer, Richard E., Herman Hattaway, Archer Jones, and William N. Still, Jr. *Why the South Lost the Civil War.* Athens: University of Georgia Press, 1986.

Berkeley, Henry Robinson. *Four Years in the Confederate Artillery: The Diary of Private Henry Robinson Berkeley.* Ed. William H. Runge. Chapel Hill: Published for the Virginia Historical Society and the Univ. of North Carolina Press, 1961.

Berrier, H. R. "Company B, Tenth Virginia Cavalry." In Clark, ed., *North Carolina Regiments* 5:627–28.

Blackford, William Willis. *War Years with Jeb Stuart.* New York.: Charles Scribner's Sons, 1945.

Blake, Joel C. "Letters of Joel C. Blake." Ed. J. Russell Reaver. *Apalachee* 5 (1957–62): 5–25.

Boritt, Gabor S., ed. *Why the Confederacy Lost.* New York: Oxford Univ. Press, 1992.

Bridges, Hal. *Lee's Maverick General, Daniel Harvey Hill.* New York: McGraw Hill, 1961.

Brown, Hamilton A. "First Infantry (State Troops)." In Clark, ed. *North Carolina Troops* 1:135–56.

Caffey, Thomas E. *Battle-fields of the South, From Bull Run to Fredericksburg, with Sketches of the Confederate Commanders, and Gossip of the Camps, by an English Combatant.* New York: John Bradburn, 1864.

Caldwell, James Fitz James. *The History of a Brigade of South Carolinians, Known First as "Gregg's," and Subsequently as "McGowan's Brigade."* Philadelphia: King & Baird, 1866.

Carman, Ezra Ayers. "The Maryland Campaign of 1862." Carman Papers. Library of Congress, Washington, D.C.

Carmichael, Peter S. *The Purcell, Crenshaw, and Letcher Artillery.* Virginia Regimental Histories Series. Lynchburg: H.E. Howard, Inc., 1990.

Chamberlayne, John Hampden. *Ham Chamberlayne, Virginian, Letters and Papers of an Artillery Officer in the War for Southern Independence, 1861–1865.* Ed. C. G. Chamberlayne. Richmond: Press of the Dietz Printing Co., 1932.

Clark, Walter, ed. *Histories of the Several Regiments and Battalions from North Carolina in the Great War 1861–1865, Written by Members of the Respective Commands.* 5 vols. Wendell, N.C.: Broadfoot's Bookmark, 1982. Cited herein as *North Carolina Regiments.*

———. "Sharpsburg." In Clark, ed., *North Carolina Regiments* 5:71–82.

Confederate Archives. Record Group 109, War Department Collection of Confederate Records. National Archives, Washington, D.C.

Confederate Veteran. 40 vols. Nashville: United Confederate Veterans, 1893–1932.

Cooke, John Esten. *Stonewall Jackson.* New York: G. W. Dillingham Co., ca. 1899.

Cowan, John, and James I. Metts. "Third Infantry." In Clark, ed., *North Carolina Regiments* 1:177–214.

Crawford, Samuel Wylie. *The Genesis of the Civil War: The Story of Sumter, 1860–1861.* New York: Charles L. Webster & Co., 1886.

Crute, Joseph H., Jr. *Units of the Confederate States Army.* Midlothian, Va.: Derwent Books, 1987.

Cuffel, Charles A. *Durell's Battery in the Civil War (Independent Battery D, Pennsylvania Volunteer Artillery): A Narrative of the Campaigns and Battles of Berks and Bucks Counties' Artillerists in the War of the Rebellion, from the Battery's Organization, September 24, 1861, to its Muster Out of Service, June 13, 1865.* Philadelphia: Craig, Finley & Co., 1901.

Cutts, Allen Sherrod. "Cutts' Battalion at Sharpsburg." *Southern Historical Society Papers* 10 (1882): 430–31.

Daly, Louise Porter. *Alexander Cheves Haskell, The Portrait of a Man.* Norwood, Mass.: Plimpton Press, 1934.

Daniel, John Warwick, ed. *Personal Reminiscences of Jefferson Davis by Distinguished Men of His Time.* Baltimore: Eastern Publishing Co., 1890.

Darter, Lewis J., Jr. *List of Climatological Records in the National Archives.* Special List No. 1. 1942. Reprint. Washington, D.C.: GPO, 1981.

Davis, Jefferson. *The Papers of Jefferson Davis.* Ed. Lynda Lasswell Crist and Mary Seaton Dix. 8 vols. to date. Baton Rouge: Louisiana State Univ. Press, 1971–.

Davis, William C., ed. *The Confederate General.* 6 vols. N.p.: National Historical Society, 1991.

DeRosset, William Lord. "Additional Sketch Third Regiment." In Clark, ed., *North-Carolina Regiments* 1:215–24.

Dinkins, James. *1861 to 1865, by an Old Johnie: Personal Recollections and Experiences in the Confederate Army.* Cincinnati: Robert Clarke Co., 1897.

———. "Griffiths-Barksdale-Humphrey Brigade and Its Campaigns." *Southern Historical Society Papers* 32 (1904): 250–74.

Divine, John E. *35th Virginia Cavalry Battalion.* Virginia Regimental Histories Series. Lynchburg: H.E. Howard, Inc., 1985.

Douglas, Henry Kyd. *I Rode with Stonewall, Being Chiefly the War Experiences of the Youngest Member of Jackson's Staff from the John Brown Raid to the Hanging of Mrs. Surratt.* Chapel Hill: Univ. of North Carolina Press, 1940.

———. "Stonewall Jackson in Maryland." In Johnson and Buel, eds., *Battles and Leaders* 2:620–29.

Driver, Robert J., Jr. *1st Virginia Cavalry.* Virginia Regimental Histories Series. Lynchburg: H.E. Howard, Inc., 1991.

———. *10th Virginia Cavalry.* Virginia Regimental Histories Series. Lynchburg: H.E. Howard, Inc., 1992.

Duncan, Richard. "Marylanders and the Invasion of 1862." *Civil War History* 9 (1965): 370–83. Early, Jubal Anderson. *War Memoirs, Autobiographical Sketch and Narrative of the War Between the States.* Ed. Frank E. Vandiver. Bloomington: Indiana Univ. Press, 1960.

Evans, Clement Anselm, ed. *Confederate Military History.* 12 vols. Atlanta: Confederate Publishing Co., 1899. Vol 2: *Maryland,* by Bradley Tyler Johnson. Vol. 3: *Virginia,* by Jedediah Hotchkiss. *Experiences of War: An Anthology of Articles from MHQ, The Quarterly Journal of Military History.* New York: Dell, 1992.

Farwell, Byron. *Stonewall: A Biography of General Thomas J. Jackson.* New York: W. W. Norton, 1992.

Ferguson, Garland S. "Twenty-fifth Infantry." In Clark, ed., *North Carolina Regiments* 2:291–301.

Fitzpatrick, Marion Hill. *Letters to Amanda from Sergeant Major Marion Hill Fitzpatrick, Co. K, 45th Georgia Regiment . . . to His Wife Amanda Olive Elizabeth White Fitzpatrick, 1862–1865.* Culloden, Ga.: Privately published, 1976.

Freeman, Douglas Southall. *Lee's Lieutenants, a Study in Command.* 3 vols. New York: Charles Scribner's Sons, 1942–44.

———. *R. E. Lee, a Biography.* 4 vols. New York: Charles Scribner's Sons, 1934–35.

Frothingham, Thomas Goddard. "The Crisis of the Civil War, Antietam." *Massachusetts Historical Society Proceedings* 56 (1922–23): 173–208.

Frye, Dennis E. "Henry Kyd Douglas Challenged by His Peers." *Civil War* (Sept. 1991): 40–46.

———. *2nd Virginia Infantry.* Virginia Regimental Histories Series. Lynchburg: H. E. Howard, Inc., 1984.

———. "The Siege of Harper's Ferry." *Blue & Gray Magazine* 5 (1987).

Gallagher, Gary W. "The Autumn of 1862: A Season of Opportunity." In Gallagher, ed., *Antietam*, 1–13.

———, ed. *Antietam: Essays on the 1862 Maryland Campaign.* Kent, Ohio: Kent State Univ. Press, 1989.

———, ed. *Lee the Soldier.* Lincoln: Univ. of Nebraska Press, 1996.

Gibson, Drury P. "Letters from a North Louisiana Tiger." Ed. Debra Nance Laurence. *North Louisiana Historical Association Journal* 10 (1979): 130–47.

Goodson, Joab. "The Letters of Captain Joab Goodson, 1862–64." Ed. W. Stanley Hoole. *Alabama Review* 10 (1957): 126–53.

Gordon, John Brown. *Reminiscences of the Civil War.* New York: Charles Scribner's Sons, 1903.

Gorman, John C. "Memoirs of a Rebel—Part I." *Military Images* 3, no. 3 (1981): 4–6.

Graham, James Augustus. "Cooke's Brigade." In Clark, ed., *North Carolina Regiments* 4:501–12.

———. "Twenty-seventh Infantry." In Clark, ed., *North Carolina Regiments* 2:425–63.

Grattan, George D. "The Battle of Boonsboro Gap or South Mountain." *Southern Historical Society Papers* 39 (1914): 31–44.

Gruber, John. *J. Gruber's Hagers-town Town and Country Almanack for the Year of Our Lord 1862.* Hagerstown: J. Gruber, 1861.

Hamilton, W. T. "Eleventh Mississippi Regiment." *Confederate Veteran* 14 (1906): 62–63.

Harris, James Sidney. "Seventh Infantry." In Clark, ed., *North Carolina Regiments* 1:361–86.

Harris, Nelson. *17th Virginia Cavalry.* Virginia Regimental Histories Series. Lynchburg: H.E. Howard, Inc., 1994.

Harsh, Joseph L. *Confederate Tide Rising: Robert E. Lee and the Making of Southern Strategy, 1861–1862.* Kent, Ohio: Kent State Univ. Press, 1998.

———. *Taken at the Flood: Robert E. Lee and Confederate Strategy in the Maryland Campaign of 1862.* Kent, Ohio: Kent State Univ. Press, 1999.

Hartwig, D. Scott. "Robert E. Lee and the Maryland Campaign." In Gallagher, ed., *Lee: the Soldier*, 331–55.

Hartzler, Daniel D. *Marylanders in the Confederacy.* Westminster, Md.: Family Line Publications, 1986.

Hassler, William Woods. *Colonel John Pelham, Lee's Boy Artillerist.* Richmond: Garrett & Massie, 1960.

Hattaway, Herman, and Archer Jones. *How the North Won the Civil War: A Military History of the Civil War.* Urbana: Univ. of Illinois Press, 1983.

Haynes, Draughton Stith. *The Field Diary of a Confederate Soldier, Draughton Sith Haynes, while Serving with the Army of Northern Virginia, C.S.A.* Darien, Ga.: Ashantilly Press, 1963.

Heitman, Francis Bernard. *Historical Register and Dictionary of the United States Army, from Its Organization, September 29, 1789, to March 2, 1903.* 2 vols. Washington, D.C.: GPO, 1903.

Henderson, George Francis Robert. *Stonewall Jackson and the American Civil War.* New York: Longmans, Green and Co., 1949.

Hennessy, John J. *Return to Bull Run: The Campaign and Battle of Second Manassas.* New York: Simon & Schuster, 1993.

Heth, Henry. "Causes of Lee's Defeat at Gettysburg." *Southern Historical Society Papers* 4 (1877): 151–60.

Heysinger, Isaac Winter. *Antietam and the Maryland and Virginia Campaigns of 1862, From the Government Records, Union and Confederate, Mostly Unknown and Which Now First Disclosed the Truth.* New York: Neale Publishing Co., 1912.

Hill, Daniel Harvey. "The Battle of South Mountain, or Boonsboro': Fighting for Time at Turner's and Fox's Gaps." In Johnson and Buel, eds., *Battles and Leaders* 2:559–81.

———. "The Lost Dispatch." *Land We Love* 4 (1867–68): 270–84.

———. Papers. Library of Virginia. Richmond.

———. Personal Papers. North Carolina State Archives. Raleigh.

Hill, Daniel Harvey, Jr. Personal Papers. North Carolina State Archives. Raleigh.

Hirsch, Isaac. Diary. Fredericksburg Area Museum and Cultural Center. Fredericksburg.

Hood, John Bell. *Advance and Retreat. Personal Experiences in the United States and Confederate States Armies.* Ed. Richard N. Current. Bloomington: Indiana Univ. Press, 1959.

Hotchkiss, Jedediah. *Make Me a Map of the Valley: The Civil War Journal of Stonewall Jackson's Topographer.* Ed. Archie McDonald. Dallas: Southern Methodist Univ. Press, 1973.

———. Papers. Library of Congress. Washington, D.C.

Hubbert, Mike M. "The Travels of the 13th Mississippi Regiment: Excerpts from the Diary of Mike M. Hubbert of Attala County (1861–1862)." Ed. John E. Fisher. *Journal of Mississippi History* 45 (1983): 288–313.

Hunt, Roger D., and Jack R. Brown. *Brevet Brigadier Generals in Blue.* Gaithersburg, Md.: Olde Soldiers Books, Inc., 1990.

Hunter, Alexander. "A High Private's Account of the Battle of Sharpsburg." *Southern Historical Society Papers* 10 (1882): 503–12; 11 (1883): 10–21.

Johnson, Bradley Tyler. "First Maryland Campaign." *Southern Historical Society Papers* 12 (1884): 500–537.

Johnson, Curt, and Richard C. Anderson, Jr. *Artillery Hell: The Employment of Artillery at Antietam.* College Station, Tex.: Texas A&M Univ. Press, 1995.

Johnson, Robert Underwood, and Clarence Clough Buel, eds. *Battles and Leaders of the Civil War . . . Being for the Most Part Contributions Based upon "The Century Magazine War Series".* 4 vols. New York: Thomas Yoseloff, 1956.

Jones, Archer. *Civil War Command and Strategy: The Process of Victory and Defeat.* New York: The Free Press, 1992.

———. "Military Means, Political Ends: Strategy." In Boritt, ed., *Why the Confederacy Lost,* 43–77.

Jones, John William. "Did Cutts' Battalion Have Sixty Guns at Sharpsburg?" *Southern Historical Society Papers* 10 (1882): 190.

———. *Personal Reminiscences, Anecdotes, and Letters Of Gen. Robert E. Lee* New York: D. Appleton and Co., 1876.

Jones, Wilbur D., Jr. "Who Lost the Lost Orders? Stonewall Jackson, His Courier, and Special Orders No. 191." In Snell, ed., *Antietam*, 1–26.

Kearney, H. C. "Fifteenth Infantry." In Clark, ed., *North Carolina Regiments* 1:733–49.

Kegel, James A. *North with Lee and Jackson: The Lost Story of Gettysburg*. Mechanicsburg, Pa.: Stackpole Books, 1996.

Krick, Robert K. "The Army of Northern Virginia in September 1862: Its Circumstances, Its Opportunities, and Why It Should Not have Been at Sharpsburg." In Gallagher, ed., *Antietam*, 35–55.

———. *Lee's Colonels: A Biographical Register of the Field Officers of the Army of Northern Virginia*. 3d rev. ed. Dayton: Morningside Bookshop, 1991.

Lane, James Henry. "Twenty-eighth Infantry." In Clark, ed., *North Carolina Regiments* 2:465–84.

Latrobe, Osmun. Diary. Virginia Historical Society. Richmond.

Lattimore, T. D. "Thirty-fourth Infantry." In Clark, ed., *North Carolina Regiments* 2:581–90.

Leach, Calvin. Diary. Southern Historical Collection. University of North Carolina, Chapel Hill.

Lee, Robert Edward. "A Lee Letter on the Lost Dispatch, and the Maryland Campaign of 1862." Ed. Hal Bridges. *Virginia Magazine of History and Biography* 46 (1958): 161–66.

———. "Letter from General R. E. Lee [to William M. McDonald]." *Southern Historical Society Papers* 7 (1879): 445–56.

———. *The Wartime Papers of R. E. Lee*. Ed. Clifford Dowdey and Louis H. Manarin. Boston: Little, Brown and Co., 1961.

Lee, Robert Edward. Lee Family Papers. Virginia Historical Society. Richmond.

Lee, Robert Edward Lee [Jr.]. *Recollections and Letters of General Robert E. Lee, by His Son*. Enlarged ed. Garden City, N.Y.: Garden City Publishing Co., 1924.

Lee, Stephen Dill. "New Lights on Sharpsburg." *Richmond Dispatch*, Dec. 20, 1896.

Lee, Susan Pendleton. *Memoirs of William Nelson Pendleton, by His Daughter*. Enlarged ed. Harrisonburg, Va.: Sprinkle Publications, 1991.

Levin, Alexandria Lee. "A Wounded Confederate Soldier's Letter from Fort McHenry." *Maryland Historical Magazine* 73 (1978): 394–96.

Long, Armistead Lindsay. *Memoirs of Robert E. Lee, His Military and Personal History, Embracing a Large Amount of Information Hitherto Unpublished*. Philadelphia: J. M. Stoddart & Co., 1886.

Longstreet, James. *From Manassas to Appomattox, Memoirs of the Civil War in America*. Ed. James I. Robertson, Jr. Bloomington: Indiana Univ. Press, 1960.

———. "The Invasion of Maryland." In Johnson and Buel, eds., *Battles and Leaders* 2:663–74.

———. Papers. Duke University, Durham, N.C.

McAlpine, Newton. "Sketch of Company I, 61st Virginia Infantry, Mahone's Brigade, C.S.A." *Southern Historical Society Papers* 24 (1896): 98–108.

McClellan, George Brinton. Papers. Library of Congress, Washington, D.C.

McLaws, LaFayette. Papers. Southern Historical Collection. University of North Carolina, Chapel Hill.

McDonald, William Naylor. *A History of the Laurel Brigade, Originally the Ashby Cavalry of the Army of Northern Virginia and Chew's Battery.* Baltimore: Sun Job Printing Office, 1907.

McGuire, Hunter. "General T. J. (Stonewall) Jackson, Confederate States Army: His Career and Character." *Southern Historical Society Papers* 25 (1897): iv n., 90–112.

McKim, Randolph Harrison. *A Soldier's Recollections: Leaves from the Diary of a Young Confederate, with an Oration on the Motives and Aims of the Soldiers of the South.* New York: Longman's, Green, and Co., 1910.

McLaws, LaFayette. "The Maryland Campaign." In *Address Delivered before the Confederate Veterans Association of Savannah, Ga.* 3:5–30.

Manarin, Louis. "A Proclamation To the People of ——." *North Carolina Historical Review* 41 (1964): 246–51.

Marshall, Charles. *An Aide-de-Camp of Lee, Being the Papers of Colonel Charles Marshall, Sometimes Aide-de-Camp, Military Secretary, and Assistant Adjutant General on the Staff of Robert E. Lee, 1862–1865.* Ed. Sir Frederick Maurice. Boston: Little, Brown and Co., 1927.

Mills, George H. "Sixteenth Infantry, Additional Sketch." In Clark, ed., *North Carolina Regiments* 4:137–219.

Mitchell, Mary Bedinger. "A Woman's Recollections of Antietam." In Johnson and Buel, eds., *Battles and Leaders* 2:686–94.

Moore, Edward Alexander. *The Story of a Cannoneer under Stonewall Jackson, in which Is Told the Part Taken by the Rockbridge Artillery in the Army of Northern Virginia.* New York: Neale Publishing Co., 1907.

Moore, Robert H., II. *The Charlottesville, Lee Lynchburg, and Johnson's Bedford Artillery.* Virginia Regimental Histories Series. Lynchburg: H.E. Howard, Inc., 1990.

———. *The Danville, Eighth Star, and Dixie Artillery.* Virginia Regimental Histories Series. Lynchburg: H.E. Howard, Inc., 1989.

———. *Miscellaneous Disbanded Virginia Light Artillery.* Virginia Regimental Histories Series. Lynchburg: H.E. Howard, Inc., 1997.

Morrison, Emmett M. "Fifteenth Virginia at Sharpsburg." *Southern Historical Society Papers* 33 (1905): 99–110.

Murfin, James V. *The Gleam of Bayonets: The Battle of Antietam and the Maryland Campaign of 1862.* New York: Thomas Yoseloff, 1965.

Murphy, Terrence V. *10th Virginia Infantry.* Virginia Regimental Histories Series. Lynchburg: H.E. Howard, Inc., 1989.

Musick, Michael P. *6th Virginia Cavalry.* Virginia Regimental Histories Series. Lynchburg: H.E. Howard, Inc., 1990.

Myers, Franklin McIntosh. *The Comanches: A History of White's Battalion, Virginia Cavalry, Laurel Brig., Hampton Div., A.N.V., C.S.A.* Baltimore: Kelly, Piet & Co., 1871.

Neese, George Michael. *Three Years in the Confederate Horse Artillery, by . . . a Gunner in Chew's Battery.* New York: Neale Publishing Co., 1911.

Nisbet, James Cooper. *Four Years on the Firing Line.* Ed. Bell Irvin Wiley. Jackson, Tenn.: McCowat-Mercer Press, 1963.

Ould, Robert. "The Exchange of Prisoners." In *Annals of the War,* 32–59.

Owen, William Miller. *In Camp and Battle with the Washington Artillery of New Orleans: A Narrative of Events during the Late Civil War, from Bull Run to Appomattox and Spanish Fort.* Boston: Ticknor and Co., 1885.

Palfrey, Francis Winthrop. "The Battle of Antietam." In *Papers of the Military Historical Society of Massachusetts* 3:1–26.

Papers of the Military Historical Society of Massachusetts. 16 vols. Boston: Various publishers, 1881–1918.

Paris, Louis Phillipe Albert d'Orleans, comte de. *History of the Civil War in America.* 4 vols. Philadelphia: Porter & Coates, 1876–88.

Pender, William Dorsey. *The General to His Wife: The Civil War Letters of William Dorsey Pender to Fanny Pender.* Ed. William Woods Hassler. Chapel Hill: Univ. of North Carolina Press, 1965.

Poague, William Thomas. *Gunner with Stonewall: Reminiscences of William Thomas Poague . . . A Memoir Written for His Children in 1913.* Ed. Monroe F. Cockrell. Jackson, Tenn.: McCowat-Mercer Press, 1957.

Ramsay, John Andrew. "Additional Sketch Tenth Regiment, Light Batteries A, D, F [E] and I." In Clark, ed., *North Carolina Regiments* 1:551–82.

Ratchford, J. W. Memoirs. Daniel Harvey Hill, Jr., Personal Papers. North Carolina State Archives, Raleigh.

Ray, Neill W. "Sixth Infantry." In Clark, ed., *North Carolina Regiments* 1:293–335.

Reilly, Oliver T. *The Battlefield of Antietam.* Hagerstown: Hagerstown Bookbinding and Printing Co., 1906.

Robertson, James I., Jr. *Stonewall Jackson: The Man, the Soldier, the Legend.* New York: Macmillan Publishing, 1997.

Ropes, John Codman. *The Story of the Civil War: A Concise Account of the War in the United States of America between 1861 and 1865.* 2 vols. New York: G. P. Putnam's Sons, 1894–98.

Ropes, John Codman. Papers. Boston University.

Roulhac, Thomas R. "Forty-ninth Infantry." In Clark, ed., *North Carolina Regiments* 3:125–49.

Sears, Stephen W. *Landscape Turned Red, The Battle of Antietam.* New Haven: Ticknor & Fields, 1983.

———. "The Last Word on the Lost Order." In *Experiences of War,* 197–210.

Sheeran, James B. *Confederate Chaplain: A War Journal of Rev. James B. Sheeran, C.SS.T., 14th Louisiana, C.S.A.* Ed. Rev. Joseph T. Durkin. Milwaukee: Bruce Publishing Co., 1960.

Shinn, James T. Diary. Edwin Augustus Osborne Papers. Southern Historical Collection. University of North Carolina, Chapel Hill.

Simpson, Richard Wright, and Taliaferro N. Simpson. *"Far, Far from Home": The Wartime Letters of Dick and Tally Simpson, Third South Carolina Volunteers.* Ed. Guy R. Everson and Edward H. Simpson, Jr. New York: Oxford Univ. Press, 1994.

Snell, Mark A., ed. *Antietam, The Maryland Campaign of 1862: Essays on Union and Confederate Leadership.* In *Civil War Regiments: A Journal of the American Civil War* 5, no. 3 (1997).

Sorrel, Gilbert Moxley. *Recollections of a Confederate Staff Officer.* Ed. Bell Irvin Wiley. Jackson, Tenn.: McCowat-Mercer, 1958.

Southern Historical Society Papers. 52 vols. Richmond: Various publishers, 1876–1959.

Squires, Charles Winder. "'Boy Officer' of the Washington Artillery—Part I." *Civil War Times Illustrated* 14, no 8 (1975): 10–24.

Squires, Charles Winder. Memoirs. W. H. T. Squires Papers. Southern Historical Collection. University of North Carolina, Chapel Hill.

Steiner, Lewis Henry. *Report of Lewis H. Steiner, M.D., Inspector of the Sanitary Commission, Containing a Diary Kept during the Rebel Occupation of Frederick, Md., and an Account of the Operations of the U.S. Sanitary Commission during the Campaign in Maryland, September 1862.* New York: Anson D.F. Randolph, 1862.

Stiles, Joseph Clay. Papers. Henry E. Huntington Library. San Marino, Calif.

Strother, David Hinter. *A Virginia Yankee in the Civil War: The Diaries of David Hunter Strother.* Ed. Cecil D. Eby, Jr. Chapel Hill: Univ. of North Carolina Press, 1961.

Summers, Festus Paul. *The Baltimore and Ohio in the Civil War.* New York: G. P. Putnam's Sons, 1939.

Supplement to the Official Records of the Union and Confederate Armies. 25 nonconsecutive vols. to date. Ed. Janet B. Hewett et al. Wilmington, N.C.: Broadfoot Publishing Co., 1994—.

Taylor, Walter Herron. *Four Years with General Lee.* Ed. James I. Robertson, Jr. Bloomington: Indiana Univ. Press, 1962.

———. *General Lee, His Campaigns in Virginia, 1861–1865, with Personal Reminiscences.* Norfolk, Va.: Nusbaum Book and News Co., 1906.

Teetor, Paul R. *A Matter of Hours: Treason at Harper's Ferry.* Rutherford, N.J.: Fairleigh Dickinson Univ. Press, 1962.

Thomas, Henry Walter. *History of the Doles-Cook Brigade, Army of Northern Virginia, C.S.A., Containing Muster Rolls of Each Company of the Fourth, Twelfth, Twenty-first and Forty-fourth Georgia Regiments, with a Short Sketch of the Services of Each Member, and a Complete History of Each Regiment, by One of Its Own Members, and Other Matters of Interest.* Atlanta: Franklin Printing and Publishing Co., 1903.

Tischler, Allan L. *The History of the Harpers Ferry Cavalry Expedition, September 14 & 15, 1862.* Winchester, Va.: Five Cedars Press, 1993.

Torrence, Leonidas. "The Road to Gettysburg, The Diary and Letters of Leonidas Torrence of the Gaston Guards." Ed. Haskell Monroe. *North Carolina Historical Review* 36 (1959): 476–517.

Trask, Benjamin F. *61st Virginia Infantry.* Virginia Regimental Histories Series. Lynchburg: H.E. Howard, Inc., 1988.

The Tribune Almanac for the Years 1838 to 1866. 2 vols. New York: New York Tribune Association, 1868.

Trout, Robert J. *With Pen and Saber: The Letters and Diaries of J. E. B. Stuart's Staff Officers.* Mechanichsburg, Pa.: Stackpole Books, 1995.

Tucker, John S. "The Diary of John S. Tucker: Confederate Soldier from Alabama." Ed. Gary Wilson. *Alabama Historical Quarterly* 43 (1981): 5–33.

Turner, V. E., and Henry Clay Wall. "Twenty-third Infantry." In Clark, ed., *North Carolina Regiments* 2:181–268.

U.S. Census Bureau. *Agriculture of the United States in 1860: Compiled from the Original Returns of the Eighth Census.* Washington, D.C.: GPO, 1864.

———. *Manufactures of the United States in 1860: Compiled from the Original Returns of the Eighth Census.* Washington, D.C.: GPO, 1865.

———. *Population of the United States in 1860: Compiled from the Original Returns of the Eighth Census.* Washington, D.C.: GPO, 1864.

———. *Statistics of the United States (Including Mortality, Property, etc.) in 1860: Compiled from the Original Returns of the Eighth Census.* Washington, D.C.: GPO, 1866.

U.S. Engineer Corps. *Atlas of the Battlefield of Antietam, Prepared under the Direction of the Antietam Battlefield Board.* 1904. 2d rev. ed. Washington, D.C.: GPO, 1908.

U.S. War Department. *The Official Military Atlas of the Civil War; Atlas to Accompany the Official Records of the Union and Confederate Armies.* Intro. Richard J. Sommers. New York: Arno Press, 1978.

———. *The War of the Rebellion: A Compilation of the Official Records of the Union and Confederate Armies.* 128 vols. Washington, D.C.: GPO, 1880–1901.

U.S. Weather Bureau. Records of Surface Land Observations, 1819–1941. RG 27, Records of the Weather Bureau. National Archives, Washington, D.C.

Vandiver, Frank Everson. *Mighty Stonewall.* New York: McGraw-Hill Book Co., 1957.

von Borcke, Heros. *Memoirs of the Confederate War for Independence.* 2 vols. New York: Peter Smith, 1938.

Walcott, Charles Folsom. *History of the Twenty-first Regiment Massachusetts Volunteers in the War for the Preservation of the Union, 1861–1865, with Statistics of the War and of Rebel Prisons.* Boston: Houghton, Mifflin, 1882.

Walker, John George. "Jackson's Capture of Harper's Ferry." In Johnson and Buel, eds., *Battles and Leaders* 2:604–11.

———. "Sharpsburg." In Johnson and Buel, eds., *Battles and Leaders* 2:675–82.

Wallace, Lee A. *A Guide to Virginia Military Organizations, 1861–1865.* 2d rev. ed. Lynchburg: H. E. Howard, 1986.

Webster's New Geographical Dictionary. Springfield, Mass.: Merriam-Webster Inc., 1984.

Weston, James A. "Thirty-third Infantry." In Clark, ed., *North Carolina Regiments* 2:537–80.

Wharton, Rufus W. "First Battalion (Sharpshooters)." In Clark, ed., *North Carolina Regiments* 4:225–42.

White, Henry Alexander. *Robert E. Lee and the Southern Confederacy, 1807–1870.* New York: Haskell House Publishers Ltd., 1968.

Wise, George. *History of the Seventeenth Virginia Infantry, C.S.A.* Baltimore: Kelly, Piet & Co., 1870.

Wise, Jennings Cropper. *The Long Arm of Lee: or, The History of the Artillery of the Army of Northern Virginia, with a Brief Account of the Confederate Bureau of Ordnance.* 2 vols. Lynchburg: J. P. Bell, 1915.

Wood, William Nathaniel. *Reminiscences of Big I.* Ed. Bell Irvin Wiley. Jackson, Tenn.: McCowat-Mercer Press, 1956.

Woodhull, Alfred A. [Letter on Antietam, July 16, 1886.] In Johnson and Buel, eds., *Battles and Leaders* 2:671n.

Worsham, John H. *One of Jackson's Foot Cavalry, His Experiences and What He Saw during the War, 1861–1865, Including a History of "F Company," Richmond, Va., 21st Regiment Virginia Infantry, Second Brigade, Jackson's Division, Second Corps, A.N. Va.* Ed. Bell Irvin Wiley. Jackson, Tenn.: McCowat-Mercer Press, 1964.

Wyckoff, Mac. *History of the 2nd South Carolina Infantry: 1861–1865.* Fredericksburg, Va.: Sergeant Kirkland Museum and Historical Society, 1994.

———. *History of the 3rd South Carolina Infantry: 1861–1865.* Fredericksburg, Va.: Sergeant Kirkland Museum and Historical Society, 1995.

Index

The following is a spare index, as befits a reference work with a detailed, classified table of contents. Not included are the almanac and climatological data from chapter 1; the regiments, battalions, and batteries from the organizational chart in chapter 2 (which are indexed in chapter 3); chapter 3 (which itself is an index); chapter 4 (which is a gazetteer); chapter 11 (which is a list of notes); or the material from any of the twenty-seven tables. Also, the items included here have fewer subheadings than the indexes to Confederate Tide Rising *and* Taken at the Flood. *Robert E. Lee, for example, who is mentioned on nearly every page in chapters 5 through 10, is indexed in only major topics.*